A HISTORY OF VENICE

THE GIANT'S STAIRCASE IN THE DUCAL PALACE.

(*From a drawing by G. Fancelli, in the Print Room at the British Museum*)

A History of
VENICE:

From its Founding
to the Unification of Italy

ALTHEA WIEL

BARNES
&NOBLE
BOOKS
NEW YORK

Originally published in 1898.
This edition published by Barnes & Noble, Inc.

1995 Barnes & Noble Books

ISBN 1-56619-682-5

Printed and bound in the United States of America.
M 9 8 7 6 5 4 3 2 1

To

MY MOTHER,

ELIZABETH, BARONESS WENLOCK.

PREFACE.

THE Story of Venice in its entirety and completeness has yet to be written. Even in Italian a perfect work dealing with the subject has not been accomplished, though documents and histories exist in abundance from which to compile such a work ; and the following pages only attempt an outline of a story whose vastness and diversity has rarely been equalled among the nations.

The strange geographical position occupied by Venice ; the extent of her commerce and wealth ; and the height of luxury and splendour to which she attained in comparatively early ages, gild her pages with a colour and vivacity alternately bewildering and fascinating. The special feature though in her story is the preponderance of the state, and the subservience of the citizen ; for Venice was an exacting mistress, and all who served her had to abrogate self and devote themselves heart and soul to her service. No individual was of account when weighed in the balance of the state's requirements ; and through every page of her history the same record of exaction and demand can be traced, side by side with a corres-

ponding supply of devotion and self-abnegation. Her
story may be divided into three periods : the first
from 697 to 1172 comprises the dawn of the ducal
power, of the councils, and of the whole process of
administration culminating in the formation of the
Great Council. The second period from 1172 to
1457 is the period of Venice's increase of might, and
the attainment of her greatest glory. It closes with
the fall of Constantinople and the end of Foscari's
dukedom, when a mistaken policy and ambition
undermined the strength and power of the Republic
by leading her from concentrating her energies on
the sea, to enlarging her domains on the mainland.
The third period from 1457 to 1797 records the slow
downward course of the story, brightened though with
occasional flashes of the old spirit and greatness
making themselves felt through the gloom of decay.
From then to the present time the story is merged
in that of France and Austria ; till finally in 1866
Venice was united to the newly-formed kingdom of
Italy.

The chief source from whence I have derived most
of the information recorded in this volume is,
Romanin's " Storia Documentata di Venezia " ;
though Daru and other writers have helped beside
to furnish whereon to descant of the "majestie of
this citie who doth deserve a farre more elegant and
curious pensill to paint her out in her colours than
mine " (Coryat's " Crudities ").

My cordial thanks are due to Commendatore
Stefani, head of the State Archives in Venice, and
to the Abate Nicoletti, of the Museo Civico, for help

and researches in connection with this work ; to Mr. Curtis (Palazzo Barbaro), for obtaining for me from Mr. Barrett Browning the use of his copy of Coryat's "Crudities." I wish further to thank Mr. Lionel Cust of the British Museum most warmly for help in reading the proofs, and for most valuable suggestions and advice throughout the work, especially with regard to art. For the help given by my husband, and through him, by the Marciana Library, my thanks can only be conveyed in a silence whose meaning is deeper than words.

CA PISANI, SANTA MARINA, VENICE.
June, 1894.

CONTENTS.

II.

RELIGIOUS AND CIVIL PROGRESS. 811–991   . 32–63

V.

XIV.

LIST OF THE DOGES.

A.D.

59. Marco Corner, or
Cornaro 1365
60. Andrea Contarini ... 1368
61. Michele Morosini ... 1382
62. Antonio Venier ... 1382
63. Michele Steno ... 1400
64. Tomaso Mocenigo ... 1414
65. Francesco Foscari ... 1423
66. Pasquale Malipiero ... 1457
67. Cristoforo Moro ... 1462
68. Nicolò Tron 1471
69. Nicolò Marcello ... 1473
70. Pietro Mocenigo ... 1474
71. Andrea Vendramin ... 1476
72. Giovanni Mocenigo ... 1478
73. Marco Barbarigo ... 1485
74. Agostino Barbarigo ... 1486
75. Leonardo Loredan ... 1501
76. Antonio Grimani ... 1521
77. Andrea Gritti... ... 1523
78. Pietro Lando... ... 1539
79. Francesco Donato ... 1545
80. Antonio Trevisan ... 1554
81. Francesco Venier ... 1554
82. Lorenzo Priuli ... 1556
83. Girolamo Priuli ... 1559
84. Pietro Loredan ... 1567
85. Alvise Mocenigo I. ... 1570
86. Sebastiano Venier ... 1577
87. Nicolò da Ponte ... 1578
88. Pasquale Cicogna ... 1585
89. Marino Grimani ... 1595
90. Leonardo Donato ... 1606

A.D.

91. Marc' Antonio Memmo 1612
92. Giovanni Bembo ... 1615
93. Nicolò Donato ... 1618
94. Antonio Priuli ... 1618
95. Francesco Contarini... 1623
96. Giovanni Cornaro ... 1625
97. Nicolò Contarini ... 1630
98. Francesco Erizzo ... 1631
99. Francesco Molin ... 1646
100. Carlo Contarini ... 1655
101. Francesco Cornaro ... 1656
102. Bertucci Valier ... 1656
103. Giovanni Pesaro ... 1658
104. Domenico Contarini ... 1659
105. Nicolò Sagredo ... 1675
106. Luigi Contarini ... 1676
107. Marc' Antonio Giustinian 1684
108. Francesco Morosini ... 1688
109. Silvestro Valier ... 1694
110. Alvise Mocenigo II. ... 1700
111. Giovanni Cornaro II... 1709
112. Alvise Sebastiano Mocenigo III. 1722
113. Carlo Ruzzini... ... 1732
114. Alvise Pisani 1735
115. Pietro Grimani ... 1741
116. Francesco Loredan ... 1752
117. Marco Foscarini ... 1762
118. Alvise Mocenigo IV.... 1763
119. Paolo Renier 1779
120. Ludovico Manin ... 1789, to
May 12, 1797

LIST OF ILLUSTRATIONS.[1]

[1] My thanks are due to M. Charles Yriarte for permission to reproduce some of the illustrations from his book, " Venise ; Histoire, Art, Industrie, &c." (Paris, Rothschild, 1877) ; and to Commendatore F. Ongania for leave to reproduce some of the drawings from his publications, " Calli e Canali " (Venezia, 1891–1892) and " Raccolte delle Vere da Pozza " (Venezia, 1889).

Several of the illustrations are from pen-and-ink drawings done by Signor Giovanni Pellegrini from the originals of the subjects in Venice.

PAGE

THE STORY OF VENICE.

INTRODUCTION.

(A.D. 421–697.)

THE early story of Venice is lost in mystery ; and legends and myths take the place of facts and assertions in the pages of her first existence. One cannot but feel however that such mystery is not out of place, and that it suits well with the romance which her later story does but emphasize ; while one is almost glad that too strong a light cannot be thrown upon the origin and rise of a city, whose charm only gathers force from the glamour cast over her by an unknown and undefined past. Her inhabitants too claim an antiquity so remote as to equal, or rather excel, not only the rest of Italy, but that of Europe itself, since they trace their ancestry back to the heroes of Troy, and to the descendants of the Gods. The most popular tradition is that the Eneti or Heneti, one of the tribes in Paphlagonia who joined the Trojan cause after the fall of Troy, came to Italy under the leadership of Antenor, a kinsman of King Priam, and

first peopled the country known to us as Venetia.
Another account connects them with the Veneti, a
race on the western coast of Gaul. Previous to the
actual foundation and settlement of the town and
state of Venice, the islands of the lagunes had served
more than once as a haven of refuge to the inhabitants of the mainland from the incursions successively
of Alaric, Radagaisus, and other northern invaders.
Again and again did these early Venetians seek
temporary shelter in a spot which offered no temptation to the cupidity of their plunder-seeking foes, and
return when all danger was over to their desolated
homes on the mainland.

When however in 452 the invasion of Attila, "the
Scourge of God," and his Huns again drove the
people to flight, they determined to fix an abiding
and permanent dwelling-place among the isles and
estuaries of the sea ; and that moment may be looked
upon as the date of the foundation of Venice. The fury
of Attila had been directed chiefly against the Roman
province of Venetia, where he closely besieged Aquileja,
the capital of the province. After a long resistance
the city was taken and given over to the mercy of the
barbarians. No safety was to be found but in flight,
and the inhabitants of Aquileja fled to Grado, those of
Concordia to Caprularia (now Caorle) ; while more still
came from Padua, Asolo and Ceneda, and settled for
the most part on the islands of Rivus Altus and Metha-
maucus, or, as they are better known to us, Rialto and
Malamocco. Nothing was to be seen on all sides but
flight, consternation and distress, the one ruling idea
being to fly from the foe and find peace and security

in a region remote from the haunts of men. The islands lying out to sea suggested a haven where nothing existed to excite the greed of the conquerors, and where a refuge at once distant and extraordinary gave promise of a protection and shelter denied them elsewhere. The strange nature of such a territory is well described by Romanin, who says : " The lagunes are those waters of the Adriatic which, penetrating towards the plains of the mainland, form a basin of shallow waters, interspersed here and there with canals, and dotted with islands. A long, narrow tongue of land called *littorali*, or *lidi* (shores or banks), constitutes, so to speak, the confine which separates the lagune from the sea. This curved tongue, or line, whose convex part is toward the present city of Venice, while its concave side faces the sea, is split up by divers openings. These again form so many ports, and through them the tides act upon the waters, preserving the purity of the air, and facilitating the entrance and exit of large ships into the bay or basin where they can anchor in safety. The shores, or *lidi*, surrounding Venice are so many ramparts created by nature for the protection of the town ; and upon these she sits enthroned like a queen." [1]

That this was the aspect presented by the islands and lagunes more than three centuries before the Christian era is proved by the records of Livy and other writers. As time went on and the number of inhabitants increased it became necessary for human aid to assist the work of nature against the encroach-

[1] S. Romanin, " Lezioni di Storia Veneta," vol. i., lezione i.

THE LAGUNES OF VENICE.

ments of the sea. This work cannot be said to have reached its consummation until shortly before the extinction of the Venetian Republic, when from 1744–1782 the *Murazzi*, or walls, were built, forming ramparts in front of Chioggia and Malamocco (two of the southernmost ports of the Lido), and serving to break the force of the waves and weaken their flow towards Venice.[1] Thus bit by bit measures were taken to secure the haven planted in the salt waves and waters, on a spot which seemed destined for any purpose sooner than for that of the building of a city, whose houses and palaces were to be renowned for the beauty and solidity of their construction, and whose glory and magnificence were to rank among the wonders of the world.

A date often given and accepted for the foundation of Venice is that of March 25, 421, when the first church, that of S. Giacomo, was built at Rialto. This date however has little beyond a legendary tradition to render it authentic ; and the date of Attila's invasion, 452, is more generally recognised as that of the first existence of Venice, when the refugees from the mainland grasped with greater accuracy the need of abandoning for ever their country homes and establishing themselves fixedly in the water-city. It must be borne in mind that for some centuries in Venetian history the year dated from the 1st of March, the months of January and February reckon-

---

[1] A fit continuation of that colossal work is now being carried on by the Italian Government off the harbours of Treporti, Sant' Erasmo, and the Lido, in the construction of dykes and ramparts, whereby to regulate the supply of tidal water into the lagunes and canals of Venice.

ing as the eleventh and twelfth months in the preceding year.

The province of Venetia was rich in rivers, there being no less than seven in number, consisting of the Brenta, the Isonzo, the Tagliamento, the Livenza, the Piave, the Adige and the Po. These rivers all flow into the Adriatic and form the lagunes and *lidi,* which encompass Venice and compose too the labyrinth of canals and streams from whence the " Ocean's Queen " rises in strength and beauty. One of these streams, known as the Rialto or Rivo Alto, flowed past the island on which the seat of government was fixed, and from this the settlement derived its earliest name.

The island of Rialto, which in early times ranked as of slight importance, had been peopled from Padua, and for some time the Paduans continued to make use of it as a handy spot whereon to store their goods and all possessions necessary for the furtherance of their traffic and commerce. There can be no doubt that Rialto and its neighbouring islands were at first under the rule of the Roman cities of the mainland—Aquileja, Oderzo (Opitergium), and Padua—and probably took from them their earliest notions of government. But in 466 they shook off the yoke of these towns and began an independent course of jurisdiction by appointing Maritime Tribunes (*Tribuni Marittimi*) to govern in each island. A kind of federation then existed throughout the isles, which, while leaving each tribune to rule over his own magistracy, afforded protection and union to the whole group of islands.

A glance at the affairs of Italy and the invasions, which successively desolated the land, will help to point out the effect that these doings on the main-land had on the rising Republic. From 493 to 526 Theodoric, King of the Goths, ruled and governed in Italy. His chancellor, the great Roman Cassiodorus, has left a series of letters describing the habits and customs of the people among whom he travelled, one of which speaks of the Venetians.[1] He alludes to the way they undertook journeys of small or great dis-tances by sea ; of the tranquillity and safety of their mode of living, and of the simplicity of their habits since rich and poor alike have but one kind of food, namely, fish ; he describes how they all live in the same sort of houses, and are above the jealousies and envies that assail the rest of humanity. He enlarges upon the wealth they derive from their trade in salt, a possession, he adds, superior to gold, since salt being a necessity required by every one is a source of never failing income and above all other riches. This record of the sixth century, and about a hundred years after Attila's invasion, is of special interest as proving how, even in those early times, the Venetians had made a name for themselves as a seafaring people, how flourishing was their trade, especially in salt ; how widespread the industry and prosperity of their state ; while the writer goes on to speak also of the art and dexterity employed by the Venetians in establishing and building their town.

In 539 the Gothic power came for awhile to an end in Italy, when Belisarius, the greatest of the

[1] Cassiod. Var. Lib. xii., Ep. vii.

Emperor Justinian's generals, overcame Vitalius, King of the Goths, and established the Greek authority in the peninsula. When from motives of jealousy Belisarius was recalled to Constantinople, and the Greek conquerors made their rule too unbearable, the Goths determined to expel them, and, choosing Totila for their leader, again invaded the country. These wars were occasionally carried into the heart of Venetia, and now and again the Venetians themselves took part in the war operations. This was the case when Narses the Eunuch, general of Justinian's forces after the recall of Belisarius, applied to them for boats wherein to convey his troops to besiege Ravenna, and the Venetians proved equal to the task. Another sign of their increasing power is also shown in the appeal made by the Paduans to Narses to stop the Venetians from trading on the Brenta and the Bacchiglione. The Venetians had established themselves on these rivers and entirely monopolised the commerce. But so completely had they asserted their sway, that Narses merely bade the Paduans be reconciled to their rivals, a clear proof that Venice had now gained supremacy, and ascendency over the older town from whence so much of her population had sprung.

In the year 568 Italy was again overrun: this time by the wildest horde that Germany had yet sent forth, in the shape of the Longobardi or Lombards under their king, Alboin. These barbarians first took possession of the province of Friuli; from there they spread over Venetia. Again were those dwellers on the mainland, who had dreamed of

GENERAL VIEW OF TORCELLO. (*From "Calli e Canali." Ferd. Ongania. Venezia*, 1891–1892.)

safety in their inland homes, forced to seek the
shelter patronised of old by their neighbours, and
repair to the lagunes. It was chiefly from the town
of Altinum (Altino) that the refugees now poured
forth, and from this exodus arose the legend of the
peopling of Torcello and its more immediate isles.
Tradition says the exiles named the isles from the
gates of their old town, and that they took in turn
the names of Torcellus (Torcello), Maiurbus (Maz-
zorbo), Boreana (Burano), Ammiana, Constantiacum,
and Anianum. The story runs that : " When Alboin
was bearing down upon the land and terror was
in every heart the inhabitants determined to seek
Divine assistance, and with tears implored for
guidance from above. A sign was granted to them
in that they saw the birds and pigeons suddenly flying from the wells, and leave their nests, carrying in
their beaks their young. This was accepted by them
as an indication that they too should seek safety in
flight. They decided to do so, and divided into three
compagnies, one going towards Istria, another to
Ravenna, while the third remained in perplexity as
to their destination. For three days they fasted, and
on the third day they heard a voice saying : ' Ascend
the towers and look to the stars.' They obeyed, and
saw before them in the distance objects resembling
boats and islands. In obedience to the heavenly
vision they embarked, taking with them their wives
and children, and all they could likewise convey of
their household goods and possessions, and preceded
by the bishop and clergy bearing the sacred vessels
and relics they sailed off to the lagunes, and there

CATHEDRAL OF TORCELLO, AND CHURCH OF STA. FOSCA. (*From "Calli e Canali," op. cit.*)

fixed their habitations." There is much to prove that these early settlers in the islands were a people of a refined and cultured nature ; a people too whose religion was of a noble and elevating kind, and who clung to that religion with a love and veneration that took palpable and abiding form in the churches now arising on all sides, adorned with the marble pillars, carvings, and decorations which the refugees were able to carry away from their forsaken homes. They were at the same time given to art and literature, and the esteem they had for letters is shown in the writings of Virgil, Livy, Cornelius Gallus, Cornelius Nepos, Catullus, Pliny, and others ; while as builders and architects they were soon to take rank in a manner that has rarely been equalled and perhaps never excelled. But their chief characteristic shone out pre-eminently in their love of freedom. The homes they had secured to themselves with such labour and difficulty they were determined to maintain free and intact. For several centuries the lesson of discipline acquired by hardship, toil, and strife was to bear fruit in a struggle for freedom and independence that, once gained, placed Venice on a height of splendid altitude, and raised her to a lofty pinnacle among the nations, where she maintained herself for nearly a thousand years, and from whence she descended only when her great mission was accomplished and Europe needed her no more.

A few years after the invasion of the Lombards the first political transaction in which Venice was engaged took place. This was in 584, when Longinus, Exarch of Ravenna, on his way back to Constantinople, visited the islands of the lagunes and, struck with the prosperity, the administration and the industry of the rising state, suggested to the inhabitants the advisability of entering into negotiations with his sovereign, the Eastern Emperor. The Venetians, fully alive to the advantages of such an offer, and aware too, that such an alliance, far from hinting at subjection or dependence would but raise their position and importance, consented to send envoys to Constantinople. These were received by the Emperor with all honour; and among other favours a diploma was granted them, assuring them of the protection of the Imperial forces, together with full liberty and safety to their trade. This is the first link in that great chain which was to bind Venice to the Levant, and was the beginning of a long series of events destined afterwards to prove of such force and interest in her story, and to colour with lines of such vivid and dazzling tints so much of her art, her history and her career. It must, however, be borne in mind that this league contained no hint of thraldom, submission, or homage on the part of Venice; on the contrary, her independence and freedom were but more fully asserted and maintained by such an act, while her position was raised still higher among other nations and states.

The question as to the dependence or the freedom of Venice in her early state is one hardly necessary to impose upon the reader. The controversy is a long and complicated one; and whereas the enemies of Venice have proved her subjection to the Emperors of the East, to the dominions of Rome, of Greece and of other states, her partisans have equally proved the absolute freedom in which she existed from the very earliest times. As in all such arguments there is probably a certain amount to be said on both sides ; and perhaps the truth can only be arrived at by holding a middle course between the two opinions. It is enough to know that Venice shook off a yoke that once bid fair to oppress her, and rose with lightened strength and activity to heights of liberty and glory gained for her by her own will and power.

LION OF ST. MARK OF THE YEAR 1600.

I.

THE FIRST DOGES.

(697–811.)

HAVING briefly considered how the town of Venice came into existence, it may be well before proceeding further to consider for a moment the manner in which the dwellings and habitations which formed the town took shape and being, and also what measures were adopted to secure the ground whereon these homes and houses were about to be established. The buildings which remain to this day attest to what a height the early Venetians attained in the art of architecture, and when the difficulties of the ground and the wildness of the spot are considered, it is strange to think how from the shifting unstable formation of mudbanks and sand-isles a city could arise, whose beauty would remain unequalled, and whose strength and solidity would seem to defy even time itself. One of the first cares of these early builders was to assure themselves of the ground chosen by them for their homesteads. From very early days they devoted themselves to reclaiming the land, consolidating the banks of the islands with piles and palisades, and protecting the edges of the soil with palings and devices of different kinds, thus securing their habitations against the encroachments of the sea and the incessant action of the water.

The houses at first consisted only of the ground floor, with a kind of attic or garret over it, but in a very short time the increasing number of the population, and the need felt to avoid the damp and near

LADY DYEING HER HAIR ON THE HOUSETOP.
(*From " Diversarum Nationum Habitus."   Opera Petri Bertelli-Patavii.   1589.)*

proximity to the water, led to the erection of upper floors and storeys.   Few houses of any size or pretension were to be found that had not on the top the *altana*, a small kind of loggia or gallery used for both household and artistic purposes, since here the linen was dried, and here too the ladies of Venice would sit in days of yore and dry their hair in the sun, so as to obtain those hues of golden auburn dye with which the brushes of Titian, Tintoret and Paolo Veronese have made us familiar. Coryat, however, tells us

STAIRCASE AND COURTYARD AT S. CASSIANO.
(*From Yriarte ; Venise, Histoire, Art, &c. Paris, Rothschild,* 1877.)

otherwise, and says : " These kinde of tarrasses or little galleries of pleasure Suetonius calleth meniana. They giue great grace to the whole edifice, and serue only for this purpose, that people may from that place as from a most delectable prospect, contemplate and view the parts of the city round about them in the coole euening." [1] The entrance to a Venetian house was generally by a covered porch, which gave on to an open courtyard, and from whence a staircase led to the upper floors, this staircase being almost always exterior and open to the air. The windows had shutters, such as those used by the Romans; and fireplaces (*camini* or *fumajuoli*) were in use in Venice at a date when they were extremely rare and almost unknown to the rest of Europe. The streets

GONDOLA. (*From a picture of Carpaccio.* 1400.)

and bridges were then few in number, and scattered at wide intervals. The approach to a house, though possible by the land way along the *fondamenta* (a sort of quay), was chiefly resorted to by the water way, this being considered an easier approach, either for intercourse or for the conveyance of wares. These— and it must be borne in mind how the nobles of Venice were also traders and merchants—were gene-rally stored in the vast cellars and spaces, which formed the ground floor and served then, as now, for storeplaces, or for housing the gondolas of the dwellers on the upper floors. The name of "gon-dola" was adopted in very early times, though the

[1] Coryat's "Crudities," London, 1611.

boat so called was different both in size and purpose, and the one so associated with Venetian life and history.[1]

The important office as to the administration of the soil was one that from the earliest times claimed the attention of the Venetians ; and at the date of the election of the first Doge at Rialto, early in the ninth century, we find that certain magistrates were chosen to superintend the drying of the land, the excavations to be made here and there, the formation of some new canals, and the closing of others. The appearance the town presented then was widely different to that which it bears now. The houses in those days were few and far between, and the winding canals betwixt gardens, orchards and patches of cultivated ground with green trees and flowering shrubs must have worn an aspect very dissimilar to the huddled together, crowded, though ever lovely Venice of to-day. The following description from Romanin [2] will help to put before us somewhat of the look of the city in those remote ages. "The sandy banks and shores were alternated with gardens, with meadows, with woods ; masts and white sails contrasted with the green of the trees, as did fishers' nets with the flocks pasturing

[1] The word "gondola," according to some writers, is derived from the Greek "kondy" and the Latin "cymbula," and was originally a large, broad boat attached for transport uses to the service of sea-going vessels. In course of time the gondola changed its shape and purpose again and again, till at the close of the last century it assumed, by orders of the Council of Ten, the sober, sombre appearance now so familiar, and discarded the bright, gaudy hues immortalised by painters in many an old picture.

[2] Romanin, "Lezioni di Storia Veneta," Lezione I.

around.   On the banks were houses of stone, or more often of wood covered with straw, or reeds, or tiles; and in front of these were short stretches of land, from whence originated the *fondamente*.   There were bridges of wood fastened on to stakes, and narrow, twisting alleys interspersed with frequent halting places, or else overgrown with grass or reeds, from whence one part of the town was called in consequence *Cannaregio*.   In front of the churches or chapels the ground opened out into wider proportions, and formed that kind of square called in Venice *Campo* (field), since from having originally been grass-grown it was afterwards set apart for the markets, as in the Middle Ages these were wont to be held in front of the churches."

As the community increased in numbers and importance dissensions arose among the tribunes appointed by the several islands, which rendered it necessary to entrust the government to the hands of a single administrator ; it being hoped in this way by restraining these dissensions to bring unity and peace to the rising settlement, and also to add dignity and importance to the post of governor itself.   This governor was to bear the title of Doge (Dux or Duke) ; and in the nature of these Doges of Venice there was an element so special and apart that some account of the fashions, habits and laws by which they were environed is necessary in order to understand the prominent part played by them in the following story.

Their power, at first almost unlimited and absolute, was cut down bit by bit, and eventually circumscribed so closely that in later days they were hardly more than lay figures of the great republic over which they were set as governors. It is also curious to note that while the Doges were gradually despoiled of power and authority, greater pomp and ceremonial was heaped about their person ; and when the inner might decayed, the outer man was adorned with a show and glitter unsupported by depth and actuality of strength within.

In all ecclesiastical affairs the authority of the Doges was great, especially in the appointment of bishops ; the military power, however, was confided to a " Master of the Forces " (*Maestro dei Militi*), subject to the will of the Doge. The ducal revenues consisted partly in tithes, partly in lands, forests, pasture grounds, rents from the salt trade, together with tributes of fish, game, vegetables, wine and fruit. They had also certain rights in regard of hunting, felling timber, and other privileges which brought them in large fortunes. Moreover, some Doges, not ashamed of their former occupations, continued after their election to pursue their trades, and owned " argosies with portly sail " and " ships of rich lading," wherewith to increase their income. It is easy, consequently, to believe in the great wealth often possessed by them ; and many proofs still exist of the noble way in which they endowed churches and monasteries, and adorned them with memorials befitting the magnificence of the donors.

The habits of the earlier Doges were active and simple. They rose betimes in the morning, even before daybreak, when after hearing mass, they attended to legal matters, and sat—always in public—for the

administration of justice, afterwards devoting themselves to the other various affairs of the state. The
dress of the Doge (at all events in those early times)
was a mantle of silk, with a gold fringe, fastened with
gold buttons or studs ; under this was a short cassock
with straight sleeves, a high ruff, and a fur collar. The
shoes and stockings were red. The earlier form of
the famous ducal bonnet was merely a cap, differing
slightly from those worn by other rulers and princes,
of a round high shape, trimmed all around with a

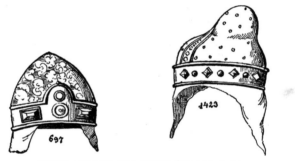

DUCAL CAPS OF THE YEARS 697 AND 1423.

wide braid, with three white knobs, sometimes pearls,
on the top, and in no way resembling the ducal bonnet
of later days. It was afterwards reduced in size, when
the high peak was altered to two smaller ones, divided
by a button ; and by degrees its whole shape was
changed and re-arranged till it took the shape generally represented in pictures. No mention is made in
the earlier records of the *Corno ducale*, indeed it is not
spoken of under that name till the sixteenth century ;
but in the documents of the thirteenth and fourteenth

centuries it is always called *birettum*, while a more
ornate cap, reserved for great occasions, was known
under the name of *zoja*, or jewel. Underneath the
ducal bonnet the Doge always wore a white cap of the
very finest linen, so that, should he have occasion to
remove the bonnet, his head, in token of his dignity,
should always remain covered. The Doges were entitled to wear the sword ; they had also a sceptre and
an ivory throne ; and when they went out in public
they were protected, as in the East, by a kind of
baldachino or umbrella, and escorted by men with
lighted torches, trumpets and standards. On certain
solemn days the Doge showed himself in public and
blessed the people, who in return acknowledged this
half-religious, half-secular character of their leaders by
offering up antiphonal prayers, as in the Greek for-
mula, for them in the churches. At the funeral of
a Doge the ceremony was half Greek and half Lombard.

The election of the Doge was at first the act of the
whole community, divided into classes, consisting of
the Greater (Majores), the Middle (Mediocres), and
the Lesser (Minores) Class ; whereunto were added
all the lowest of the people as well (" et magna Venetorum conglobatio "). Thus the entire population took
part in the nomination of their Doge, and from this
can be traced that spirit of democracy which entered
so largely into the government of the Republic, and
played so prominent a part in her early history. The
part taken by the populace in the choice of their
supreme magistrate is a mark of great note in Venetian
story, and one much dwelt on by all her chroniclers.

But it will be seen how gradually this power was withdrawn from the people, till in 1423, at the election of Doge Foscari, the harangue (*arengo*), whereby the public had been wont to assert their voice for or against the candidate to the dukedom, was entirely abolished ; and from thenceforward all share taken by the people in the nomination of their Doge was swept away for ever. It does not appear that the powers of the first Doges were very clearly defined, though it is certain that the tribunes still existed as assistant magistrates. But no great or important question such as war or peace, the fixing of taxes, the passing of laws, or any other affairs of moment, could be concluded without the unanimous voice and consent of the people.

The Doge's sway extended in those early days over a territory restricted to twelve townships and islands that constituted the Dogado ; and consisted of Grado, Bibbione, Caorle, Heraclea, Jesolo, Torcello, Murano, Rialto, Malamocco, Poveglia, Clugia Minor, and Clugia Major or Chioggia. Of these some have disappeared, swept away by war or time, while others again played an important part in the history of Venice. The first point of historic interest is centred in Heraclea, where the seat of ducal government was first fixed, and where for some years it flourished. The town partook of an essentially aristocratic nature, and was a fierce rival of its neighbour, the democratic town of Jesolo or Equilius, so called from its celebrated breed of horses. Heraclea, situate at the mouth of the river Piave, was founded about 688 by the refugees from Oderzo, who, under the guidance of their bishop, Magno, fled for safety from the invasion and persecution of Rotari, King of the Lombards. In 805 Heraclea was destroyed by Obelerio, Tribune of Malamocco, but it rose again under the name of Citta Nova. In 903 it was destroyed by the Huns, and at the present day no traces of it remain.

The actual date when the first Doge of Venice was chosen is uncertain, but the year 697 is the one most generally accepted, when Paolo Lucio, or Paolucio Anafesto, a native of Heraclea, was elected to the dignity. When the unanimous voice of the people had confirmed the Doge's election, and he had received from them the oath of allegiance, the Doge was carried on the shoulders of his new subjects round the square to the Church of St. Theodore,[1] where he swore to observe the laws, and devote himself to the welfare of his people. The Pope was after this informed of his nomination, and there is reason to think it was announced to the Greek Emperor as well.

The reign of Anafesto was far from peaceful. A fierce war was raging between Ravenna and Constantinople, both of them towns on whose good-will much of the prosperity and trade of Venice depended. In order to secure a firm ally in these troublous moments, the Doge formed a league, the first on record of such a nature, with Luitprand, King of the Lombards, by which numerous advantages were secured to Venice.

---

[1] The Church of St. Theodore stood where that of St. Mark now stands, and was, with the Church of St. Geminiano which stood opposite it, erected in 552 by Narses, in fulfilment of a vow, and to celebrate his victory over the Goths.

The extent of her territory on the mainland was enlarged, its limits, marked by dykes and ditches, were
well defined, and she on her part undertook to pay an
annual sum as a just equivalent for the many privileges
vouchsafed to her.

Doge Anafesto died in 717, while engaged in quell-
ing some of the many tumults raised against him by
internal jealousies and factions, and was succeeded by
Marcello Tegaliano.   Marcello was the head (*maestro*)
of the army, and on his nomination to the ducal
throne, this office was merged for the time being in
the higher dignity of Doge.   His reign of nine years
was a peaceful one, only disturbed by a religious controversy between the sees of Aquileja and Grado, the
rights of which were referred for settlement to both
the Pope and the Doge.

On the death of Marcello in 726, Orso Ipato was
chosen to be Doge, who like his two predecessors was
a native of Heraclea.   The reign of Orso is celebrated
for the part taken by him and his people with Leo III.
the Isaurian, Emperor of Constantinople, against their
former ally, Luitprand, King of the Lombards, and
the Pope.   Gregory II. had called on Luitprand to aid
him in resisting the arrogance of Leo, whose command
for the destruction of images, and overweening attitude
towards Italy, alarmed the Pontiff.   Venice, who was
steadily rising to a position of moral and political
importance, determined now to come openly to the
front and to throw in her lot with the power most
calculated to help her attain her desired end of becoming a great state.   She joined forces with the
Emperor Leo, and sent a large supply of men and

ships to assist him in wresting Ravenna from Luitprand. The allies were entirely successful ; and to
mark his sense of the services received by him, Leo
granted to the Venetians numerous privileges and
concessions as to their trade, and bestowed on the
Doge the title of Hypatos [1] (Consul) for the personal
share he had taken in the war.

But hardly was this war at an end before disturbances and riots broke out in the home
administration, which resulted in the murder of
Orso (737) and in a change as to the government.
It was thought that the late Doge had shown proclivities of too warlike a nature, and to avoid the
recurrence of such an evil it was settled to abolish
the office of Doge, and appoint instead *Maestri dei
Militi*, who were to remain but one year at the head
of affairs. This rule lasted for only five or six years,
when the dignity of Doge was reinstated, and the
seat of government transferred from Heraclea to
Malamocco. The new Doge was a son of the late
Orso, by name Deodato. He was elected in 742, and
had already ruled as Master of the Forces.

Under the reign of Doge Deodato the commerce
of Venice was carried on with increasing vigour and
success, but the Doge was unable to escape the jealousies and factions, which raged between the rival townships and proved a source of constant bloodshed and
disturbance to the rising state. Deodato, though a
Heraclean, had been forced to dwell and govern at
Malamocco, which, together with Jesolo, shared the

---

[1] From the Greek, signifying superiority, and also denoting specially
the office of consul.

democratic tendencies opposed to those of aristocratic Heraclea. While the Doge was engaged in forti-fying a castle at Brondolo, close to Chioggia, he was attacked by Galla Gaulo, a native of Jesolo, who seized him and caused his eyes to be put out in the barbarous Greek fashion often adopted at Venice. This consisted of exposure over a brazier of burning coal. Galla then seized on the throne and took possession of Malamocco, where for a year he was able to maintain himself at the head of affairs ; but at the end of that time the people rose in rebellion against him, deposed him from office, and meted out to him the same measure he had dealt to his prede-cessor.

Domenico Monegario, the first citizen of Mala-mocco who was advanced to the dignity, was named Doge in 756, on the deposition of Galla, and an effort was now made to curb and limit the ducal power by the appointment of two tribunes, who were to be associated with the Doge. This step however led only to fresh disputes and wranglings, and for the eight years of his reign the Doge had to endure this annual nomination of the tribunes. In 764, after an ineffectual struggle to establish peace and quiet, Monegario suffered the fate of his two prede-cessors : his eyes were put out, and he was deprived of the dukedom, while the office of the tribunes was abolished for ever.

His successor was Maurizio Galbajo, of Heraclea, a man of high lineage and noble family, with a mind and intellect fitted for his position, and able to cope with the difficulties of his situation. The stride that

Venice made during this reign towards consolidating still more her advance as a state and power is shown in the determination now resolved upon to nominate a bishop to administer to the spiritual wants of the growing city.   A vast concourse of the people met at Grado to elect their bishop.   The Patriarch of Grado, in his capacity of metropolitan of the province, presided over the assembly, and the seat of the new diocese was fixed at Olivolo, now Castello, when Obelerio of Malamocco was appointed as first bishop. The bishops of Castello continued to hold office till the middle of the fifteenth century; their title was then merged in that of Patriarch of Venice, when the metropolitan see was transferred from Grado to Venice, where the title and dignity of Patriarch remain to this day.

Galbajo, in his old age, feeling the cares of office weigh heavy on his shoulders, associated his son Giovanni with him in the government, and at his death in 787 this son Giovanni became Doge.   He in his turn associated his son Maurizio with him, and father and son remained in power till 807, when they were overturned by a rebellion headed by Fortunato, the Patriarch of Grado, who was bent on avenging the murder of his uncle and predecessor Giovanni. This Giovanni had been basely murdered by the Galbaji, and Fortunato, his nephew and successor, stirred up the people with such effect that the Doge and his son were deposed, driven out of the realm, and with difficulty escaped alive to Mantua.

After their deposition Obelerio, Tribune of Malamocco, was appointed Doge, and his reign proved an important one in Venetian annals, as the question now arose whether Venice should place herself under the dominion of the Franks—who, under the rule of Charlemagne and his son Pepin, had driven the Lombards out of Italy and settled themselves in their stead—or under that of the rulers of Constantinople.   Space does not allow of detailing the way in which the Venetian Government hesitated alternately between the King of the Franks and the Emperor of the East.   Suffice it to say, that Venice proved true to her traditions of liberty and independence, and chose the more perilous, but far more glorious, course of shaking off alike the two contending powers, and asserted her own liberty and line of action in a manner, which henceforward proclaimed her free of both king and emperor.   It was now too that arose the legends as to the battles fought by the Venetians for this liberty against the Franks, and though it is difficult to tell where fiction ends and fact begins, there exists sufficient foundation for the story that tells of one great encounter, when the Franks were defeated with such terrible loss that the canal between the islands of S. Servolo and S. Clemente, where this fight took place, was called in consequence the "Orphans' Canal" (*Canal Orfano*), from the number of children left fatherless on that day.   It is said the Venetians craftily allured the Franks into the shallow canals, and assaulted them when the tide was out, and the heavy vessels were unable either to manœuvre or escape.   The actual date of the battle against the Franks is uncertain, but there is little doubt that it occurred during the reign of Obelerio. This Doge had early associated his brother Beato with him on the throne, and a few years after (808) a third brother, Valentino, was also joined to the ducal power. The three brothers were the last Doges who reigned at Malamocco. In 810 they were found conspiring to bring their country under the dominion of the Franks, and were deposed as traitors from office. It was then determined to remove the seat of government to Rialto, that island being looked upon as a safer and more central spot for the administration of office, and one removed from the danger of assault and invasion, to which the more outlying town of Malamocco had been exposed. With this important action of the transfer of the seat of government the first epoch of Venetian history comes to an end ; an epoch full of uncertain traditions and doubtful legends, but still outlining to some extent the rise and origin of the Venetian people and of their weird watery home.

CAPITAL OF COLUMN.
(*From a drawing at the Marciana.*)

II.

RELIGIOUS AND CIVIL PROGRESS.

(811–991.)

THE history of Venice has now reached a period when a clearer light shines in upon her records, and when the characters and actors in her story assume by degrees a stronger personality, beginning with Agnello (or, as he is sometimes wrongly called, Angelo) Partecipazio. By many historians he is reckoned as the first Doge of Venice, whereas, counting his predecessors at Heraclea and Malamocco, he ranks actually as tenth on the list. It was by his advice and judgment that Rialto was chosen in preference to Malamocco as the seat of government, and subsequent events were to prove the wisdom of such a decision. Apart from the geographical and political advantages secured by this choice, there was also a religious side to the question, which in those times ranked of as much, if not more, importance as the other two. A legend ran that some centuries previously, when St. Mark had sailed from Alexandria to Aquileja to preach the Christian faith, he had been overtaken by a storm and forced to put in on one of the islands of the lagunes (said to have been that where the Church of S. Francesco della Vigna now stands). Here an angel appeared to him, and greeting him with the words, " Pax tibi Marce Evangelista meus," told him that near to that place where he now found shelter his bones should one day rest and be held in veneration. The fulfilment of this prophecy was ever present in the expectation of many a Venetian mind, and the religious argument did but confirm the secular one in establishing their hopes as well as their church and government around Rialto. The prediction was to be accomplished ere long ; but first a glance must be given at the affairs leading up to that fulfilment, together with an outline of the story of the Partecipazio family.

In 811 the General Council (*General Concione*) had unanimously appointed Agnello Partecipazio Doge of Venice. He was a noble of Heraclea, and several of his ancestors had been tribunes at Rialto, where the family had settled when they came to Venice. One of his first cares was to rebuild his native town of Heraclea, which now rose again under the name of Città Nova. He also lost no time in inviting the people who had fled before the Franks to return and repeople the places left desolate by the foreign invasion ; and at the same time urged on progress and development in every direction, appointing architects, engineers, and overseers for the embellishment and improvement of the town of Rialto, and for providing in every way against the encroachment of the waters, and for the security of the soil. He laid the foundations of the first ducal palace, though fires and alterations have left no traces of his work in the

glorious building now familiar to us.   Close by stood
the Church of St. Theodore, and served then, as St.
Mark's did for so many centuries after, as the private
chapel of the Doges.   In the reign of Agnello's son,
Giovanni, St. Theodore had to give way to St. Mark
as the patron saint of the town, which from hence-

WINGED LION ON THE COLUMN IN THE PIAZZETTA.
(*From a photograph made when the Lion was taken down for repair.*)

forward adopted the emblem of the winged lion as
the badge of the Republic.

The external government of Doge Agnello was
marked by the friendly relations he maintained with
Charlemagne and also with the Greek Emperor, with
whom he renewed old treaties and formed new ones,

confirming to Venice fresh privileges, and establishing even more decidedly her freedom and independence. In spite of the peace and prosperity secured by Agnello both within and around his dominions, he was unable to promote tranquillity in his own family; and the jealousies between his two sons, Giustinian and Giovanni, both of whom were alternately associated with him in the ducal power, proved a source of constant trouble and difficulty to him. After numerous disputes and rivalries between the brothers, Giovanni saw prudent to retire to Constantinople, while Giustinian remained to share his father's throne. This habit of associating a son or a brother in the dukedom was of frequent occurrence in the early annals of Venetian story. The tendency which the practice involved of making the dignity hereditary in one family always met with determined opposition from the people, whose plea that they had fought for the liberty of being governed by a ruler of their choice, not by a succession of hereditary monarchs, was generally supported by stern measures of revolt and bloodshed when any danger imperilled a disregard of their rights.

The spirit of this age was eminently religious, and the Doges, both father and son, availed themselves of this to establish their power and popularity, and at the same time indulge their own pious tastes. They founded and endowed the convent of S. Servilio, or Sèrvolo, on the island of the same name,[1] and also that of Sant' Ilario; while about the same time the Emperor, Leo the Armenian,

[1] Now a lunatic asylum for men.

although an iconoclast, sent them the body of San Zaccaria,[1] and other relics, an act of courtesy for which the Venetians undertook to pray for the well-being of the Emperor and of his heirs.

In 827 Agnello Partecipazio died, and his son Giustinian succeeded his father as sole Doge. He was then far from young, and the first part of his short reign was disturbed by differences between the patriarchs of Grado and Aquileja. These differences involved not only an ecclesiastical question, but, still more, a political one between the Empire of the Franks and Venice ; and in after times these disputes led occasionally to arguments which were only settled by the sword.

The event of most importance, however, in the reign of Giovanni Partecipazio was the acquisition of the body of St. Mark, and consequent foundation of the church called after the saint, and built to receive his remains. We have seen how the Venetians were on the look-out, so to speak, for the bones of the Evangelist, and the way in which they obtained the longed for treasure was as follows : Two Venetian merchants, Bono of Malamocco and Rustico of Torcello, were trafficking, or, perhaps, smuggling, at Alexandria, when they heard

[1] The Church of S. Zaccaria, as we now know it, was built in 1456, but the first church that originally stood there is attributed to St. Magno in the seventh century. It was famed for the privileges granted to it by popes and emperors, for the wealth of its revenues, and for the annual visit paid by the Doge. Eight Doges were buried in the original building, namely, Pietro Tradonico, 864 ; Orso Partecipazio, 881 ; Pietro Tribuno, 912 ; Tribuno Memo, 991 ; Pietro Orseolo II., 1009 ; Domenico Flabanico, 1042 ; Vital Michiel I., 1102 ; Vital Michiel II., 1173.

CHURCH OF S. ZACCARIA. (*From "Calli e Canali," op. cit.*)

of the depredations committed by the Saracens on
all Christian edifices. Rumour also said that the
temple of St. Mark, rich beyond most other
churches in marbles and precious stones, and containing beside the body of the saint, was in danger
from their cupidity. Knowing the legend that fore-
told how St. Mark's bones were to rest in Venice,
and well aware of the credit that would accrue to
them could they return home with so coveted and
eagerly expected a possession, they determined to
gain it. By means of eloquent arguments and large
bribes, the two merchants persuaded the guardians
of the church to part with the saint's remains, and
finally found themselves owners of the desired relic.
Their next puzzle was how to convey their prize
out of the country, and pass unchallenged the
scrutiny of the Custom House. But having overcome the difficulty of acquisition, they were not to
be defrauded of the enjoyment of possession, and
craftily hid the body at the bottom of a basket,
covering it entirely over with pork. The horror of
the Moslems on being confronted with what was to
them the acme of abomination can be imagined.
Exclaiming with disgust, " Khanzir, Khanzir," they
averted their eyes from the defiling spectacle of
" swine's flesh," little dreaming of the treasure which
lay beneath. The basket with its precious contents
was removed out of their sight, and transferred in
safety on board the merchant vessels, and after a
stormy and perilous journey arrived in Venice on
January 31, 828. The joy that reigned throughout
the town at the acquisition of such a treasure was

untold ; and the Doge lost no time in setting to work to construct a resting-place for the saint's bones, now come, according to the old prophecy, to find rest and honour in the heart of the lagunes. The Square of St. Mark presented a very different aspect then to what it does now, and it is not easy to present it to one's imagination when it was simply a green field, planted with trees and called in consequence, *brolo*, or *broglio*, *i.e.*, "garden " or " orchard." The Canal Batario divided the Square, and the Church of St. Geminiano formed its boundary at that date, but was afterwards moved further down, when Doge Vitale Michiel II. (1156–1172) enlarged the Piazza to its present dimensions, and covered in the Canal.

Close to the palace begun by his father, and adjoining the small church of St. Theodore, Doge Giustinian Participazio laid the foundation of the ducal chapel, or Church of St. Mark, afterwards to become so famous for its riches and beauty, and laid the body of the saint to rest under the high altar. St. Mark was now proclaimed patron of the town in the room of St. Theodore, who had occupied that position for so many years, and who had now to resign his high office. His statue erect on a crocodile was still allowed to remain on the column in the Piazzetta, opposite the one where the emblem of his successor stands triumphant ; perhaps to prove how the saints had agreed to bury their rivalry and watch in harmonious union and charity over the welfare and interests of the city committed, in turn, to their protection.

WELL HEAD IN THE COURTYARD OF THE PALAZZO CORNARO AT
S. SAMUELE.

(*From " Raccolte delle Vere da Pozzo," Venezia, Ongania,* 1889.)

The Doge did not live to see the work of his chapel begun ; he died in 829, leaving large legacies to the monasteries of Sant' Ilario and S. Zaccaria, as well as gifts of money, marbles, and precious stones for the building of St. Mark. He was succeeded by his brother Giovanni, whom he had recalled from Constantinople a short time before, and associated with him in his office.

The Church of St. Mark was consecrated during the reign of this Doge, but, with the exception of this auspicious event, fortune does not seem to have smiled on this third of the Partecipazii. He was ever fighting and contending to keep peace and order in his dominions, and that with small success. A powerful league was formed against him, headed by Obelerio, the Doge who had been deposed in 810, and who, backed by his supporters at Malamocco and Vigilia, threatened to overturn Giovanni. But the Doge acted with promptness and vigour. The rebellion was suppressed, Obelerio beheaded, and his head exposed on a pole as a warning to traitors. The seeds were not stamped out, but bore fruit in a fresh revolution, this time headed by one Pietro Caroso, who, on the plea of putting an end to the Partecipazio dynasty, endeavoured to make himself Doge. He succeeded in so far that Doge Giovanni had to fly ; and for six months Caroso remained at the head of affairs. At the end of that time the lawful Doge was reinstated, and Caroso deposed, blinded, and exiled. Partecipazio could not, however, turn the tide of events or stem the current surging so strongly against him. In 836 he was arrested when leaving the cathedral church of Olivolo, and forcibly made to enter a monastery at Grado, where he soon after died.

The faction opposed to the house of Partecipazio, and to the succession that had almost become a rule in their family, resolved to adopt an altogether different line of action. They chose as Doge, Pietro Tradonico, whose ancestors belonged to Jesolo, the rival town of Heraclea, from which sprang the Partecipazii, and opposed in every way to the aristocratic traditions clinging around this latter town. The unanimous applause that hailed Tradonico's appointment proved that the people were in favour of such a choice, and that they, too, were opposed to the hereditary tendency, which had crept so insidiously to the front in so short a time. The new Doge was a man of energy and power, and his talents were called into play by the wars he had to wage against the pirates of Croatia and Dalmatia, as well as against the Saracens and Turks, whose forces and numbers overcame the Venetians on more than one occasion. The Doge's son, Giovanni, was associated with him in the dukedom; but he had a more powerful aid and ally in the person of the Eastern Emperor, who had invoked his assistance against the Saracens, and who entered with him into a league offensive and defensive against these formidable foes.

Doge Tradonico also signed a treaty with Lothair, Emperor of Germany, and this treaty is of special interest, since it is the first document relating to Venetian diplomacy which has come down to our times. It was drawn up at Pavia in 840, and in it the limits of traffic and trading, both for Venetians and for Lothair's subjects, were defined, together with other mutual and numerous advantages. On the death of Lothair in 855, the Venetians sent deputies to his successor, Louis, to confirm the treaty and the other friendly relations into which they had entered with his predecessor ; and soon after Louis decided to visit in person the city whose alliance was now beginning to be an important object to kings and emperors, and whose position as a power and a state was daily growing in the political world around. Louis was accompanied by his wife, Engelberga, and received by the Doge with all the pomp and ceremonial befitting such an occasion. The royal visit lasted three days, when the Emperor stood sponsor to the Doge's grandson, inspected the town, and departed, having greatly strengthened the links of friendship and cordiality with its ruler and its people.

In spite of the outward appearance of prosperity presented by such doings, things were far from settled in Venice. A plot was forming against the life of the Doge, who was accused of having become haughty and overbearing. Some acts, which his foes ascribed to pride and despotism, led to a rebellion against him, and he was treacherously murdered on Easter Tuesday, April 2, 861, as he was leaving the Church of S. Zaccaria. His body, abandoned and neglected amid the confusion and tumult that ensued, was found by the nuns of the Convent of S. Zaccaria, and by them laid to rest in the vestibule of this

church, of which, during his lifetime, Doge Tradonico
(or Gradenigo, as his family name afterwards became)
had been a constant and generous patron. It was
he who instituted one of the well-known festivals
(*feste*) of Venice, that of the annual visit of the
Doge and Signory to this church. The Lady
Abbess of this convent (at that epoch one of those
most in vogue among the Venetian patricians) was
a member of the afterwards great family of Morosini,
and to mark her sense of the benefits conferred by
Doge Tradonico on her abbey, she presented him
with a diadem, or, more truly, a " Corno Ducale." To
quote from the authoress of " La Feste Veneziane," [1]
this ducal cap " was entirely of gold, the rim being
adorned with twenty-four pear-shaped Oriental
pearls. On the top sparkled a diamond with eight
facets, of marvellous weight and brilliancy. In front
was a ruby, also of great size, the brightness of whose
colour and fire was dazzling. But how to describe
the great cross which stood in the centre of the
diadem? This was composed of precious stones,
specially twenty-three emeralds, five of which forming the arms surpassed in beauty all that could be
seen of the sort." It was then decreed that this gift,
which, our authoress tells us, delighted the Doge,
should only be used on the Doge's coronation day.
" But," she adds, " in order that the good nuns should
not be deprived of the pleasure of again beholding it,
. . . it was besides decreed that every year, when
the visit to S. Zaccaria took place, it should be taken

[1] Giustina Renier Michiel, "Origine delle Feste Veneziane,"
Milano, 1829.

from the public treasury, and presented by the Doge himself on a ewer, and shown to the sisters ; all of which was faithfully carried out." [1]

The confusion consequent on Doge Tradonico's murder was followed by summary justice on his assassins, and quiet was restored by the appointment (864) of Orso Partecipazio to the dukedom. He distinguished himself greatly in his wars against the Slavs of Dalmatia, and though he met with some reverses, he also gained some brilliant victories, and

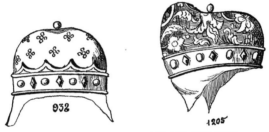

DUCAL CAPS OF THE YEARS 932 AND 1205.

remained in possession of numerous prisoners and much booty.

The struggles that frequently arose between the popes and the Doges in regard to the see of Grado

[1] This account of the ducal bonnet is not considered exact by many writers ; and it was not till after the lapse of some centuries that the jewelled diadem came into use. Up till 1174 the Doge wore simply a circlet of gold ; at the close of the thirteenth century this circlet had become a crown of gold with precious stones ; and in 1367 it had increased to such a weight, orders were given to reduce it, in order to make it light enough to be worn. A coloured drawing of the " Corno Ducale," of great beauty, executed by J. Talman in 1719, is in the Print Room at the British Museum.

were renewed at this period. Doge Orso had determined that a certain Domenico Caloprino should be named Bishop of Torcello, in spite of the Patriarch of Grado, Pietro Marturio, pronouncing him unfit for the post. The matter was referred to Pope John VIII., who sided with the metropolitan, and cited all the Venetian bishops to appear at a council held at Ravenna to settle the question. The bishops, who, with the people of Venice, espoused the cause of the Doge, refused to attend ; and the difficulty was only solved by Caloprino being appointed bishop. The Doge gained his point, regardless of the inefficiency of his nominee, and of the opposition offered by the head of the Church and by the Patriarch. This is but one instance out of many proving how great the power of the Doges in those days was in affairs spiritual, as well as temporal, and how firmly the principle existed in the ruler and in the people of Venice alike to allow no stranger or outsider to meddle in matters relating to the state. It was also the first instance of resistance to the dictates of Rome, and in the course of this history there will be frequent occasion to notice the supreme indifference Venice showed to the orders of the popes when those orders came in opposition to her own views and interests.

Doge Orso did much for the improvement and adornment of the town ; he caused palaces and houses to be built at Rialto, besides attending to the drying and reclaiming of the soil ; he also provided for populating the island of Dorsoduro, which from that date was reckoned among the *sestieri* or sections of the town. His relations also were friendly on all sides ; he was beloved and looked up to by his subjects ; respected and honoured by Basil, Emperor of Constantinople, whose niece he married ; and was happy, too, in his children, all of whom rose to different high positions, especially the eldest, Giovanni, who was associated with him in the dukedom. Orso Partecipazio died after a glorious reign of seventeen years, when his son and associate, Giovanni, was chosen to succeed him.

During the reign of Giovanni Partecipazio II. (881), Venice was engaged in disputes with the town of Comacchio, which, situate on the Adriatic coast, to the north of Ravenna, threatened at one moment to assume maritime importance, an assumption not to be tolerated by Venice in so near a neighbour. The Doge's brother, Badoer (the name taken by the Partecipazii in after times as their surname, and by which they are most generally known in history), was sent to suppress the claims and arrogance of the town. In a conflict against the inhabitants he was so badly wounded that he returned to Venice only to die, and his fellow citizens, to avenge his death, sent a large force against Comacchio. The town was assaulted and reduced to such a state by fire and sword, that all its prospects of importance were swept away for ever, while the Venetians returned home crowned with spoils and victory.

This reign was signalised by extraordinary meteoric disturbances : strange sights and sounds were said to have been observed in the heavens ; the storms of rain, wind, and yellow dust were such as to threaten annihilation to the islands, and to cause the old chroniclers to observe that strong indeed must have been the love of liberty in a people, who were willing to risk their habitations and lives sooner than renounce the freedom and independence assured to them by sojourning in so strange and so unstable a spot.

Doge Giovanni associated all his brothers in turn on the ducal throne ; but feeling the cares of state too heavy, he resigned his high post and, transferring the ducal office to Pietro Candiano, who was chosen to succeed him, he retired into private life.

It was in 887 that Pietro Candiano I. became Doge for the brief space of five months, when he died fighting valiantly against the pirates of Dalmatia, at the age of forty-five. His body, rescued by one Andrea Tribuno from the enemy, was said to have been buried at St. Eufemia at Grado ; and an old tomb is pointed out by the inhabitants of the country not far from the spot where the engagement took place, which tradition has handed down as that of the slain Doge. His loss was looked upon as a great and public calamity, as, apart from his warlike prowess, he was also extremely religious, liberal, and wise. The perplexity as to who should succeed him was great, and the only way that presented itself out of the dilemma was to entreat Doge Giovanni Partecipazio to resume the reins of government. This he consented to do till Candiano's successor should be unanimously appointed ; as this happened soon after, the old Doge again withdrew and shortly after died.

In 888 Pietro Tribuno was named Doge. He was the son of Domenico Tribuno,[1] and Agnella or Angela Tradonico, granddaughter of the Doge who was murdered in 864, when leaving the Church of S. Zaccaria. His reign is famous for the gallant resistance made by him and his people against the Hungarians, whose invasion of Italy had carried widespread terror and ruin, and who resolved to possess themselves of the treasures and riches, for which Venice was fast becoming celebrated. No pains were spared to fortify and protect the town against the threatened danger; new forts were erected and old ones reconstructed, whereof some traces have come down to us in the names still in vogue, such as Castel forte near S. Rocco, Castello, till then Olivolo, and the like. The outlying forts were put in order; at Rialto no stone was left unturned to provide for the safety of the capital; a strong wall was built, extending from Olivolo (now Castello) along the present Riva degli Schiavoni to Sta. Maria Zobenigo, while a great chain was drawn at night across the Grand Canal. Preparations were also made to pull up the piles, which standing out in the lagunes serve to guide the vessels and ships among the sandbanks, and thus to destroy the marks and indications of the waterway through the tortuous passages leading out to sea. The inhabitants from the more distant districts collected for greater safety at Rialto, and this increase of numbers and population in the centre has gained for Doge Tribuno the credit of having planted

---

[1] The family of Tr.buno are better known under their subsequent name of Trono or Tron, and exist to this day.

a city at Rialto. The conflict with the expected foe took place at Albiolo, a port between Venice and Chioggia, and ended after a fierce fight in a great victory for the Venetians. The Doge was universally hailed as the saviour of public freedom, and the expeller of the barbarians ; and when he died in 912 another Partecipazio, Orso II., reigned in his stead.

This Doge was a man of high intelligence, at the same time famed for his goodness, his justice and his generosity. The twenty years of his government were noted for the peace and quiet, which reigned throughout the length and breadth of the land—a marked contrast to the wars and disputes at this time disturbing the rest of Italy. In 932 Doge Orso withdrew from public life, and retired to the monastery of S. Felice on the island of Ammiana, a monastery founded thirty-two years previously by the monks of St. Stephen of Altino, when they fled from the invasion of the Hungarians.

The reigns of Doge Pietro Candiano II., 932, and Pietro or Badoerio Partecipazio, 939, who succeeded him, were uneventful, and were followed by that of Pietro Candiano III., who became Doge in 942.

It was under this Doge that the famous " Rape of the Brides" took place, and the " Festival of the Maries" was instituted.[1]   Most writers dwell at some

---

[1] The actual date of this "Rape of the Brides " is a much disputed one, and one still uncertain and unsettled.   Some historians place it in the reign of Pietro Candiano II., others under that of Pietro Tradonico, others again as far back as the time of the Tribunes.   I have followed Romanin, and two or three other writers, who, though admitting the uncertainty of the date, seem to have good reasons for placing it about this period.

length in describing these two events, and though the accounts are far from agreeing in all points, there is enough wherefrom to glean how important they were, and how closely linked with the story of Venice. The ceremony of marriage was one of great weight and importance, and one day in each year was set aside, when in one church all the pending marriages were celebrated as a national feast, and with universal pomp and rejoicing. The day fixed for the rite was that of the Purification of the Blessed Virgin (February 2nd), and the church where the ceremony took place was S. Pietro in Castello, then the cathedral church of Venice.[1] The brides, each carrying her marriage portion in a small casket, were accompanied by a train of relations and friends, and together with the appointed bridegrooms attended mass, after which the bishop preached a sermon and invoked a blessing on each couple. This function ended, they returned home, followed by their train of friends, and the rest of the day was passed in quiet feasting and gladness. When the city had increased in wealth and population, the festival became more elaborate and magnificent; it was patronised by the Doge, who attended in person with all the pomp and retinue belonging to his state, and nothing was omitted to enhance the splendour and gorgeousness of the rite. It was then decreed that twelve maidens of irreproachable conduct, and generally chosen from among the poorer families, "dressed as in olden fashion in white, with their hair thrown over their shoulders, and interwoven with

---

[1] This church was the cathedral of Venice from very early times, and remained as such till 1807, when St. Mark's took its place.

threads of gold," [1] and adorned also with jewels, should be presented to the Doge, who accompanied them to the altar, and gave them over to their respective bridegrooms. But in 943 an event happened which gave a new and different character to the festival. Some pirates, either of Trieste or Dalmatia, concealed themselves among the reeds and bushes, at that period covering much of the island of Olivolo, and at the moment when the brides were approaching the cathedral with their caskets in their hands, rushed from their hiding-place, and with drawn swords and daggers succeeded in carrying off the maidens and their treasures. This assault, in the midst of an unarmed and merry-making company, aroused the wrath and indignation of all, including Doge Candiano, who was present and called on the bereft kinsmen and bridegrooms to arm and prepare for revenge. His appeal met with immediate response, and the Venetians quickly put to sea, resolved at any price to wipe out so dire an insult, and regain so dear a prize. They overtook the foe in the small port of Caorle (called ever after in remembrance of the event, " Porto delle Donzelle "), and fell upon them with fury. After a sharp struggle they gained a complete victory, and returned to Rialto crowned with success, and bringing with them the rescued brides.

To commemorate this triumph it was settled that annually on February 2nd, the day on which the Venetians had returned from the overthrow of the pirates, the Doge should visit the Church of Sta. Maria Formosa, and endow twelve poor maidens with

[1] Sansovino.

a marriage portion from the Government, while processions of schools and corporations added dignity and solemnity to the whole performance. This ceremony, remarkable in early times for its simplicity and unostentation, became by degrees so costly that laws were passed by the Council of Ten restricting the sums to be spent on the festival ; and at the close of the fourteenth century wooden figures were substituted in place of the damsels whose appearance in public had given rise to grave scandals.[1] There is a tradition that explains why the Church of Sta. Maria Formosa was chosen in preference to any other for the commemorative visit of the Doge. On the occasion of the successful rescue of the brides, the cabinet-makers — whose trade comprised that of making the caskets wherein the maidens carried their portions, and who lived chiefly in the parish of Sta. Maria Formosa — had been foremost in lending their boats and their services to avenge the audacity of the pirates. The Doge, to show his appreciation of their zeal, demanded of them how he should requite such valuable aid? They requested the favour of an annual visit from him to their parish church. To this the Doge com-

[1] This innovation was hated by the people, who showed their resentment by hurling turnips, radishes, and other missiles at the wooden effigies to such an extent that in 1349 a decree was passed by the Great Council, forbidding the throwing of any roots during the time of the " Feste," under penalty of a heavy fine. To show their contempt for the figures, and to avenge themselves for the loss of more active insults, the populace instituted a proverb, still in vogue, and pronouncing " Maria di legno " (wooden Mary) any woman who is skinny. dull or unattractive. The etymology of " marionette " has been held by some writers to be deduced from these wooden effigies of the " Marie."

plied, inquiring, however, what should happen if the heat were too great? "We will give you withal to refresh yourself," was the reply. "And should it rain?" asked the Doge. "We will provide you with hats," they said. And in consequence the Doge was ever after presented at this festival with gifts of Malmsey wine and hats of gilded straw, in remembrance of the compact made between his predecessor and the cabinet-makers of "St. Mary the Beautiful." In 1379, when the war with Chioggia had drained all resources and the public mind was entirely engrossed with this struggle, the Festival of the Maries was done away with, but the annual visit of the Doge to the church was continued until the fall of the Venetian Republic.

Doge Pietro Candiano III. had associated his son, also called Pietro, with him in the government, but the youth, full of ambition and vanity, organised a conspiracy against his father and against the state. He was taken, found guilty, and condemned to death, but, owing to the prayers and entreaties of his old father, his life was spared. He was exiled, however, from Venice, and an oath registered against his ever becoming Doge. This occurred in 960, and was the first instance in Venetian annals of the whole community uniting in one to enforce a decree. The decree enforced that neither during his father's life, nor after his death, should this rebellious son be recognised as Doge, and it was signed by the entire body of the bishops, the lower clergy, and the common citizens. This first example of a popular and **unanimous** vote was made only to be broken in a short time, and the record of it would seem only ironical were it not a curious instance of the mutability of a united people. Pietro the younger was for ever waging war against his country ; and a fearful pestilence which now devastated Venice, and caused the interference of all trade and the deaths of thousands of people, was looked upon as the signal vengeance of Heaven for allowing so treacherous a citizen and son to remain alive. This pestilence was so awful that all the schools were shut, trade languished, and all movement and life in the city seemed at an end. To propitiate the wrath of Heaven and to restore energy and confidence, processions paraded through the town, large sums were spent in charity, churches were erected—among others those of S. Simeone, San Basilio or Baseggio, Sta. Maria del Giglio or Zobenigo, all of which belong architecturally to this date. These cares and anxieties so weighed on the old Doge that they hastened his end, and he died in 959 after a reign of seventeen years.

The disorders which broke out after his death were infinite, and the state of misrule and confusion on all sides great. No fit ruler for the state presented himself in Venice, and all eyes were turned to the man, who but so short a while before had been exiled, and debarred for ever from attaining to the highest dignity. Pietro Candiano was now chosen to a position from which his misdeeds and failings should have irrevocably excluded him ; the sentence of exile was revoked, and he was escorted from Ravenna with all the zeal and enthusiasm of a people, who but a few months before had sworn never to acknowledge him

as their head.   At first his rule gave hopes that order
and discipline would be restored in the islands, and
his first acts seemed to betoken a spirit of justice and
equity.   He deposed Mirico Tribuno, who by means
of simony had been elected Bishop of Torcello ; he
strove hard to suppress the slave trade which at that
date had made great strides in Venice ; and he
formed a league with Otho I. of Germany, confirming
old and new privileges to Venice and to her trade.

But Pietro could not, or would not, go on in the
way wherein he had begun.   His personal ambition
was boundless, and he was unscrupulous in the attainment of his aims.   He divorced his wife Giovanna, a
Venetian by birth, to marry Waldrada, the daughter
of Ugo of Tuscany, who brought him a rich dowry
of lands and money.   He forced Vitale, his son by
his first marriage, to become a priest, and soon
after appointed him Patriarch of Grado.   After his
marriage with Waldrada he assumed royal airs and
magnificence; he kept large bands of foreign servants
and retainers to guard both himself and his house,
and oppressed his subjects in a way that roused them
at last to wild and open rebellion.   In August, 976,
the people rose against him, and set fire to the ducal
palace.   The flames spread to St. Mark's, burning it to
the ground, and causing a wholesale conflagration as
far as Sta. Maria Zobenigo, where the fire was only
extinguished after it had done irreparable damage.
In the palace the Doge, no longer able to endure the
heat of the fire and the suffocation of the smoke, says
Sagornino, endeavoured to escape with his youngest
child, an infant in arms, by one of the doors of St.

Mark's. He was seized upon, however, in the vestibule of the church, and although he begged hard for his life, and promised to accede to all that might be required of him, he was cut to pieces on the spot. The indignation against him was so great that the murderers tore his innocent son out of his nurse's arms and killed him too ; after which the two bodies were dragged to a butcher's shop, in order, said these human tigers, that dogs should devour them. From such ignominy they were however rescued by the entreaties of Giovanni Gradenigo, a man of saintly life, who succeeded in saving the victims from such brutality, and caused the remains to be collected and given honourable sepulchre in the Abbey of Sant' Ilario di Fusina. The foreign guards were all massacred, while the misery and destruction wrought by the fire spread desolation and dismay throughout the town.

The widowed Dogaressa fled to the Court of Otho II., who had succeeded his father in 973, and cried for vengeance on the murderers of her husband and innocent babe, and for redress for the loss of her fortune. This appeal, in which Vitale, the eldest son of the slain Doge, also joined, was espoused by the Emperor, who sent to Venice to plead Waldrada's cause. The plea met with a prompt response in regard of the Dogaressa's fortune ; all her possessions and monies being restored to her intact. It is evident that her mind was a contented one, as on the receipt of her fortune she pronounced herself fully satisfied, and wrote to the state expressing her gratitude, promising never to dream of vengeance either against

the ruler of Venice, his heirs, or the Venetian people.
And as it is recorded she did this of her own free
will, no pressure of any sort being put upon her, it
may be concluded that she was easily satisfied !

Before this, however, on August 12, 976, the choice
of the people had proclaimed Pietro Orseolo Doge.
The enmity between the houses of Candiano and of
Orseolo was great, and some opinions hold that
Pietro Orseolo was the author of the fire that had
so disastrous an effect on the ducal palace and on
St. Mark's. He is otherwise described as a man of
holy and irreproachable life, and on his nomination
to the dukedom he set to work to restore order
and quiet, to remit the fortune of the widowed
Waldrada, and to rebuild St. Mark's. This church
had been burnt almost to the ground and there
can be little doubt that the body of the patron
saint was entirely consumed,[1] though a pious fable
maintains that it still rests under the high altar.
In this work of rebuilding St. Mark's and the
ducal palace the Doge spared neither pains or expense. He devoted the whole of his fortune, luckily
a large one, to this purpose, and, the public exchequer having been much drained of late, he
instituted the payment of tithes on all property, and
devoted this revenue to the needs of the state and
the buildings for public offices and for churches.

For the restoration of St. Mark's, Orseolo sent for
the cleverest builders and workmen from Constantinople, and a legend is extant that the architect who

[1] " The body of St. Mark had, without doubt, perished in the conflagration of 975," Ruskin, " Stones of Venice," vol. ii. chap. iv.

DOORWAY INTO ST. MARK'S.
(*From "Calli e Canali," op. cit.*)

superintended the whole work was a dwarf of distorted proportions and bowed legs, who agreed to erect an edifice of unequalled form and beauty on condition that his statue should be placed in the most conspicuous spot in the church. The bargain was struck, but one day when the Doge was watching the rising of the building, he overheard the dwarfish architect say that owing to certain obstacles thrown in his way, he could not, and would not execute the work in the manner he had intended. "In that case," broke in the Doge, "we are absolved from our promise"; and instead of erecting the statue in a spot where all could see it, the story says it was put in a corner of one of the archivolts. There it stands at the close of a series of figures representing different trades and crafts; and is a quaint effigy of an old man on crutches, with his finger on his lip, to denote doubtless regret for an indiscretion that had cost him his exalted position, and for which he was to mourn in stony silence for ever.

Besides these works of art and magnificence the Doge also built a hospital for the poor, which stood at the base of the belfry of St. Mark's, and was named after the saint; but in 1581 it was removed to make way for the Procuratie Nuove,[1] and transferred to the Campo San Gallo.[2] It was this Doge who ordered from Constantinople the famous Pala d'Oro, or reredos, so to speak, of gold, enamel, and

---

[1] The Procuratie Nuove form the line of buildings on the south side of St. Mark's Square.

[2] This Campo, almost opening out from St. Mark's Square on the north side, was formerly called Rusolo, a corruption of Orseolo.

precious stones, displayed on high days and festivals at the back of the high altar of St. Mark's. This work was not completed or erected till the reign of Ordelafo Falier in 1105, while the actual church rebuilt by Orseolo I. was not finished till 1071.

In spite of these outward signs of prosperity and splendour the Doge's reign was far from serene. The supporters of the house of Candiano were always plotting against the peace of the Government, and against the life too of the Doge. These plots served probably to strengthen the tendencies always shown by Orseolo towards a monastic life. His ascetic tastes had already been indulged in as far as was possible in his exalted position ; he separated himself from his wife Felicia, by whom he had but one son also called Pietro, who afterwards became one of Venice's most famous Doges ; he led in every respect a monk-like existence, and longed to put into practice the habits of discipline and self-denial for which he yearned. On the 1st of September, 978, he at length accomplished his purpose. He escaped or rather fled from Venice, and retired to the monastery of Perpignan in France, where he lived for nineteen years, and after his death was canonised. He was only fifty when he abdicated the throne, and it is said that, when some time after his son visited him in his seclusion, he predicted to him his eventual elevation to the dukedom and the glory that would accrue by his reign to Venice.

The dismay was great in Venice at the desertion of a Doge, whose short reign of only two years and one month had augured so well for the state. The partisans of the Candiano faction were quick to profit by the opportunity thus afforded them, and put forward Vitale, brother of the murdered Pietro Candiano, as claimant to the throne. He was declared Doge the same year, but his reign, unmarked by any great event, lasted only fourteen months, when he too sought the quiet of the cloister, and retired to Sant' Ilario near Fusina, where four days after his arrival he died.

Another member of the Candiano faction was appointed in his stead, in the person of Tribuno Memo, whose wife was a daughter of the murdered Pietro, and in whose reign Venice was the scene of violent and disgraceful divisions and strifes between the houses of Caloprini and Morosini. The Doge was supposed to favour the latter, while the Caloprini sought the aid of the Emperor Otho II., to whom in the most scandalous way they were ready to betray their country. The Venetians had sided with Basil and Valentine, Emperors of the East, against Otho; so, to avenge himself for this help given to his foes, Otho listened to the overtures of the Caloprini, and prepared to wage war upon Venice. From such a danger the state was delivered by the death of Otho at Rome in 983; while the death of Stefano Caloprini, the ringleader of that house, in the following year, seemed to annihilate the hopes of his party, who were consequently pardoned and allowed to return to Venice. But in 991 fresh murders and assassinations between the Morosini and Caloprini —when three of the latter were murdered by the Morosini—roused the people to action. They deposed Memo, who was considered incompetent, and who was even thought to be concerned in the murder of the Caloprini, and insisted that he should retire to the monastery of S. Zaccaria, where six days after his forcible entrance he died. The people then proceeded to choose for their ruler a man in every way qualified to put down the dissensions in the town, and to raise Venice to the position which for centuries she was to fill in so glorious and remarkable a manner.

This man was Pietro Orseolo II., son of that Doge Orseolo who entered a monastery in France, and whose prophecy as to the greatness of his son's reign we shall now see so fully carried out.

MURAL DECORATION OF PEACOCKS AT STA. MARINA.

III.

INTERCOURSE WITH CONSTANTINOPLE.

(991–1096.)

THE authors of a valuable work on Venice [1] describe the opening of Doge Orseolo II.'s reign by declaring that "when the future historian of Venice relates the actions of this great Doge his soul will swell within him"; for they say, and say truly, that Venice now arose from insignificance to greatness, and that she now sprang into all the power and importance of a nation developing vast resources of wealth and strength.

The Doge's first act was to regulate among the lower classes. Their turbulence and rioting had brought much confusion and disorder into the government, and with a strong hand he now reduced them to order. He then turned his attention to foreign affairs, and renewed the leagues and treaties relating to the intercourse and trade of Venice with neighbouring states, especially with Otho of Germany, and with the Eastern Emperors. From these he obtained the Chrysobol, or Golden Bull, which confirmed to Venice privileges and conces-

[1] "Venezia e le sue lagune," Venezia, 1847.

sions as to her Eastern commerce far exceeding any yet vouchsafed to her. To the German Emperor the Doge appealed for the adjustment of some trading difficulties with the bishops of Treviso and Belluno. Otho decided in favour of Orseolo, and granted to the Venetians the right of holding ports, and of trafficking on the rivers Piave and Sile. He also allowed a line of communication to be opened between German and Venetian territories, and so greatly facilitated the intercourse and commerce of the two countries.

But Orseolo's dealings were not limited to his neighbours and accepted allies. With a wide-mindedness and foresight much in advance of his age, he entered into a treaty with the Saracens, who till now had been looked upon as infidels and heretics, unworthy of being dealt with by civilised Christians. It must be borne in mind that Venice was now developing as a commercial power in a remarkable way, and as such every device and stratagem that could be turned to her advantage in this respect had to be employed on all sides. Her fleet, too, was rapidly and steadily gaining size and power, and the exigencies of her position and trade only tended to increase still more the number and quality of her vessels. Though, as one of her most recent historians has said, "the Venetians never were nor became an industrial people, their position as importers and distributors was great," [1] and as at that moment, and for long after, she was the only

[1] H. F. Brown, " Venice, an Historical Sketch of the Republic." London, 1893.

state who could furnish ships, whether for transport
or for war, her importance in that capacity was untold ; and gave her weight and influence among other
nations even when her rank as a first-class power
had declined. Doge Orseolo realised fully the
need of furthering the cause of Venice as a commercial, ship-sailing, and ship-building state ; he
neglected no means whereby to increase her rank
and position in every one of these respects.

But the Doge's chief work, and the one which
reflects most fame and glory on his reign, was the
conquest of Dalmatia. The Dalmatians had implored his aid against the Narentines, pirates who
infested their coasts, and devastated their rich
and prosperous lands. On Ascension Day of the
year 998, a date that was to be for ever famous in
Venetian annals, the Doge sailed from Venice to
the relief of the oppressed country. He received on
starting a consecrated banner from the Bishop of
Castello, and again at Grado, at Parenzo, and at Pola
the dignitaries of the Church blessed his fleet and enterprise. Everything smiled upon a voyage undertaken
under such holy and happy auspices. On his arrival
in Dalmatia most of the province acknowledged his
sway, and placed itself voluntarily under his command ; but he had a hard fight before conquering
the island of Curzola, and a harder one still awaited
him at Lagosta. This fortress of the Narentines,
placed on the summit of a high rock, was almost
impregnable, and it was not till after a long and
bloody battle that the Venetians remained in
possession of it. The victory was complete ; the

supremacy of St. Mark was acknowledged throughout the country, which in return received from Venice a treatment and consideration both wise and moderate. The laws of the country were respected and preserved honourably and scrupulously; and only a small tribute imposed on each town according to its produce and trade. The benefits gained to the Republic by this conquest were numerous: her commerce both by land and sea profited enormously; the direct communications now open to the East were to prove of lasting advantage; while the woods and forests of Dalmatia were to furnish timber and fuel to Venice of an excellence and abundance renowned to the present day.

The Doge on his return to Venice was greeted by the applause and rejoicing of the whole people; the title of Duke of Dalmatia was conferred on him, a title borne henceforward by all successive Doges, and, to celebrate so auspicious an event, the festival of the "Sposalizio del Mare" was instituted, and performed annually on the Feast of the Ascension for many a year to come.[1] In later days the ceremony was as follows:

On the vigil of Ascension Day, the *Bucintoro*[2] was

---

[1] It was not known by this name till 1178, when under the dukedom of Doge Ziani and the patronage of Pope Alexander III. it became more elaborate in ceremonial. The theory, however, was the same, as when the performance was simpler, and when it was spoken of only as "the going out of the Doge from the Lido to wed the sea."

[2] The etymology of "Bucintoro" seems lost in doubt; but among many opinions the one that commends itself most is the one that holds it to be derived from *buzo,* a ship, both of war and trade, as described by Tal in the "Archéologie Navale," and from whence came *buzin d'oro* and *bucintoro.*

THE BUCENTAUR. (*From Yriarte, op. cit.*)

launched from the Arsenal, taken to the Piazzetta, and prepared for the reception of the Doge and his suite. The *Bucentaur* was divided into two floors, or decks, in the lower one were seated the one hundred and sixty-eight *arsenalotti*, who worked the forty-eight oars by which the boat was propelled. These *arsenalotti* were the workmen of the Arsenal, who claimed the privilege of rowing the Doge on this special occasion ; their masters in the meanwhile being placed on the upper deck around the Doge and the Signory. This upper deck, covered with crimson velvet, trimmed with gold braid and tassels, formed a saloon ornamented with bas-reliefs representing the Arts and Sciences, and extended the whole length of the ship. At the stern was the small window from whence the Doge threw the ring into the sea. A richly adorned ducal chair stood in front of this window, and was raised on two steps, with a canopy overhead in the form of a shell, supported by two cherubs, and having on each side two wooden, gilt figures representing Prudence and Strength. Near the steps were gorgeous seats for the Patriarch, the Ambassadors, the dignitaries of state, and the governors of the Arsenal. Here again were other bas-reliefs of Apollo and the Muses, and classical decorations, while the whole effect was heightened and coloured by an abundance of gold lavishly used in all directions. The *Bucentaur* was met at S. Nicolò del Lido by a barge, covered with cloth of gold, on which were assembled the clergy, all in full canonicals. This barge contained a pail of water, a jar of salt (for purification), and a holy water brush of olive-wood ; two canons intoned the litany, after which the bishop repeated in Latin the following prayer : " Vouchsafe, O Lord, that this sea appertain unto us. And to all those who sail over its waters give peace and quiet. We beseech Thee to hear us." He then blessed the water and the ring ; and on the approach of the Doge, a deacon read aloud : " Purge me, O Lord, with hyssop and I shall be clean." After this the bishop sprinkled the Doge and those who were with him, and poured the rest of the water into the sea, the Doge throwing the ring, at the same time exclaiming : " We wed thee, O Sea, in token of true and lasting domination." The religious function ended, the Doge returned with the same pomp to the capital, where the day was observed as one of universal rejoicing and thanksgiving. Religion at that period was so inwoven with the government and all its acts and ceremonies, that this blending of worship and festival had a meaning and import of untold depth and significance to the people and their rulers alike, and united them in heart and feeling with bonds of a powerful and abiding nature.

In the year 1000, soon after the institution of this festival of " La Sensa " (as the Venetians call it), the mysterious visit of Otho III., Emperor of Germany, to Venice took place. The Emperor, evidently prompted by a desire to make the acquaintance of the Doge, whose deeds filled him with admiration, determined to come in person to Venice, and un-fettered by public receptions and entertainments, see for himself what manner of man Orseolo really was. Otho had been on a pilgrimage to Ravenna, and from there announced his intention of spending some days in retreat at Pomposa, an island not far removed from the Venetian territory. Arrived here he ordered his room to be prepared, and then, at dead of night, attended by only six followers, he secretly embarked for Venice, where he landed after a stormy passage, being met by the Doge at S. Servolo. He was lodged at the monastery of S. Zaccaria, and during his stay in Venice, which lasted only three days, numerous interviews took place between him and the Doge. Among other matters settled by them was the remittance of a tribute till then paid by Venice on the accession of each emperor; and privileges of free entrance to certain neighbouring ports and other trading advantages were conceded by Otho to the Republic. The Emperor also stood sponsor to an infant child of the Doge, and then returned to Ravenna, the secret of his visit to the lagunes having been kept inviolate, and only transpiring after his departure. The explanation as to the need of this mystery and secrecy remains unanswered, but when the news of it, together with the concessions and advantages obtained for them by the Doge, came to light, the people of Venice could not sufficiently applaud their prince, or testify their gratitude for all he had done and gained for them. As a proof thereof it was universally decreed that his son Giovanni should be associated with him, and at his death succeed him as Doge.

In 1004, fresh glories accrued to the Venetians and their Doge from the share taken by them in the siege of Bari. The Emperors of Constantinople, Constantine and Basil applied to Orseolo for help to defend this town against the Saracens. The appeal met with a prompt response, the Doge himself sailing with a well-equipped and numerous fleet to the defence of the town. His stratagems both by land and sea proved so effectual, that when after desperate fighting the Saracens retired, and victory remained with the Greeks and Venetians, the Doge was hailed as the deliverer of the city, and his praises were in every mouth. The news of this triumph was greeted with joy at Constantinople, where, to recompense the Doge for the important service rendered them, the joint Emperors invited his son and colleague, Giovanni, to Constantinople, and bestowed on him the hand of their niece, Maria, in marriage. He was also presented with an abundance of gifts, and the wedding was celebrated with a pomp and magnificence worthy of even Oriental splendour. These nuptial rejoicings were repeated soon after on the arrival of Giovanni and his bride in Venice, when, says Sagornino, the town was in untold gaiety, the like whereof had never been equalled. This glory and rejoicing were soon to be clouded over by sorrows and distresses also unequalled in their way. The contact and intercourse with the East brought in its train the scourge of the plague, an illness till then unknown in Venice. What with the difficulty of contending with a malady of whose nature they had no experience, against which they were in no wise provided, and whose subtle force added to their difficulty, the citizens were in a sorry plight; the pestilence gained ground daily, and thousands of victims died. Among the number were the Doge's son, Giovanni, his young bride and their infant son Basil, who all succumbed in a short time, and were all buried in one tomb at S. Zaccaria. The plague was followed by a famine, so that to the Doge's private sorrows was added the grief of seeing his people decimated and brought to the depths of misery and ruin. Against such appalling troubles the Doge could no longer make head ; crushed by so heavy a weight of public and private sorrow his heart seemed broken, and feeling his end approaching he made every preparation to meet death with calmness and courage. After a reign of seventeen years and a half, he died in 1008, at the early age of forty-eight, and bequeathed his large fortune equally between the poor and his family.

Pietro Orseolo II. may well be reckoned among the greatest of the Venetian Doges ; his conquest of Dalmatia and subsequent government of the country were a gain and importance to Venice that cannot be overrated, while the advantages he obtained for his country from the Emperor of Germany and other sovereigns are proofs of his wisdom and sagacity as a ruler and a patriot. He was succeeded in the dukedom by his son, Ottone Orseolo, who by the public voice had been associated with his father on the death of his brother Giovanni two years previously.

Otho, or Ottone, Orseolo was only eighteen years old, when in 1008 he succeeded his father as sole Doge of Venice, and he would probably have left a name and reputation equal to his, had it not been for the jealousies that arose against his family, and that swept him and them away in one wholesale ruin. The eminence to which most of Pietro Orseolo's children had attained was, it must be allowed, dangerous for one family in a state professing republican government.   Of his five sons the eldest, as has been said, died when yet his father's associate ; the second, Orso, was first Bishop of Torcello, and then raised to the Patriarchate of Grado ; Ottone, the third, after being his father's colleague, was appointed sole Doge ; while the next brother, Vitale, was made Bishop of Torcello on his elder brother's promotion to Grado. All these high offices heaped upon members of one family raised open and violent sedition ; and although Ottone had waged successful war against Adria, and conquered the province of Croatia, he was unable to stem the tide of envy and dissension raised against him by his own subjects. The cry of dissatisfaction arose at Grado, and swelled so powerfully that the Doge and his brother could only find safety in flight and withdrew to Istria.   The enormities committed by their chief enemy, Poppone, or Pepone, Patriarch of Aquileja, against the town of Grado proved a powerful factor for good in the cause of the fugitive brothers ; and the fickle multitude who had clamoured for their deposition, now as ardently insisted on their re-institution to office, and entreated them to return.   This they accordingly did ; but on the Doge declining to appoint a youth of the Gradenigo family, aged only eighteen years, to the bishopric of Olivolo, the faction of Gradenigo, supported by another powerful family, the Flabianico, rose against him, deposed him, and banished him to Constantinople.

After stormy debates the dukedom was conferred

upon Pietro Centranico; but order was far from being restored by his election, and the partisans of the Orseoli used every device to bring about the recall of the exiles. These machinations together with renewed strifes in the see of Grado, and an insurrection against Venice by some of the cities of Dalmatia, created intense discontent against Centranico. He had also incurred the displeasure of Conrad II., Emperor of Germany, who withdrew many of the privileges granted by Otho II. to Venice, and this damage to their commerce, joined to the other disasters—for which perhaps the Doge should not be held responsible—exasperated public feeling against him. After four years of government he too was deposed and exiled to Constantinople, while Ottone was invited to return. Death, however, had put in a prior claim; and when the deputation headed by Vitale, Bishop of Torcello, the exiled Doge's brother, reached Constantinople, they found they had come in vain, for Ottone Orseolo was dead.

The throne was seized by one Domenico Orseolo, who strove to assert himself as Doge, and took possession of the ducal palace; but the people, furious at this act of usurpation, drove him with violence out of the country, and chose Domenico Flabianico as their Doge.

An important movement took place soon after his appointment, when a law was passed, abolishing for ever the nomination of any colleague or associate to the ducal power. Another measure was also now brought about in the re-institution of the "Consiglieri

Ducali," [1] who were appointed to advise the Doge in matters of slight importance.   In graver questions the most learned and wise among the nobles were invited to assist him with counsel and wisdom ; and from this form of consultation originated the Council so famous in after times under the name of Consiglio dei Pregadi (*Pregati*, " invited ") or the Senate, which took definite shape in 1229, under the dukedom of Jacopo Tiepolo.

Beyond disturbances between Venice and the turbulent see of Grado, no marked events signalised the ten years of Flabianico's reign, and he died in 1042, when Domenico Contarini succeeded him. Contarini's reign of twenty-eight years is strangely devoid of incident, as, beyond the revolt of the town of Zara and its recapture, there is little to record.

The election of Domenico Selvo on the occasion of Doge Contarini's funeral, at the Church of S. Nicolò del Lido, was remarkable as having been prompted by absolute spontaneity and unanimity on the part of all present, when but one mind and one desire reigned in the hearts of the people as they shouted with one voice, " Domenicum Silvium volumus et laudamus." Selvo refused at first to believe in his nomination, but yielded to the insistency of the people and of his friends, and, on being borne in triumph to St. Mark's, received there the pledges and insignia of sovereignty.

One of the chief events in Doge Selvo's reign was the completion of St. Mark's Church, and the lavish

---

[1] These ducal councillors were two, then four, and then six in number, and together with the Doge and the three heads of the " XL al Criminale," formed the " Lesser Council " or " Signoria."

decoration of this church with marbles and costly stones from the East. The relations between Venice and Constantinople had been much strengthened at this period by the Doge's marriage with a Greek princess, the daughter, according to some, of Constantine X. (Ducas), according to others, of Nicephorus III. (Botaniates) ; and one of the results of this increased intercourse was the abundance of marbles brought to Venice for the adornment of St. Mark's. A law existed forbidding any vessel trading in the Levant to return to Venice without bringing marbles or precious stones for this purpose ; and the proof of how faithfully this law was fulfilled is evident to all who enter St. Mark's and gaze on the porphyry, verde antique, alabaster, and marble, which decorated every corner and give an effect of wealth and colour, blending beauty and devotion in one harmonious whole.

This Eastern Dogaressa also introduced into her adopted home a luxury and lavishness hitherto unknown in Venice. The old chroniclers all agree in giving minute accounts of her use of scents and perfumed waters. They enlarge on the " gold sticks " employed by her to convey food to her mouth ; on the Eastern balsams and unguents sprinkled over her clothes ; the gloves which always covered her hands ; the order given to her handmaidens to collect every morning the fresh dew with which to bathe her face and improve her complexion ; the marvellous quantity of perfume she indulged in, and which, it is said, was so excessive that ladies often fainted away in her presence in consequence. It is said that the inordinate use of these scents and essences undermined her

health and materially hastened her end, besides producing so loathsome a disease that no one could
approach her without severely offending that sense,
to which during her lifetime the poor lady had been
so ardent a devotee.

In the meantime events had been going on in Italy
which were now to affect and influence Venice to
no small extent. The Normans, under their leader,
Robert Guiscard, had conquered most of Apulia,
and now threatened to carry their victorious arms
still further. They attacked the coast of Dalmatia,
on which the inhabitants appealed for help to Doge
Selvo, addressing him as: " Duke of Venice and
Dalmatia, Imperial Protopedro, and our Lord." The
help given by Venice did not tend to create a friendly
feeling towards her by the Normans, and this enmity
was further increased when the Doge refused to join
his forces to those of Duke Robert, and elected
instead to support the cause of Alexius Comnenus
against the invaders. Alexius had been crowned
Emperor of Constantinople in 1081, when he founded
the dynasty which bore his name, and which for a
whole century swayed the tottering throne of the
Eastern Cæsars. To him Guiscard opposed all the
strength and strategy of his forces, and commenced
operations by besieging the town of Durazzo. Alexius
turned to the Venetians for support, which was
promptly given, and the Doge sailed in person at
the head of a large fleet to the rescue of the city.
The allies at first gained some successes, but after a
fierce encounter on the land side of the town, they met
with a crushing reverse. The same fate awaited them

at a somewhat later date, when Alexius again implored
their aid. This aid was again gladly given, though
the result was another severe defeat. On the news of
this fresh disaster reaching Venice, the popular grief
and fury knew no bounds, and, urged on by Vitale
Falier, a patrician inimical to the Doge and ambitious of the sovereign power, the people forced Selvo to
resign the throne and enter a monastery. This was in
1085, and Vitale Falier was named Doge in his place.

The first act of the new Doge was to make prepa·
rations to wipe out the stain inflicted on the Venetian
arms by the Normans. Once again did Alexius plead
for help to Venice against the foe, and, thirsting for
vengeance, the Venetians responded eagerly to the
appeal. At last fortune smiled on the allies, and a
great victory was gained by the Greek and Venetian
armies near the island of Corfu. The death of Duke
Robert occurred soon after this victory ; he died of the
plague while engaged in besieging Cephalonia, and his
death freed Venice and Constantinople from a dreaded
and formidable foe.[1] The Greek Emperor was not
slow in recompensing his allies for the help they had
given him. He renewed and confirmed to the Doge
the titles of Duke of Dalmatia and of *Protosebaste*,
i.e., Most August Prince, together with a large sum of
money ; another Chrysobol, or Golden Bull, granted
to all Venetian ships free entry and exit for themselves
and their cargo into every Eastern port ; and in
Constantinople and other towns a large number of
shops, warehouses, and magazines were set apart for

[1] See The Story of the Nations, "Byzantium," chap. xxi. p. 259, by
C. W. C. Oman.

the merchandise and traffic of Venetian traders exclusively.

Together with this increase of affluence and these advantages to the state, there arose a dread lest the Doge, too, would seek to extend the power allotted to his office ; and to restrain any ambition that might be surging in his brain, it was decided to appoint three nobles who were to sit in judgment with him, and who, since they also resided in the ducal palace, were called "Judges of the Palace," or of "the Doge's Court." They formed the "Magistracy of Right" (*Magistrato del Proprio*), and their functions consisted in restraining the free action of the Doge, though their office did not extend beyond the city.

Another event, though of a more legendary nature, belongs to this period in the supposed re-discovery of St. Mark's body. There is no doubt that this relic had perished in the fire which had occurred in 976, but, as the saint's body was needed to aid the devotions of the faithful and to attract rich visitors to its shrine, it was judged expedient to recover it. The Emperor of Germany, Henry IV., took part in a ceremony to which the Doge convened all the clergy and people, ordering a fast of three days' duration, together with prayers, processions, almsgivings, and other pious measures to propitiate the Almighty and to intercede for aid in the discovery. These intercessions were not in vain. On June 25, 1094, while High Mass was being celebrated, and the congregation in St. Mark's were intently awaiting the miracle, some pieces of stone were heard to fall from a pillar supporting the altar dedicated to St. James, and an arm was seen to project from the column, which was speedily recognised as that of the saint. The joy of the multitude can be imagined ; and whatever doubts may have lingered in any sceptical bosom were speedily dispelled by a sweet fragrance which emanated from the spot, and, it would seem, wafted all disbelief away for ever. The body of the saint, found hid in this column, was now deposited in the crypt or "*Sotto-Confessione*," where the tomb was re-discovered in 1811, together with several coins, a ring, some other small objects, and a block bearing the date of Doge Falier's reign. For years after the anniversary of this blessed recovery was observed with great devotion and ceremony. The consecration of St. Mark's was also solemnised in 1094, during Vitale Falier's reign ; and two years after this event he died. He was buried in the vestibule of St. Mark's, where a rude tomb, standing immediately to the right on entering, is shown as his resting-place, and is said to be among the earliest specimens of Venetian architecture.

He was succeeded by Vitale Michiel I., but before passing on to record his reign and the events at that moment engrossing all Europe, it may be well to speak of the fortunes of Venice, and the position she had acquired for herself in regard of matters commercial and political. Her chief commerce naturally was by sea, but on the land side also she carried on a brisk trade, and the rivers in the provinces around, the Brenta, the Bacchiglione, the Sile, the Piave, the Po, the Adige, &c., facilitated her means of conveyance to Padua, Vicenza, Treviso,

Belluno, Ferrara, Mantua, Verona, and other towns. To the centre and south of the peninsula her merchandise was transported in caravans, and found sure and ready markets. Another source of income was the hire of her boats and ships. The advantages reaped by this traffic were twofold ; for the Venetians who sailed to distant ports and countries not only enlarged their knowledge as to ship-building, but they also learned new arts and inventions for the improvement of their navy and the embellishment of their town, which they were not slow to put into practice. The skill of the Venetians as sailors and navigators is well known ; the voyages they undertook for trade and for discovery were unequalled then, and have perhaps only been excelled since by English ships and seamen ; while the wars in which their fleets engaged, raised their importance throughout the known world.

Side by side with the thrifty and business life of the town was to be found a keen love of pleasure and pageant. The festivals, religious and secular alike, in which one and all of the inhabitants partook, form a peculiar feature in Venetian story, while the jousts and aquatic sports developed the strength and vigour of the population in a different though as effective a way as games and races on *terra ferma.* The legislation and government of Venice differed also from those of other towns, and were as equally adapted to the requirements and peculiarities of the sea-girt city as her regattas and water-games. The Venetians were never guided by either the Lombard or the Frankish laws ; the feudal system was unknown among them, and the appeals to judicial duels or to the " Judgment of God" they never used. One and the same law was enforced for clergy and laity alike ; and the administration of justice was carried on by judges appointed for that purpose throughout the state. To all questions concerning the well-being of the entire state the voice of the populace was consulted in early days, and their wishes studied together with those of the upper classes ; but as the aristocracy grew in number and power the *vox populi* waxed fainter and fainter till by degrees it faded away entirely.

WELL HEAD IN A HOUSE ADJOINING THE CHURCH OF STA. MARIA FORMOSA. (*From " Raccolte delle Vere da Pozzo," op. cit.*)

IV.

THE CRUSADES.

(1096-1172.)

THE hour had now come when Venice was to make
open confession, as it were, of her devotion to religion
and her love of sacred rights and traditions. The
whole of the Christian world had been aroused by
Pope, or conscience, or public opinion, to arm in
defence of Christ's sepulchre, and fight for the
rescue of the Holy Land. For two years the Venetians found reasons for excusing themselves from
joining the Crusades; but now they could no longer
remain neutral, for the Pope and the leaders of
Christendom appealed to them to aid the cause of
the Cross with their ships, and convey the Crusaders
to Palestine, and on no account could they refuse.
Doge Vitale Michiel convoked a general assembly
when he pointed out the claims of religion, and the
advantages that would accrue to their commerce if
they acceded to the proposal. His words ended by
arousing universal enthusiasm, and inducing numbers
to prepare to share in the sacred undertaking. A
fleet of over two hundred ships of war and of transport was fitted out, and sailed under the command of
Giovanni, the Doge's son, and of Enrico Contarini,

Bishop of Castello. A solemn service was held at St. Mark's, when the consecrated banners were delivered to the two leaders, spiritual and temporal, and amid the acclamations and good wishes of all the people collected on the Lido, the armament sailed away and wintered at Rhodes.

Here for the first time Venice was to find herself face to face with a new foe, and to measure forces with the Republic of Pisa. The maritime powers of Pisa and Genoa had for some time been gaining in strength and importance, and their supremacy on the element, where Venice meant to " reign alone," was a very present dread to the Ocean-Queen, and one she had now to combat in real earnest. Genoa and Pisa were both establishing relations in the East too firmly and swiftly for Venice's peace of mind ; and the Crusades, apart from the religious aspects they wore, presented Venice with an opportunity not to be neglected of asserting herself over these rivals, and of forcing them, if possible, into a subordinate position. The first engagement between Venice and Pisa took place at Rhodes, when the two republics, equipped and eager for the rescue of the Saviour's sepulchre, turned their arms against each other, and after a bloody fight Venice remained victorious. Different reasons have been ascribed for this encounter ; some writers ascribe it merely to the jealousy between the combatants ; others again say it was a dispute over the body of S. Nicolò. The Venetians had possessed themselves of the body, and the Pisans claimed that it should be divided between them ; but the origin of the dispute had probably nothing to do with the saint, as it was not till the following spring when the Venetians continued their course and arrived at Mira, that they obtained the coveted relic of his remains.

The Christian host were prepared to pass through the territory of the Emperor of Constantinople, a passage which that monarch could not but view with dismay ; and he resolved to use all his arts and wiles to glean what advantages he could from their presence, while he did his utmost to detach the Venetians from their new allies. It has been alleged that one explanation of the lukewarmness of Venice in regard of the Crusades can be found in her friendship and alliance with Constantinople ; but against that statement must be urged the fact of the refusal made by Doge Michiel to listen to Alexius's offers, and his steady adherence to the soldiers of the Cross, once he had thrown his lot in with them. And too it was in this direction that Venice's true interests now lay. The necessity existed for her to enter the ranks of the Crusaders, if only to exclude any possible competitors in her Eastern markets, and maintain absolutely and entirely in her own hands the monopoly of trading in the Levant. With this purpose before her, and doubtless also with much of the devotion and romance which fired many a Crusader, Venice ordered her fleet to advance to the support of Godfrey of Bouillon and his brother Baldwin. The Venetians' first exploit was at the siege of Jaffa, where they rendered efficient service ; afterwards they sailed home, bearing with them the spoils and trophies of their Syrian campaign, their special prize being the body of S.

Nicolò, which they calmly carried off by right of their own good will, and placed in the church already prepared for it on the Lido.

A different kind of warfare shortly after engaged their troops, when they were called on to support the countess Matilde of Tuscany at the siege of Ferrara against the German Emperor, Henry IV. The countess was warring on behalf of the Pope ; her arms and those of her allies proved successful ; and to reward the Venetians for their prompt and effectual help numerous privileges were granted them in Ferrara as to free trade and other advantages, which they possessed for many a year to come. In another direction, namely in Hungary, similar rights were vouchsafed them by Caloman, King of Hungary, for the help given him against the Normans, who were again infesting the coasts of Dalmatia and Croatia. These negotiations were the last acts of Doge Vitale Michiel I., who died shortly after and whose successor was Ordelaf Faledro,[1] or Falier.

This was in 1102, and two years after the Doge prepared a fresh armament to help Baldwin, King of Jerusalem, in the Holy Land. This force was successful against Sidon, which the Venetians captured, and where they were allowed a church, a street, and a market place ; also the right to use their own weights and measures, and to legislate for their own subjects. This was the first kind of colony established by Venice in the East, and served as a model for many

[1] It is curious to observe how the Christian name is simply the surname spelt backward.

others planted by her along her victorious path. These colonies claimed from the parent city a care and protection often onerous to discharge, although it cannot be denied that they added largely to the prestige and wealth of the great trading Republic.

Their rivals, the Pisans and Genoese, were also active and successful in this war ; and Baldwin was not slow to recompense all who helped in the good cause, though the rewards and gifts he granted with equal justice and generosity to the two powers, did but fan the flame of jealousy already existing between them, and sowed the seeds of war and bloodshed to be reaped so terribly in future ages.

The glory of the Venetian arms abroad was sadly counterbalanced by disasters at home. Awful storms of wind and rain swept over the islands of the lagunes, spreading universal terror and desolation. The havoc caused throughout the town was unprecedented, and so great was the violence of the hurricane, that the whole island of Malamocco was submerged and swept completely away. The Doge ordered that the bishopric, which had existed on the island, should be transferred to Chioggia, but the survivors clung to re-establishing as far as could be the old order of things ; and settled down not far from where their old habitation had been, though on a spot more secured against the rage of the elements, and where the present Malamocco now stands. Soon after this tempest two fires threatened to annihilate the desolated town ; the churches of the Santi Apostoli, SS. Ermagora e Fortunato, S. Cassiano, Sta. Maria Formosa, S. Zaccaria (in which more than a hundred nuns were suffocated), S. Moisè, Sta. Maria Zobenigo, S. Barnaba, S. Trovaso, and several others were burnt, and even the ducal palace and St. Mark's did not escape intact. The prosperity of Venice however was sufficient to make head speedily against such misfortunes ; and preparations were started to take vengeance on the King of Hungary, who had judged the moment a fitting one to break the treaty existing between the two countries, and had incited the Dalmatian subjects of the Republic to revolt. Doge Falier determined to quell this revolt in person, and in 1114 he led an expedition against Dalmatia, from whence he returned home covered with victory and honour, and was received at Rialto with joyful triumph. Two years later fresh rebellions broke out again in Dalmatia, and the Venetian fleet, once more commanded by Falier, sailed to the scene of action and laid siege to Zara. The result however was far different to the former experience. The Venetians met with a severe defeat, and a severe loss in the person of their Doge, who died fighting valiantly, and whose death utterly dispirited his followers. His dead body was carried back to Venice, and universal lamentation was the tribute paid to him who, in the words of the old chronicler Dandolo, had so "gloriously ended his days."

It was in this reign that the Pala d'Oro was completed, that reredos of gold and precious stones and enamels to which allusion has already been made (see p. 60). Another important event under Doge Falier's rule was the foundation of the Arsenal, that cradle, so to speak, of so much of the power and wealth and glory of Venice, and from whence for so many centuries her ships were to go forth "conquering and to conquer."

On the death of Ordelafo Falier in 1116, Domenico Michiel was chosen to succeed him, and inaugurated his reign by a treaty with Stephen, King of Hungary, which secured peace to the two countries for five years. His next act was to prepare another expedition to the East, where affairs wore a threatening aspect for the Crusaders, and where Pope Calixtus II. was urging all Christendom to repair and rescue the armies of the Cross. A fleet of not less than two hundred vessels under the command of the Doge set sail for Syria ; and at Jaffa a fierce battle was fought between the Saracens and Venetians, when the latter remained victorious. But the strife was a desperate one, and the slaughter so great that one historian [1] states the victors stood ankle deep in blood on their decks, while the sea for a circuit of two miles (some say four) was red with blood. The Doge, having settled his navy in safety at Jaffa, went on to Jerusalem, where he was warmly welcomed by the Council of Regency, with whom he concluded a treaty securing many advantages to his republic. One-fourth of the town of Acre had on a previous occasion been allotted to the Venetians ; now a new grant assured to them an entire street in each city of the kingdom of Jerusalem, as well as a bath, a bakehouse, a market and a church. All their imports were to pass free of duty ; they were exempt from taxes ; their

[1] William of Tyre, L. xii. §. 22.

magistrates were assigned almost paramount authority, and whenever any questions arose between Venetians they were tried by their own courts of law, and only when they appeared as prosecutors had they to appeal to the king's court. Other privileges and concessions beside were granted them, and in the forthcoming conquests (of which the Crusaders already made sure) a third of Tyre, Ascalon, and their dependencies was to be theirs. The siege of Tyre had been settled upon by the Crusaders, not from any facility offered for taking it—for its position was almost impregnable—but from the hazardous expedient of drawing by lot the name of the town to be assaulted. Probably no other fortress could have offered such difficulties or proved of such importance. It was defended by both Saracen and Egyptian forces by land, where a circuit of fortified walls with numerous and strong ramparts presented obstacles of a most serious nature. On the sea side the town was considered well-nigh unassailable, but here Doge Michiel occupied a narrow space which blocked the harbour, his object being to cut off from the besieged all communication or assistance from without. The siege dragged on for three long months, and in that time the land forces had many a weary and arduous fight with the Saracens, who showed no sign of surrendering. The allies, dispirited by their want of success, were greedy, querulous and suspicious, and rumours arose in their camp that the Venetians, secure in their ships, not only escaped the ills to which the land forces were exposed, but that should a general engagement take place they would sail away and leave their allies to

perish on land. This accusation, as foul as it was
unfounded, was answered by the Doge with a noble-
ness of language and behaviour that reveal the high
character of the man. He ordered every one of his
ships to be dismantled from bow to stern, and proceeded in person to the camp bearing with him the
masts, sails, rigging, rudders and oars, of his fleet.
"You have called in question," he said, "the loyalty of
ourselves and our services. Here is the guarantee of
our good faith. Deprived of these equipments we could
not, even if we wished it, leave our post, where now we
shall remain exposed to perils far beyond what you
may be called on to endure." This proof of devotion
and self-sacrifice brought the allies to their senses,
and to atone for the injustice done to the Venetians, they insisted on the fittings being restored to
the ships and all put into order again. The siege
lasted another two months after this, when a lucky
stratagem enabled the Crusaders to possess the town.
They captured a carrier-pigeon flying into Tyre and
bearing under its wing a message of speedy help and
deliverance from the Sultan of Damascus. This
message was instantly turned into one of discourage-
ment, saying that succour was impossible, and advising the besieged to surrender. The plot succeeded
perfectly. The bird flew on its errand with the forged
news and counsel, and the inhabitants settled to
yield. The victorious troops entered in triumph ;
and, as had been previously determined, one-third of
the town was ceded to the Doge, who immediately
took possession of his rights. Shortly after Ascalon
was besieged and taken ; the Venetians again received

their allotted portion, and after this they sailed home. There is a story extant, that during the siege of Tyre Doge Michiel's funds ran short, when to satisfy his

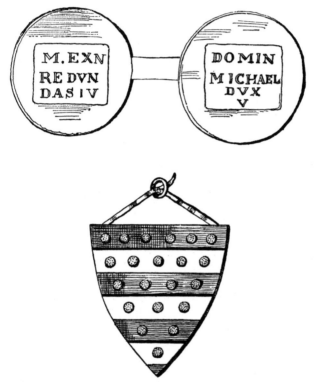

SHIELD AND COINS OF THE DOGE, DOMENICO MICHIEL.

followers he ordered a leather coin to be stamped and given to the troops with the promise that on their return to Venice they should receive the full value in money. The promise was kept, and in recollection of the fact the Michiel arms to this day carry on their shield a bar azure and argent with twenty-one coins.

In Tyre the Venetians lost no time in building three churches, and establishing their commercial houses, and the new and brisk trade which they now plied with Syria, was a dire offence and injury to the Greeks at Constantinople, who saw their commerce languish and their wealth diminish to an alarming extent. To quote a modern writer : " The commerce of the West with Persia, Egypt, Syria, and India, ceased to pass through the Bosphorus. Genoa and Venice became the marts at which France, Italy, and Germany sought their Eastern goods. It is probable that the trade of Constantinople fell off by a third or even a half in the fifty years that followed the First Crusade." [1] This state of things was not to be endured, and the bitterness aroused in Constantinople at the supremacy gained by Venice and the position lost to herself was keenly felt. Venice had been for awhile more or less subject to the Greek power ; from that she had raised herself to a level of equality and friendship ; then for years the two states had been powerful and faithful allies. Now Venice had left her former protector and friend in the lurch, and regardless of old times and of old links had developed new interests, new privileges, new advantages, on her own account which meant ruin and decay for her ally. No wonder that Constantinople was now turned into a bitter foe, and that she determined to strike a blow and utter a protest against such a fate. An order was issued to

[1] Story of the Nations, " Byzantium," chap. xxi. p. 268. C. W. C. Oman

interfere with the trade of Venice, and to seize all her merchant vessels and ships wherever they were met with in Grecian waters. This was in 1125, and the Doge at once set to work to avenge such a decree, and defend his country's rights. He sailed for the Archipelago, and the expedition was one long series of triumphs. He besieged and conquered Rhodes, Scio, Samos, Paros, Mitylene, Tenedos, and Lesbos ; he carried destruction and terror along all the coast of the Morea, where, with regret it must be said, he stained his victories by carrying off numerous slaves from among the fairest of both sexes ; from there he proceeded to Dalmatia, and put down with a strong hand the towns of Zara, Spalato, and Trau, which had joined the King of Hungary in revolt against their suzerain of Venice. Covered with glory and spoils Michiel returned home, and retired soon after to the monastery of S. Giorgio Maggiore, where he died in 1130, and where his monument speaks of him as the " Terror of the Greeks," in the words : " Terror Graecorum jacet hic." It was this Doge, who instituted small tabernacles to be placed at the head of the narrow dark streets of Venice, wherein a lamp was to be set to lighten the glory of the saint enshrined within, and illumine the traveller on his way.

Under the dukedom of his son-in-law and successor Pietro Polani, 1130, a short and successful campaign took place against Padua, which is of interest merely as being the first occasion on which Venice made use of mercenary troops for her wars on the mainland. Numerous and petty warfares also occupied the arms of the Republic against Pisa, and the rivalry and enmity between these two powers were fanned by uncertain victories, which left the supremacy of each doubtful, and only intensified their jealousies. A more important war occurred in 1147, when friendly terms were for awhile resumed with Constantinople on the occasion of the Emperor Manuel applying to Venice for aid against the Normans, who under their king, Roger of Sicily, were threatening the coasts of Greece and Dalmatia. The Venetians, who had equal cause with the Greeks to fear the Normans as foes, espoused without delay the Emperor's cause, who confirmed to them the golden statute and other privileges granted of old by his grandfather Alexius. The Doge set out to lead the expedition, but was taken ill before reaching Corfu, and only came home to die, when Domenico Morosini was named as his successor.

The reconciliation between Venice and Constantinople was of short duration, and in spite of the efforts made to keep the peace, the two states broke out anew into furious hatred and fighting. The Venetians were overcome, but soon after avenged themselves by seizing an Imperial galley, which they adorned with cloth of gold and gorgeous hangings, and dressing up an Ethiopian slave distinguished for his ugliness, they saluted him as Emperor of Constantinople, in ridicule of Manuel's swarthy complexion. The Emperor was too sorely pressed by necessity to pay any apparent heed to the insult ; he made every preparation for action, and bided his time for vengeance. The island of Corfu was taken by the allies after a long and stubborn resistance, and soon after the Doge signed a treaty with King Roger, which was confirmed by his son William, wherein the interests of Venice were not forgotten. The seven years of Morosini's reign were chiefly marked by treaties with different powers in regard of the commerce and trade of the state ; and the marvellous advantages secured to Venice in all these treaties must be borne in mind when her riches and prosperity excite surprise. At every port, where she traded to any considerable extent, she had free entrance and exit for goods, whether imported or exported. Special privileges were granted to her citizens and merchants ; and the enormous facilities thus opened to her enabled her with ease to attain to those heights of splendour and wealth, which arouse our eulogy and wonder. Still it must be remembered what difficulties she overcame before this condition was reached ; and it is impossible to withhold one's admiration as one contemplates the obstacles surmounted, the opportunities never neglected, the enemies repulsed, and the glorious fight for liberty (that origin and mainspring of Venice's existence) nobly sustained from one generation to another.

In Doge Morosini's reign it is also said that the campanile or bell tower of St. Mark's was finished. Its foundations had been laid in 912 during Doge Pietro Tribuno's reign, and some ascribe its termination to this period, others to a later date.[1]

---

[1] An odd form of torture took place of old in this belfry. A strong beam projected half way up the tower, from which was suspended a cage, wherein were placed ecclesiastical offenders guilty of grave delinquencies. The cage was lined with wood, and the criminal

CANAL SHOWING CAMPANILE OF ST. MARK'S.
(From " Calli e Canali," op. cit.)

Vitale Michiel II. was chosen to succeed Morosini in 1156, at a moment when affairs in Italy were rife with importance and interest. The peninsula was torn in two by one of those frequent struggles between Guelph and Ghibelline which so often devastated her land, bringing ruin and evil in their train. Frederick Barbarossa, Emperor of Germany, had finally dominated Milan, and now prepared to avenge himself on the Venetians for the aid given by them to his enemy, Pope Alexander III. He first stirred up the inhabitants of Padua, Verona, and Ferrara against Venice, and supported Ulric, Patriarch of Aquileja, in his claims to the see of Grado, to which see the Pope had granted the adhesion of all the Dalmatian bishoprics. Ulric waited for what he considered a favourable moment when Venice was harassed with other foes, to summon the barons of Friuli to his aid ; he then invaded Grado, drove out the patriarch Enrico Dandolo, and appropriated to himself all the plunder whereon he could lay his hands. He was busy in this way when the Venetians, headed by the Doge, bore down upon him and, after defeating his troops, carried him off. prisoner to Venice in company with the twelve canons of his chapter. He was only released after much time and deliberation, and after he had sworn to send annually to Venice a tribute of a boar and twelve pigs. This fine (a humiliating representation of the patriarch and his canons) was to be sent every year on the first

remained in it for the term allotted him, sometimes for his whole life. His food was conveyed to him through a tube, and this form of punishment, known as "*La Cheba*" (*Gabbia*), remained in use till 1518, when it was abolished altogether.

Thursday in Carnival. A famous festival was instituted in consequence, when the Doge assisted at the
slaughtering of the animals, and at the destruction of
certain wooden erections in the *Sala del Piovego*,
representing the Friulian castles and fortresses overthrown by him when he took Ulric prisoner. This
festival, celebrated on the day known in Venice as
that of *Zioba grasso*, was continued till the time of
Doge Andrea Gritti in 1524, when both the humiliation and the buffoonery were judged to have lasted
long enough, and were done away with.

Affairs in the East now engrossed public attention
in Venice in a fearful way. The vengeance vowed
long ago by Manuel at the siege of Corfu was to be
paid, and paid with interest. The Emperor organised
a secret plot, by which all the Venetians throughout his
dominions were to be seized, their goods confiscated,
and their property handed over to the Greeks. Some
hint of this scheme found its way to the ears of
Sebastiano Ziani and Orio Malipiero, ambassadors
from the Republic at the Court of Constantinople,
but the Emperor was able to allay their suspicions
till the 12th of March, 1171, when the conspiracy
broke out in full execution, and hardly a Venetian
escaped. The fury and indignation aroused by the
news in Venice was intense ; and all hope that the
report of so dire a calamity had been exaggerated
was dispelled by the arrival in Venice of a few ships,
which had miraculously evaded the wholesale capture
and brought confirmation of the tidings. The consternation throughout the city was great; " War, war!"
was the cry heard on all sides, and no pains were

spared to prepare an armament wherewith to liberate their countrymen, and wipe out the insult inflicted on their name. The public coffers, however, had been drained by former wars, and could not bear the strain now brought to bear for the equipment of the fleet. The Doge consequently determined to raise a loan on the six different districts (*sestieri*), wherein the city was divided,[1] and an interest of four per cent., payable twice a year, was to be paid on them by the State revenues. This transaction led to the foundation of the Chamber of Loans, which paid half-yearly an interest of four per cent. to its contributors. The holders of these bonds from the chamber could sell, bequeath, or mortgage them as they chose ; and in the method now adopted for repaying their loans "the earliest instance is on record of the funding system, and the first example of a permanent national debt." [2]

The loan, and the interest paid on it (a rate far below the standard of the age), were most unpopular in Venice, and added to the personal feeling against the Doge, soon to be manifested in a fatal way.

In the meanwhile a powerful fleet had been prepared ; each Venetian family had strained every nerve to contribute of its best and bravest, the Giustiniani alone devoting every member of their house to their country's service. This gallant host sailed under the command of Doge Vitale Michiel in September, 1171, to a fate alike undeserved and

[1] These *sestieri*, or districts, exist to this day, and are—Castello, San Marco, Cannaregio, Santa Croce, San Polo, Dorsoduro.

[2] "Sketches from Venetian History," vol. i. chap. i.   Murray, London, 1831.

tragic. Their only conquests were those of some towns along the Dalmatian coast, which submitted almost immediately to the superior forces brought against them. On nearing the shores of Negropont they were met by some embassies of the Greek Emperor, who proposed that they should send some deputies to settle their differences by negotiation. The Venetians had all to lose, and the Greeks all to win by such a suggestion, but the Doge consented to it, and Manuel spun out the conferences till the winter was over. Then the Venetian contingent found themselves with their troops disheartened by delay, discontent and discord spreading through their ranks, and a worse evil awaiting them in the shape of the plague which now broke out among them. It is a matter of surprise and distress, and one not easily explained, how the Venetians, generally so wide awake and crafty in all questions of diplomacy and intrigue, can have let themselves be hoodwinked and duped in this way. To allow their forces, panting for revenge and honour, to eat their hearts out with delay and hope deferred, is a puzzle not to be solved, and one cannot but blame the Doge severely for his want of acumen and discernment. At Scio, where the fleet was anchored, the plague broke out in all its horrors; it was said that Manuel had poisoned the wells and waters, and though this accusation has been called in question, the fact remains that the Venetians perished ignominiously, without striking a blow for their country—mown down in thousands, the victims of inaction, despair, and the pestilence. Of the whole family of Giustinian, who had volunteered so nobly in their country's cause, not one survived; and this house, one of the oldest and noblest in Venice, was only saved from extinction by the sole remaining member, Nicolò, then a monk, being released from his vows and given in marriage to Anna Michiel, the Doge's daughter. This union was crowned with the birth of several sons ; the parents then retreated to monastic life, and renewed the vows interrupted for so just a reason. All that remained of the Venetian host set sail homewards, conveying with them on board ship the pestilence which had stricken so many abroad, and now spread with deadly rapidity through the city. This new evil, joined to the loss of such thousands of their fellow citizens, and the destruction of their fleet, drove the people to madness. They rose up against their Doge, to whose unpopularity in the finance question was added the failure of the expedition to the East, and he fell a victim to the fury of the populace, who murdered him close to the Church of S. Zaccaria on May 28, 1172.

The state of Venice had reached a climax when vigorous measures were needed, if the Republic was to hold up her head as a power in Europe, or sink beneath the troubles and seditions now threatening her dissolution. One of her finest armaments had just been annihilated ; her ranks were thinned by disease and pestilence ; to the loss of many among her noblest and best was joined the mortification of defeat and discomfiture ; while to set the seal to all these griefs and distresses, her ruler, called by the popular voice and raised by unanimous election to the throne, had been hurled from that height to die a cruel and undeserved death. Some extraordinary means were clearly required to restore confidence and order, reforming at the same time both the powers of the governing bodies, and the mode whereby those governors were elected. The task was no slight one ; but notwithstanding the risks and perils it involved, leading men in Venice did not shrink from their duty. They set to work to remodel the system by which the General Assembly till then had been governed, and effect more order and dignity in its action. It was decided to name twelve electors, two from each of the six districts, who in their turn appointed forty of the ablest among their citizens, thus forming a council of four hundred and eighty individuals. These were to be renewed every year by fresh electors, chosen from out this same council by nomination and by ballot. Thus was laid the basis of that famous body known as the "Great Council," or *Maggior Consiglio*, to whom the supreme authority, both distributive and deliberative, was entrusted, and whose voice was paramount in all affairs of state. Eventually in 1296 it developed into more abiding shape and prominence, when at the epoch known in its history as the *Serrata del Gran Consiglio* (closing of the Great Council) it assumed the characteristics and features which distinguished it for so many years.

Restrictions were also made in regard of the Doge's power. His councillors, originally two in number, had proved themselves simply puppets in his hands, echoing and seconding his every wish. They were now increased to six—one from each district—and without their consent the Doge might not insert any special clauses in foreign treaties ; nor might he act in the free and independent way that till now his predecessors had done. From henceforward the Doges of Venice were to be surrounded with greater external pomp and ceremonial, but their position was changed in actual essentials, and instead of an almost absolute sovereignty they dwindled down more and more to the decorated but empty figure-head of a vast oligarchy. The dignity that wrapped the person of the Doge was now to be largely increased ; when he went out he was not to be accompanied only by his servants and retainers as heretofore, but by an escort of nobles and people ; after his election he was to be carried, in Eastern fashion, round the piazza in a circular chair, in later times called *Pozzetto*, scattering money to the people. This alteration as to the Doge's power was not distasteful to the generality of the citizens ; it promised on the whole greater tranquillity to the Republic, and it also removed their fears of a despotic governor. But another clause had been added as to the Doge's election, not equally to their liking, and which was as follows : The Doge had to be chosen by eleven electors, all members of the Great Council, and only on the suffrage of nine votes could he be duly nominated Doge. After this actual appointment a form was gone through of presenting him to the people in the Church of St. Mark to ratify the decision already taken. This however was far from satisfying the populace, who accused the councillors of tyranny, and of depriving the people of their liberty and freedom of choice as to their ruler. Feeling ran so high that tumult and bloodshed threatened to interrupt the proceedings ; and to appease the anger of the crowd it was decreed that after the Doge's nomination he should be presented to them in the church with the words: " This is your Doge, an it please you," and that the election should only be valid when the people had sanctioned by their approval the choice of the electors. In this way calmness and harmony were restored, and this order of things lasted till the time of Doge Foscari, when even this concession was withdrawn, and the aristocracy established more fully their power and authority to the exclusion of that of the masses. The change here mentioned in the mode of ducal election closes the first period of the personal sway of the Doges ; a period that had lasted from their foundation down to this date (1172), and during which they had been possessed of well-nigh unlimited power, not to say despotism. This was now to fade from their grasp, and external show and ostentation were to replace real authority and administration.

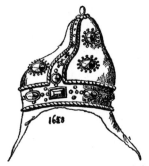

DUCAL CAP OF THE YEAR 1658.

V.

GERMANY, ROME AND VENICE.

1172–1193.)

THE first Doge appointed under the changes mentioned above, and with diminution of power, was Sebastiano Ziani, a native of Altino, and a man of peculiar ability and intellect, possessed too of a large fortune. His first care was to wreak vengeance on the murderers of his predecessor. He next devoted himself to the finances of the state, which had fallen into disorder and confusion, and by the advice of the *Pregadi* he decided to remit for the time being the payment of interest on the national debt. Peace being sorely needed for the readjustment of the financial difficulty, he despatched ambassadors to the courts of Constantinople and Naples to offer terms to the respective sovereigns. With Manuel this proved impossible, but with William II. of Sicily a league was signed for twenty years.

Shortly afterwards the arms of the Republic were invited to co-operate against the Greeks as to their possession of the town of Ancona. This town was one much coveted by the Venetians, who grudged the advantages gained by so important a foothold in

Italy to the rulers of Constantinople ; and when
Christian, Archbishop of Mayence, by order of the
Emperor Frederick, besieged the town and invited
the Venetians to help him, they gladly consented
and, forgetting their former differences with Frederick,
sent a fleet to assist his forces. The allies however
were compelled to withdraw, for the garrison made a
gallant defence, and, after enduring all the horrors
of scarcity and famine, were relieved in time to save
their town and their honour, and drive the Germans
and Venetians from their walls.

The dukedom of Doge Ziani is crowded with
events of wide and stirring interest, but the confusion
as to exactitude of dates, together with much dis-
crepancy as to detail, is extreme, and few accounts
agree in their statements or attempt any chronological
order. The meeting in Venice of the Emperor
Frederick Barbarossa and the Pope Alexander III.,
though related by most historians, is not enlarged on
by all, while the accounts as to how the Pope arrived
in Venice and his behaviour to the Emperor are
many and varied. Venice had been chosen as the
place where the reconciliation between Frederick and
Alexander could take place, as she alone in Italy
presented the neutral ground necessary for such an
act. When Frederick Barbarossa had entered Italy
at the head of a large army, the chief towns of Lombardy had formed the well-known Lombard League
against him, in which they received the support of
Alexander III., who maintained his right to the tiara
against Victor IV., the creature and *protégé* of the
Emperor. But in that league Venice as yet had

forborne to enter, having taken no part in the battle
of Legnano, when the Imperial forces had been
defeated by the Leaguers ; and her speedy acknowledgment of Alexander as Sovereign Pontiff had
gained her the goodwill of the Pope. The account
of the manner in which Alexander III. came to
Venice is veiled in mystery, and the secrecy of the
whole transaction has cast over it a veil of doubt and
unreality difficult to unravel. Some writers say that
the Pope arrived in disguise, and was only discovered
after he had passed several days—it is even said,
months — in the town, when news was conveyed
to the Doge that he was serving as a menial in
one of the monasteries. Ziani, having ascertained
the truth of this rumour, treated his guest with
the honour due to his rank and position, and despatched ambassadors to Frederick to sue for peace
and reconciliation between him and the Head of the
Church. These ambassadors were treated by Frederick with extreme scorn, and sent back to Venice
with the following message : " Return to your Prince
and Senate, and tell them that Frederick, Emperor
of the Romans, claims from them a fugitive who is
his foe. If he is not speedily delivered up, the
Venetians will prove themselves enemies to the
Empire, an insult I will avenge by assailing you by
land and sea, and spite of their incredulity, I will
plant my victorious eagles before the Basilica of St.
Mark." These words were backed by deeds as well.
A fleet, aided by Genoa and Pisa, was made ready
against the Republic, commanded by the Emperor's
son Otho, a lad of eighteen years. The Venetians

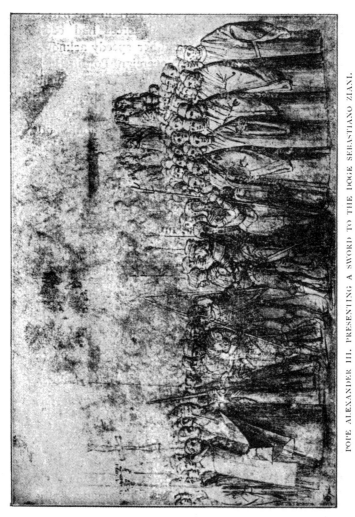

POPE ALEXANDER III. PRESENTING A SWORD TO THE DOGE SEBASTIANO ZIANI.

(*From a drawing by Gentile Bellini (in the Print Room at the British Museum); original study for one of the Paintings in the Ducal Palace, destroyed by fire in 1577.*)

were far from ready for the attack, but though they could bring only thirty ships to the fore, they sailed out against their invaders, headed by Doge Ziani, who had received from the Pope a golden sword and his blessing. Armed with these spiritual and temporal advantages, the Venetians obtained a signal victory. They captured no less than forty-eight galleys, besides a host of prisoners, including the youthful commander. The Doge generously sent the captive Otho at once back to his father with twelve ambassadors to renew the proposals for peace, and the Emperor, struck with the noble conduct of Ziani, agreed to come to Venice and make terms with Alexander. The meeting between the Vicar of Christ and the Emperor of Rome and Germany took place in St. Mark's Church, the Doge and a crowd of nobles and courtiers being present. The Emperor, in token of his penitence and humility, took off his royal mantle, which, together with his regal decorations, he laid before the Pope, himself kneeling to kiss the feet of his spiritual lord. Alexander, carried away by pride and exultation, placed his foot on Frederick's neck, exclaiming, "Thou shalt go upon the lion and adder ; the young lion and the dragon shalt thou tread under thy feet." With an indignation not to be smothered by any amount of humiliation, the Emperor retorted, "Not to thee, but to St. Peter." Whereat the Pope, to enforce still more his triumph and his foe's abasement, placed both his feet upon the Emperor's neck, rejoining, "Both to me and to St. Peter." He then raised the prostrate monarch, the kiss of reconciliation was given and received, and for the moment harmony was restored between the sovereigns. In the vestibule of St. Mark's is still to be seen a slab of red marble marking the spot where this memorable scene took place, and though many of the details are exaggerated and enlarged beyond their original actuality, the fact remains that in 1177 the interview took place on that site.

Other writers—perhaps, too, the most trustworthy—make no mention of the Pope's secret stay in Venice. They talk of his arrival and open reception with due honours from the Doge, of his residence for some months at the palace of the Patriarchs of Grado at S. Silvestro, and of the reconciliation between him and the Emperor, without any of the additions of arrogance and wounded pride related above. But whatever may have been the smaller incidents and details in the scene, no one can deny that it was a strange and an important episode ; and while the story of it is to be seen to this day in glowing colours on the walls of the Hall of the Great Council, the record of the advantage and gain it brought to Venice is to be found in her archives and in the increased liberty and greatness now attendant on her story. For Pope and Emperor alike were ready to give proof of their gratitude to the Republic and her rulers for the part they had played in bringing about so needed and so longed for a reconciliation ; and while Frederick renewed old privileges in regard of commerce and conferred new ones as well, Alexander added spiritual advantages as to indulgences, consecrations of churches, and rebuilding of chapels. He also presented to the Doge the Golden Rose,[1] and confirmed to Venice her authority as queen and sovereign of the Adriatic. It was in consequence of this latter grant that from henceforward the rites of the "Sposalizio del Mare" became more elaborate, that espousal of the ocean which gave to Venice one of her most poetic titles, and also enhanced so greatly her position and rank among maritime powers.

The simple ceremony introduced at the time of Doge Orseolo II. was now supplemented by one far more splendid and ornate. The Pope presented Doge Ziani with a consecrated ring with the words, " Receive this as a sign and pledge of the sovereignty which you and your successors will possess for ever over the sea." The Doge then set out in the *Bucentaur,* surrounded by an innumerable company of dignitaries, ambassadors and nobles, escorted by boats and galleys crowded equally with high officials, and followed in their turn by masses of the people. Arrived at the island of Sant' Elena, the Doge was received by the Bishop of Castello, while the monks of the island offered him a bunch of damask roses in a silver vase.[2] Of these the Doge kept one for himself, and distributed the rest to his suite. The procession then moved on to the entrance of the harbour of the Lido, when the *Bucentaur* was turned toward the sea,

---

[1] The Golden Rose presented by Alexander III. to Doge Ziani is in use to this day, when it is placed on the high altar of St. Mark's on the great festivals of the Church.

[2] The spot where the roses once grew, and which till lately boasted a lovely garden and vine-covered paths, has been reft of its beauty, and is now a blank space of ground devoted to military exercises.

THE DOGE SETTING OUT IN THE *BUCENTAUR* TO ESPOUSE THE SEA.
(*From Giacomo Franco's* " *Habiti d'Huomeni et Donne
Venetiane,*" &c. *Venice,* 1609.)

and the nuptials were consummated by the Doge throwing the consecrated ring into the ocean. This act had a meaning and significance to the Venetians of old far beyond what the bare recital of it might lead us nowadays to imagine; for, apart from the almost feudal ownership and suzerainty implied by the ceremony, it spoke to them of courage, hope and venture, and in a mysterious manner blessed to them their every enterprise and undertaking "in the mighty waters." The sanction conferred on the ceremony by the Pope had also the effect of proclaiming to the rest of Europe the supremacy of Venice over the waters of the Adriatic; and this act, together with its material use in exalting her in the eyes of her neighbours, insured her position as ruler on that element over which she had attained so strong and widespread a dominion. The concourse, too, of strangers and foreigners, who flocked to Venice to witness this pageant, gave an impetus to trade and to business, by no means one of the least of the advantages that accrued to the town from this festivity.[1]

The Pope had not been forgetful to bestow on Ziani outward tokens of his gratitude as well as the spiritual advantages already showered upon his town.

---

[1] The only record now left of the old ceremonial of the "Sposalizio" is the quaint procession in the clock tower of St. Mark's before the image of the Madonna and Child, when at the striking of each hour the three Eastern Magi come out of a side-door and offer obeisance, as they totter before the Holy Mother and Son in grotesque solemnity. This function begins every year on Ascension Day, and lasts for a fortnight. It dates from the year 1172, when it ranked as one of the sights at the "Festa della Sensa."

The Doge had accompanied Alexander to Rome after the reconciliation at Venice, and was lodged in the Pope's own palace, and treated with the same hospitality so lately extended to the fugitive Pontiff. Alexander conferred on him certain marks of royalty and imperial rank, adopted henceforward by the Venetian Doges: and from this period a lighted taper, a sword, a canopy, a chair of state, a footstool covered with cloth of gold (these two latter he was allowed to use even in the Pontifical Chapel), silver trumpets, and embroidered banners proclaimed the presence of the Doge.

On his return home Ziani busied himself largely in matters of commerce, and in embellishing the town. He improved the Square of St. Mark by re-building the Church of St. Geminiano, which stood opposite St. Mark's till 1810, when it was demolished by Napoleon to build an extra wing to the royal palace; he was also the first to pave the square, and this with a sort of flint-stone, replaced in 1264 by large flat stones. It was also now that the two columns were erected on the Piazzetta. They had been brought to Venice in the reign of Doge Domenico Michiel, and remained buried in the mud till this date, when they were placed in their present position. The story runs of how they were set up by one Nicolò Barattieri,[1] a Lombard, who directed the erection by causing the ropes with which they were hoisted to be

---

[1] There seems some uncertainty as to the name of this Lombard, some writers insinuating that his passion for gambling gained for him his sinister surname; others speaking of him as "*Nicolò Staratoni, maestro dei Baradori.*"

kept constantly wet. Being told to name his reward for the work so successfully accomplished, he claimed the right to keep gaming tables between the two columns. Such a pursuit was then strictly forbidden by the laws of the state, but his request could not be refused, so to counteract the carrying out of the prohibited entertainment, a decree was passed that on that spot all public executions should take place. The decree became law; the gallows remained masters of the field, and for ever ousted from that fair situation the chances and hazards of the lottery boards.

On these columns were placed, some few years later, the two statues representing the two patron saints of the town—the winged lion of St. Mark, and St. Theodore on the crocodile.[1] The labours of Barattieri did not cease with the erections of the columns; he is said to have designed the first bridge built across the Grand Canal at Rialto, which was of wood, and was known then as the *Ponte della Moneta* or *del Quartarol,* from a small coin paid for crossing it. It is also supposed that he invented the sort of cage or suspended scaffolding, wherein to hoist workmen and materials on high for any

[1] Some opinions hold to this latter being St. George of Dalmatia, and not St. Theodore; but this opinion is not generally accepted, and popular proverbs and sayings have asserted that it is the old patron of their city, not the protector of their vanquished dependency, who stands thus on high. There were originally three columns, one of which fell into the water and could never be recovered. Within the last two years both the Lion and St. Theodore have been taken down for restoration, and after undergoing thorough repair, have been replaced on their heights.

building requiring repair or alteration, an invention
still used at the present day.

On the 12th of April, 1178, after innumerable acts
of piety and devotion, and large almsgiving to the
poor, Doge Ziani abdicated the throne, and retired to
the monastery of St. Giorgio, where he died at the
age of seventy-six. Before his abdication he enforced
some alterations as to the election of his successors,
which were henceforth adopted, and were as follows :
Instead of the eleven electors who had been appointed
at his nomination, four were to be chosen from the
Great Council, who in their turn should choose ten,
and from these Forty the Doge, according to the
majority of votes polled by him, was to be elected.
The process resulting in the ultimate choice of the
Doge was changed and readjusted more than once,
but as the changes introduced by Sebastiano Ziani
became the ruling order of things for almost a century,
it will be well to describe here briefly the process of
election. As soon as the Forty were chosen they
withdrew to a special chamber, from whence they
could not emerge till a unanimous choice had been
agreed on ; and meanwhile no hint was to escape to
the outside world of the deliberations passed in that
secret chamber. In front of a table, on which stood
a ballot-box and an urn, a president with two secretaries took their seats. The secretaries presented to
each elector a slip of paper whereon he recorded the
name of his candidate. The slips were then placed
in the urn, and one drawn at hazard. Should the
name drawn happen to be that of one of the electors,
he was requested to withdraw, when a discussion

arose as to his merits, qualifications, or shortcomings, all of which were recorded by the secretaries. The person in question was then recalled and allowed to defend and excuse himself, and if successful in so doing, and also in obtaining the twenty-five votes needed for election, he was declared Doge ; if not, the process began again till the necessary qualifications had been attained. When this point had been reached, the Signory were informed of the event, and the new Doge escorted by the electors went to St. Mark's, where, standing in the pulpit on the north side of the choir, he was presented to the people. After this he walked up to the high altar, where he took the coronation oath, and where the standard of St. Mark was given into his hands. The great west doors were then thrown open, and the Doge at the head of a long procession filed round the square, afterwards passing through the *Porta della Carta*,[1] and ascending the great stairs into the ducal palace. At the top of the stairs the ducal bonnet was placed on his head by the eldest ducal councillor. He then went into the *Sala del Piovego*, where his predecessor had lain in state a few days before, and where he too would be laid in the same way when his earthly course was run.[2]

On the retirement of Doge Ziani the new mode of

---

[1] So called because through this gateway the secretaries passed to their offices in the ducal palace.

[2] Most of this account is taken from " Venetian Studies," by Horatio F. Brown (London, 1887), whose study on the Venetian constitution, drawn from the chief documents and archives in Venice, is a fund of information on this and other points in Venetian history.

election was put into practice, when Orio Mastropiero
or Malipiero was appointed in his stead. He had
already been named to the ducal chair in 1172, but
had declined the post, declaring that Ziani, who was
then elected, was more fitted for the dignity than
himself. The fourteen years of his dukedom passed
unmarked by great or stirring events ; and but for a
revolt in the town of Zara, not very successfully
quenched by the Venetians, and an expedition made
by their fleet to the support of the besieged town of
Acre, there is little to record. In 1192 Doge Malipiero retired, like his predecessor, to a monastery,
when the quietude that marked his reign was startled
into life and activity by the elevation to the dukedom
of a Doge whose name and doings have been sung
and chronicled by poet and historian in well-nigh
every nation.

But before passing on to speak of "blind old
Dandolo," mention must be made of some new laws
and institutions now introduced into Venice, and
which formed a vital part of the government and
administration of the Republic. Among the new
offices now called into being was that of the *Procuratori di San Marco*, whose original number of one
was at this time increased to three, in order to
administer the wealth and legacies bequeathed by
Doge Ziani to the poor of the town and to the
Church of St. Mark. Their numbers gradually
swelled to six, and in 1442 to nine ; and at this
number they remained till the fall of the Republic.
The dignity of procurator ranked immediately after
that of the Doge, and was conferred on patricians,

who as ambassadors or generals had deserved well of their country. Their dress was a gorgeous one, of red damask, with large capacious sleeves, which figure again and again in historical paintings. In early times the Doge himself was often chosen from their ranks;

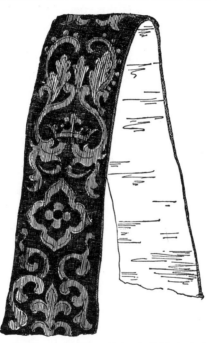

STOLE OF A PROCURATOR. (*From Yriarte's " Venise," &c., op. cit.*

while their duties were to superintend the church and treasures of St. Mark's; to watch over the safety of the members of the Great Council when that council was sitting; to act as guardians for orphans, and as executors to whatever Venetian chose to appoint them in that capacity. Their privileges were numerous; they were exempt from serving on foreign embassies, and inhabited a fine palace in the Square of St. Mark, where they were obliged to hold audiences three times a week. Another body who were also created at this period (1187) were the *Avogadori*, who were employed in all civil and criminal cases, and who watched jealously over all legal matters, punishing with vigour any offenders of the same. Their business was also to suppress all illegal and forbidden publications; and eventually they acted as keepers and guardians of the *Libro d'Oro*, or Peerage, so to speak, of the Venetian nobility. The *Libro d'Oro* was not instituted till 1569, and was an official record of marriages and legitimate births of every high-born Venetian. In it were also stated the qualifications attendant on names eventually to be submitted for ballot and admission to the Great Council; and once a name was entered in its pages, the owner on attaining the age of twenty-five might apply for admission to that council.

The law that watched over the safety and well-being of each citizen was a peculiarity and characteristic of that age in Venice; no undue privilege or concession was granted to class or rank; the same justice was meted equally to high and low in a manner much to be admired, and not generally practised at that date in the other towns and states of Italy.

Such was the condition of affairs when in 1193 Enrico Dandolo was proclaimed Doge. His appoint-

ment was greeted with universal rejoicing, though
beyond the fact that he had taken part in an embassy
to Constantinople some years previously, he had not
otherwise figured in his country's services, while the
fact that so long a life should have passed with so
little incident would seem almost to infer that he was
not specially fitted for the post he was now called on
to fill. Events were to give a strong contradiction to
such an hypothesis. Dandolo was eighty-four years
old at the time of his election, and afflicted beside
with almost total blindness, which has alternately been
ascribed to the cruelty of the Emperor Manuel, who,
it is said, himself applied red-hot irons to his
(Dandolo's) eyes when ambassador at his court ;
and, again, with far more probability, to a wound
received in battle. He was the first Doge who on his
succession subscribed to the form known as *Promissione*, a kind of written oath, re-formed on the succession of each new Doge, and signed by them in earnest
of their duties and obligations to the state. The
Promissione ducale is an important item, and one of
frequent recurrence in the history of the Doges. It
was the equivalent of the coronation oath of other
countries, though the alterations it underwent at each
fresh succession and the restrictions that hedged in
in ever-closing limitations the powers and privileges
of the Doges, is a thing peculiar to Venice.

Dandolo's first care was to adjust some differences
in regard of commerce between the Venetians and
the Veronese ; but the interest that centres round his
reign lies in the history of the Fourth Crusade and
the siege and capture of Constantinople. The part

that Venice took in these actions has been often told,
and ranks as one of the brightest and most important
pages in her story, no matter in what aspect it is
viewed.

VENETIAN GALLEY OF THE YEAR 1618.
(*From an engraving at the Museo Correr of a naval fight.*)

VI.

THE FOURTH CRUSADE.

(1193-1205.)

THE reproach of folly and error must ever attach to Venice for the share taken by her in the Fourth Crusade, but the events and incidents that surround that period make it one of absorbing interest equally with one of profound reflection as to the consequences brought about by such a course of action.

The condition of things in the Holy Land had aroused fresh zeal and ardour on behalf of the Crusaders in Europe, and most of all in France, where Louis, Count of Blois, Thibaut, Count of Champagne, and Baldwin, Count of Flanders and Hainault, espoused the cause of the defenders of the Holy Sepulchre with all the devotion and chivalry of high-minded, generous partisans.[1] Having determined to shorten their journey by going by sea instead of undertaking a toilsome march across foreign countries and unknown lands, they despatched an embassy to Venice to request the Doge

[1] The story of this Crusade is related by Villehardouin, a subject of the Count of Champagne, and an eye-witness and actor in the whole affair, in so graphic and straightforward a manner, that I have borrowed his words and ideas very frequently in the following record.

and his Council to further their cause by the loan
of transport ships and vessels for their hosts, and
by this means expedite a journey otherwise fraught
with labour, difficulty, and expense. The ambassadors were given absolute liberty as to terms ; they
might treat with the Doge as freely as though their
lords were present in person, and every bargain
concluded by them was to be honourably and scrupulously maintained. Dandolo answered their demand
for ships by requesting that eight days should be
granted to him and his council wherein to consider
the proposal. At the end of that time another audience was held, when the subject was freely discussed
on both sides, and the Doge set forth the conclusions
arrived at by his party, which were as follows : That
the Venetians should furnish vessels for the transport of four thousand five hundred horses, nine
thousand esquires, and twenty thousand foot soldiers,
with provisions for nine months ; to date from
the day wherein they should sail from the port of
Venice to whatever part of the world their enterprise should lead them. The sum to be paid for the
hire of the ships and the expense of providing for
and equipping such an armament was to be eighty-
five thousand marks of silver—a sum not out of
proportion to the requirements demanded by the
contractors.[1] The town of Venice undertook to
contribute as her share in so great and glorious
a cause, fifty galleys, on the condition that one

---

[1] Sismondi calls the contract a just one; Michaud, on the contrary,
speaks of the transaction as a far more avaricious than generous one on
the part of the Venetians.

half of every conquest made by the allies, whether on land or by sea, should be ceded to her. After some hesitation this proposal was accepted ; and then to allow the populace to have a voice in a matter already settled by their rulers, a great assembly was convened in St. Mark's Church, where, after a celebration of the mass of the Holy Ghost, the citizens were invited to express their approbation or condemnation of their leader's actions. Many pious tears were shed on all sides, and amid a commotion and excitement that must seriously have stirred every heart, a great cry arose from the Venetian people of consent and exultation, as with one voice and one mind they agreed to throw in their lot with the warriors of the Cross.

The Pope Innocent III. was an ardent supporter of this Crusade ; it was an undertaking whereon he had set his whole heart, and for whose furtherance he was ready to strain every nerve. He held out the inducement of special indulgences to all who joined in it, and everything seemed to smile on an enterprise for whose success "prince, prelate, potentate, and peer" were ready to stake life, property, and honour. But this fair prospect clouded over quickly : Count Thibaut of Champagne, the chosen leader of the forces, the most high-minded and noble perhaps of all those gallant Paladins, was stricken with mortal sickness, and died before the expedition started on its way, bequeathing his fortune to its fulfilment, and enjoining on his many followers to persevere in the service in which they had enrolled. Boniface, Marquis of Montferrat, was appointed in his stead—a knight who had distinguished himself in the siege of Acre, but who lacked the higher qualities possessed by his predecessor. Some delay had been caused by this re-arrangement of chieftains, and of this many of the Crusaders took a base advantage to forswear their oaths. Instead of arriving in Venice at the time appointed, they set sail for Palestine by other routes, forsaking their leaders and comrades, and acting with an independence fraught with mischief and damage for themselves and their party. The Venetians meantime had not been backward in fulfilling their part of the bargain; transport ships were ready, provisions provided, the galleys voluntarily contributed for the good cause equipped, and all in readiness for the embarcation of a host no longer forthcoming. The Marquis of Montferrat and the Counts of Flanders and of Blois repaired to Venice, but with only a small part of the following who had promised to accompany them, and whose defalcation was painfully felt in regard of the debt owing to Venice. This debt fell heavily on those who had kept their appointment, and who tried hard to keep honourably the engagement contracted by all alike as to money. The generosity of these Crusaders is worthy of all praise; they paid as far as they could the sum owing, and despoiled themselves of their personal possessions and of their plate and jewels to compensate to the utmost for the shortcomings of their faithless comrades; but spite of all their efforts and self-denials the sum still owing to the Republic was thirty-four thousand marks. The moment was a critical one: Venice, according to the strict terms of the compact, might have declined to fulfil her share of the covenant, and left the Crusaders stranded on her shores. On the other hand, the eyes of the world were upon her; she had spared neither cost nor trouble in making ample preparation for the war; doubtless, too, some of the zeal that had fired other nations was kindling in her veins as well; and beside all this she saw in the present dilemma a stroke of business to be effected for her own concerns and interests, of which she was not slow to take advantage.

The town of Zara on the Dalmatian coast, though subject to Venice, had endeavoured several times to throw off her allegiance; she had now put herself under the protection of the King of Hungary, and set the Republic at defiance. To punish her rebellious subject as thoroughly as she longed to do would tax the powers of Venice somewhat heavily; but with the aid of the Crusaders the task would prove a slight one, Zara would be brought into proper subjection, and, in recompense for the help given, Venice would overlook the debt still owing till such time as she and her allies could recover the sum. Dandolo accordingly laid this proposal before the leaders of the undertaking, to whom however it was not wholly acceptable. They demurred that they had taken arms against the Infidel, not against the King of Hungary, a monarch who himself had taken the Cross; that they had sworn to deliver the Holy Land, not a city in revolt against its suzerain; while to these protests was added a sharp injunction from the Pope forbidding altogether the expedition against Zara, declaring such an act nothing less than sacrilege. Dandolo, however, was not a man to be moved from a purpose on which he had set his heart, or swayed by threats from what he considered his country's advantage. He dwelt on the absolute need of securing to the cause the town of Zara, whose position, he asserted, was all-important, and able to work equal weal or woe to the Crusaders, according to its being held by friend or foe. But to persuade them still more to accept his counsel, the Doge proposed to enroll himself in the ranks of the Crusading forces, and share with them their toils and perils. With this object in view he assembled his subjects in St. Mark's, and in a touching speech declared to them his intentions. " Seigniors," he said, " you are associated with the finest people in the world, for an enterprise of the very highest order. I am an old man, in failing health, and in need of rest ; but I see that none could govern and direct you in like fashion as I your lord. If you consent that I take the sign of the Cross to guard and command you, and are willing that my son stay in my stead to protect the country, then gladly will I go to live and die with you and with the pilgrims." The people on hearing this exclaimed with one voice: " We beseech you in God's name so to do, and to go with us." Great was the emotion excited by such an act, and many were the tears shed over this aged warrior, for whom repose seemed so necessary, " for very old he was, and although the eyes in his face were beautiful he could see nothing, from a wound he had received in his head. Very great of heart he seemed. Ah! how widely those differed from him who had sailed from other ports to escape the dangers of the way! He then descended from the pulpit and went to the altar and knelt down, weeping copiously, and there they fastened the Cross to his large cotton bonnet, for he willed that all should see it. And the Venetians began to join the Crusades in great fashion and plentifully on that day."[1] From that moment preparations went on actively; the Doge's son Renier was appointed as Vice-Doge, and all was in readiness to sail for Zara, when a fresh interruption again delayed the start of the Pilgrims.

This interruption came from Constantinople, where affairs had taken a turn pregnant with importance for Venice and the Crusaders, and which led the soldiers of the Cross far from their original course, and brought about results little contemplated by the originators of the Crusades. A few years previously (1195) Isaac II. (Angelus), had been dethroned by his brother Alexius, who seized on the crown, caused his brother to be blinded and thrown into prison with his son, a youth also named Alexius. This latter managed to escape, and fled from Constantinople to Philip of Swabia, who had married Irene, a daughter of Isaac Angelus. From his brother-in-law's court Alexius appealed to the Pope and to other potentates for aid against the oppression and injustice of his uncle; and hearing of the armament preparing at Venice for a religious war, he hastened there in person, and implored the Crusaders to sail for Constantinople sooner

[1] Geoffrey de Villehardouin, " De la Conquête de Constantinople." Traduite par M. Natalis de Wailly. Firmin Didot. Paris, 1872.

than for Zara, to redress his own and his father's
wrongs. His entreaties did not fall on altogether
deaf ears, but the Doge was set on first reducing
Zara, and Alexius was despatched for the present
with only words of hope and encouragement.

This insistence on the part of the Venetians to
regain Zara was a source of intense annoyance to the
Pope, who sent the Cardinal of Capua to remonstrate
with Dandolo, and dissuade him from the undertaking. It is a matter of great interest and note to
observe how the Venetians even at so early a date
disregarded the orders and threats of the Holy See
whenever the desires of the latter were contrary to
the aims and ambitions of the Republic. While other
powers and states trembled before the successor of
St. Peter, Venice behaved with an indifference and
disdain that brought down on her head excommunications and anathemas, treated by her with a contempt
and an unconcern as surprising to other nations as
it was mortifying to the Holy Father. And Dandolo
set the fashion, so to speak, of this behaviour. The
Pope's wishes, his anger, his messages, were alike
unheeded; and when the cardinal appeared in the
capacity of papal legate, and as such desired to
assume the directorship of the fleet, the Doge calmly
informed him that his presence among them as a
Christian preacher was welcome, but should he
attempt any temporal authority he would not be
admitted on board their ships. Such a rebuff the
cardinal could not endure; he withdrew to Rome,
and as fresh messages from the Eternal City proved
equally futile, Innocent placed the Venetians under

an interdict. This sentence met with absolute indifference; and the French barons, astounded at the behaviour of their allies and their disregard as to the wrath of the Church, strove to effect a reconciliation between the two; a reconciliation that Venice certainly took no pains to procure, and for whose attainment she was altogether callous. The fleet accordingly sailed from Venice, and on November 10, 1202, arrived at Zara, where strong reinforcements had been sent from Hungary, and where all was in readiness for an obstinate defence. The inhabitants having refused to obey Dandolo's summons to yield, the Crusaders proceeded to besiege the town ; they broke in two a strong chain swung across the entrance to the harbour, sailed into the port, and began to assault the town. Upon this the citizens, regardless of an oath they had taken to die sooner than surrender, sent ambassadors to Dandolo to treat for peace. The Doge offered them terms of mercy on condition of their entire and absolute submission ; but some of the Crusaders, hinting to the ambassadors that they had no cause to yield, and that from the French they had nothing to fear, the terms were refused, and the siege began anew amid gathering murmurs and complaints in the allied camp. The discontent was quieted though for the moment by the leaders of the expedition, who reminded their followers how they were pledged to succour the Venetians ; and after a fierce assault, which lasted five days, the city was taken, and the booty equally divided between the French and the Venetians. The bad feeling however that existed between the two

nations broke out immediately after, and caused
more bloodshed and loss than even the siege had
done. The reason for this quarrel was as follows.
Winter was advancing, and Dandolo pointed out the
impossibility of continuing their journey at such a
season ; the town of Zara offered good accommoda-
tion for wintering in, and he suggested that they
should divide the town between them, each nation
residing in the half allotted to it, and there await
the spring, when they could pursue their route. This
was agreed to, but an accusation—perhaps not a
false one—was brought forward by the French that
the Venetians had chosen the best quarters for themselves, and left the least commodious for their allies.
From complaints they came to blows, and to such
serious fighting that all the efforts of their leaders to
maintain order was in vain, and only after a week of
terrible slaughter was peace restored. In the midst
of these disturbances a letter was received from the
Pope, again reprimanding the Crusaders in severe
terms for their behaviour in besieging Zara, and
urging them to make amends for the impiety and
sacrilege they had committed. This letter aroused
nothing but contempt among the Venetians, while
the French received it with real penitence and distress.   They sent off messengers to Innocent to
entreat for pardon and reconciliation, explaining that
they had had to submit to the law of necessity, and
were ready to atone as far as possible for their iniqui-
ties. This conduct highly gratified the Pope. He
sent back a message of forgiveness, urging them to
march immediately for Syria, without turning to the

right hand or to the left; and enjoining them, though the Venetians were excommunicate, to profit by their services till they came to the Holy Land, and then to decline all further dealings with them should they still prove rebellious. The injunctions of Innocent were far from obtaining the consideration he had fondly desired for them; while the power and influence exercised over the French barons by the domineering master-mind of Dandolo, must have filled him with gall and bitterness. While awaiting at Zara the approach of spring to continue their journey, the Crusaders were again visited by the young Alexius, who pleaded more eloquently than before the cause of his blind, imprisoned father, and urged certain advantages to be gained by the Crusaders should they espouse that cause, which proved too powerful a plea and too strong a temptation to be resisted. He promised to divide among the Pilgrims the sum of two hundred thousand marks of silver; to send at his own expense ten thousand men for a year to Egypt; and to keep a troop of five hundred always ready for the wars in Palestine; then finally, to silence all religious scruples, and to give a character of sacred gain and advantage to the enterprise, he undertook to bring about the union of the two Churches, and place the Church of Constantinople once again in harmony and concord with that of Rome. There was much division in the camp as to what answer to give the young prince. Many of the Crusaders were averse to the undertaking; they saw in it greater and longer delays in reaching Palestine; they recalled how this same Isaac whom they

were asked to defend was himself a usurper, and had
been one of the keenest foes of the Christians and
warmest supporters of the Turks in the last Crusade;
they pleaded the disgrace of turning their arms—
vowed to the recovery of Christ's sepulchre—against
Christians; and they pointed out the folly of trusting
the promises of a prince as to subsidies and men who
had neither a coin in his possession nor a soldier at
his command. But against these many and weighty
arguments were to be set those of the Venetians,
headed and impelled by Enrico Dandolo; and Dandolo was not a man who brooked opposition, or could
be swayed from any object on which he had set the
energies of a will blended with selfishness, courage,
ability, self-reliance, and patriotism. He was now
ninety-four years old, but time seemed only to excite
more keenly his ruling passions, and to stimulate him
to overcome obstacles and dangers from which a
younger man might well have shrunk. His political
foresight judged very truly of the advantages that
might accrue to Venice by closing with Prince
Alexius's offer; his hatred against Constantinople,
and his desire to be avenged for the personal wrongs
he had suffered there, prompted him, it is said, to
make war against the Greeks. Nor must it be forgotten that the Venetians had many injuries to be
smoothed away, and many insults to wipe out, that
made the idea of assaulting Constantinople an acceptable one to them and to their leader. Among the
Crusaders, too, were several who were fully persuaded
of the wisdom of possessing themselves of Constantinople. They argued that once the town was theirs

the route to Palestine was both swifter and surer; their chivalry led them to see an act of right and justice in the liberation and restoration of Isaac Angelus; and they believed they would further the cause of God and of religion in effecting the union of the Eastern and Western Churches. Supported by these opinions, Dandolo succeeded in over-ruling those antagonistic to his views; and almost the whole army agreed to throw in their lot with the Greek prince, though a few declined to do so, and made out their own way to the Holy Land, among them being the Abbot of Cerin, who had opposed from the first the siege of Zara, and who in council and debate combated the policy of the Doge; and Simon de Montfort, father of the Earl of Leicester.

While these preparations were making to over-throw his kingdom, Alexius, Emperor of Constanti-nople, awaited the result with all the indolence and apathy of an ignoble and besotted character. His total neglect of all that could insure the safety of his empire was extraordinary; the fleet, which but a few years previously was said to have numbered 1,600 vessels of war, was now disabled, the rigging, masts, sails, all had been sold; and the suggestion to refit the ships and supply timber for that purpose from the royal forests, was pronounced impossible, since these forests were reserved for the Emperor's hunting, and all that conduced to the royal pleasure out-weighed any other consideration. Alexius III. con-sequently closed his eyes and ears to the dangers encompassing him; he devoted his mind to designing

and laying out new gardens on the shores of the Propontis, and believed in nothing but his own security.
In the meanwhile the younger Alexius with his Crusading allies was approaching daily nearer to the
capital, and receiving on all sides the homage and
obeisance of towns and subjects ready to bow to
whatever master happened to be in the ascendant.
At Durazzo, at Corfu, at Negropont, and at Andros
the young prince had been hailed as lord, and recognised as sovereign, and the skilful navigation of the
Venetian pilots now conducted him and his following
under the very walls of Byzantium, where so much
glory and misery was to befall them. The hearts of
the Crusaders must have alternately swelled and sunk
within them as they approached the city whose fair-
ness impresses every eye, whose fortifications seemed
to proclaim her inviolable and invulnerable, and
whose population of over four hundred thousand men
of arms bade fair to annihilate at one blow the Latin
force of not more than twenty thousand. The
advance of this small force was directed by Dandolo
with consummate skill ; his former residence in Constantinople had given him a knowledge of its
approaches and defences about to prove of untold
value to the invaders, and to save them more than
once from defeat and even from destruction.

The first attack against the city was made on the
land side by the French, who were outnumbered to
a fearful extent by their foes, while the Venetians
attacked by sea. The Doge had ordered his fleet to
advance in two divisions ; in the first were set the
galleys in battle array, with the archers and engines

of war aloft ; in the second were the heavy ships, on
which were erected towers "higher"—according to
the Venetian historian Cappelletti—"than the highest
towers in Constantinople." As soon as the soldiers
on board the galleys had set foot on land they
planted ladders, while the heavier ships, advancing
more slowly, threw flying bridges from the masts,
which communicated with the ladders and seemed
to make a passage through the air to convey the
soldiers to the topmost ramparts. In the thick of
the fight the old blind Doge was to be seen standing at the prow of his galley, which he had had
secured close under the walls, with the banner of St.
Mark waving in his hand, alternately threatening,
entreating, commanding ; and insisting that he should
be carried on shore, so as better to encourage his men
to follow where he led. And to so noble an example
his people were not slow to respond. Inch by inch
they disputed the ground with their adversaries, and
when the standard of St. Mark suddenly floated
triumphantly from one of the heights (probably
planted there by some warrior who immediately paid
for his valour with his life) the Venetians ascribed
the action to a miracle, and broke into a mighty
shout of rejoicing. Confident of victory they swept
all before them, and remained masters of the field,
and of no less than twenty-five towers as well.
To secure their position and to prevent any unexpected assault the Venetians fired all the buildings
between themselves and the Greeks, and, if Nicetas
is to be believed, the fire was so grievous that had
it but been beheld by pious souls they would have

wept rivers of tears sufficient to have extinguished it.[1]

In the midst of his successes news was brought to Dandolo that the French were being beaten back on land by overwhelming numbers. The Doge turned at once from his own conquests to succour his allies, whose position was one of extreme peril. The cowardice however of the Greeks proved the salvation of the Latins. At the sight of this unlooked-for relief the Greeks, though outnumbering their foes to a large extent, turned from the field and fled, leaving the allies to congratulate themselves on a victory as complete as it was unexpected. The news of the discomfiture of his troops utterly disheartened Alexius ; he sought safety in flight and escaped from Constantinople, carrying with him his daughter Irene and a large sum of gold. The allies lost no time in placing the blind old Emperor Isaac on the throne, who, rescued from the dungeon where he had languished for eight years, received the allegiance and homage of subjects who but a few hours before were equally ready, had his allies been defeated, to have clamoured for his life. The Crusaders called on him to confirm the promises made to them by his son, which he was by no means minded to do, knowing well the impossibility either for himself or for Alexius to carry out these promises, or satisfy the claims of his deliverers. These latter however succeeded in overcoming his scruples and hesitation, and he ended by ratifying the conditions and affixing to them the golden seal. Upon this the father and

[1] Nicetas, Choniates Annales, L. iii., p. 288.

son were restored to each other, and shortly after crowned joint Emperors of Constantinople. The allies were quartered in the suburbs of Pera and Galata, it being considered wiser to establish them at some distance from the Greeks, whose mortification at the presence of a victorious foe can be well understood ; the more so as the foes were treated by their sovereigns as friends, and implored by them not to abandon the neighbourhood or to leave them to the mercy of their treacherous subjects. The Angeli found themselves in an awkward and intricate position: on the one hand were the Latins, who called on them to fulfil the promises made in regard of the union of the two churches, and of the payment guaranteed for their services ; on the other were their Greek subjects maddened by the idea of submitting their religious rights to the Church of Rome, and further irritated by the conduct of Alexius, who lived with his deliverers on terms of familiarity and intimacy derogatory to his position. But Alexius lowered himself still more in the eyes of his subjects by levying new taxes on them and melting down the sacred vessels of his own church in order to pay off the debt owing to his friends. This state of things could not go on, and an awful fire, which broke out in the town and was ascribed, both by the Greeks and Latins, to the hostile faction, widened still further the breach between them. This fire raged for eight days, and exceeded any that had occurred before in Constantinople ; churches, palaces, warehouses filled with the most costly goods, whole streets of houses and buildings, were swept away before the fury of a conflagration presenting a front of fire no less than three miles in length. The loss of life and property was fearful ; the animosity increased on both sides, and matters finally reached a climax.

The Crusaders, seeing that Alexius wearied of the demands which neither he nor his father could satisfy, sent an embassy to him to ask for an explanation. The envoys consisted of three Venetians and three Frenchmen, among these latter being Geoffrey de Villehardouin, whose simple and graphic chronicle gives double interest to a scene in which he was both an eye-witness and a partaker. After describing how the ambassadors found the Emperors and the Empress surrounded with much pomp and magnificence, he adds how they calmly told Alexius that if he and his father chose to ratify the covenant made between them, well ; if not, then from henceforward they, the Pilgrims, would regard him neither as lord nor friend, and would enforce their rights in every possible way. Having hurled against him an open defiance, they concluded by saying : "You have heard well what we have said ; ponder on it as seems best to you." The indignation and fury of the Greeks may be imagined ; never before had an Emperor of the East been bearded in like fashion in his own palace, or been insulted by such words and behaviour. A tumult arose, and had it not been that the envoys wisely slipped out of the presence chamber, and were off and away on their steeds before their exit was discovered in the confusion, it is certain not one would have escaped with his life. On their return to the camp they related the failure of their undertaking, and on both sides preparations were immediately commenced for war. The Greeks began by endeavouring to fire the fleet; seventeen rafts filled with pitch and every kind of combustible material were launched at night towards the spot where the Venetian ships were anchored. A favourable wind carried the destroying vessels on their way, and had it not been for the vigilance and dexterity of the Venetians the fleet must inevitably have perished. But they leaped into their light boats, and with long grappling irons hooked the burning rafts away from their ships, and drifted them, still alight, out into the waters of the Propontis. This effort to destroy the fleet and so cut off for the allies all possibility of escape in case of defeat having failed, the Greeks resolved on other measures, but determined before all to choose an emperor less effete than Alexius, and who would espouse their cause against that of their hated foes. Their choice fell upon Alexius Ducas, surnamed Murtzuphlus, from his thick, shaggy eyebrows, and the way, although hopeless, in which he strove to inspire his countrymen with discipline and courage and to make head against their invaders, proves him to have been worthy of their choice. He stained the beginning of his reign though with an act of treachery, and inveigled the young Alexius into his power, only to put him to a cruel death. The allies determined to avenge his death and that of his old father, for on hearing of his son's end Isaac died of a broken heart, and war was declared against Murtzuphlus.

Before embarking on this second attack on Constantinople the allies drew up a treaty among themselves, subscribed to by all the leaders, and bearing the impress of confidence and success. This treaty was dated March 7, 1204, when it was determined that three parts of the spoil of the city were to be handed over to the Venetians, the rest to be given to the French; all the grain and other provisions were to be equally divided; the Venetians were to retain all their old rights and privileges; six Venetian and six French electors were to choose the new Emperor of Constantinople, to whom one-fourth of the empire should be ceded, the other three-fourths to be divided equally between the French and Venetians. A patriarch was to be chosen out of the nation, from which the Emperor had not been appointed, and both French and Venetians were to remain for a year in the service of the new monarch to establish him firmly in his dominions. Other laws and regulations were drawn up by the allies as to ecclesiastical rights, and feudal obligations regarding the new Emperor.

This strange partition of one of the world's greatest empires was thus deliberately planned before it was in the hands of its confident pilferers, and it has generally been ascribed to the craftiness of Dandolo, whom even Venetian writers call "a most expert negotiator," [1] as, indeed, the terms made by him clearly prove. The assault began on April 9th, when the allies were beaten back; and many among them were for relinquishing an undertaking on which they were certain Heaven did not smile. But the undaunted

[1] "Venezia e le sue lagune."—Venezia, 1847.

Dandolo would not hear of withdrawing; and owing to his insistence and determination the attack was renewed after three days had been spent in repairing the damage done to the fleet. The ships were now lashed together in couples, that their increased weight might make head against the showers of stones and other material hurled down on them by the defenders. The van was led by the bishops of Troyes and of Soissons on board two galleys bearing the auspicious names of the *Pilgrim* and the *Paradise*, and the third attack upon Constantinople was thus begun, when a long and desperate fight ensued. In this engagement the town was again fired, and night fell upon the combatants, leaving the Latins in possession of the north-west angle of the city. Next day the allies expected to meet with still more resistance, and had prepared for a desperate opposition. Their surprise was consequently great when they found the town delivered over without another blow, and realised that they were the undisputed masters of Constantinople. Murtzuphlus had done all that lay in his power to induce his soldiery to fight, but years of laxity and disorganisation had taken too strong a hold upon his subjects ; he was unable to lead them to battle, and had no choice but to fly.

The conduct of the allies in regard to their conquest is one over which every writer would fain draw a veil, for the brutality shown by French and Venetians alike is a foul blot on the fair name of each nation, and one admitting of no excuse. For three days the city was given up to the butchery, greed, and licentiousness of a soldiery over whom their leaders could not, or would not, exercise any restraint. No sex was respected, no age spared ; churches and nunneries were desecrated ; thousands of unarmed citizens massacred in cold blood ; while the injury done to treasures of art was one never to be repaired. The profanities committed by the soldiery were of every sort and kind ; a harlot was enthroned in the Patriarch's chair in Sta. Sophia, from whence her ribald songs and obscene dances delighted her audience, who testified their approbation by scattering the sacred Elements on the ground, rifling the most precious shrines, and joining in orgies and desecrations in a way not equalled even by barbarians.

The ruin and havoc involved upon works of art were incalculable. Constantinople had received since the days of Constantine all the treasures collected by him and his successors ; she had been the seat of learning for centuries ; the storehouse where the chief glories of Greek art were to be found ; the home of all that was beautiful. Now all this was to be swept away ; "marbles, pictures, statues, obelisks, bronzes ; the whole literature of the time ; prizes which Egypt, Greece, and Rome had supplied, and which had justly rendered Constantinople the wonder of nations, perished indiscriminately beneath the fury of the marauders."[1] The few works of art which did escape this wholesale destruction were those saved by the Venetians, and brought home by them to decorate their town, among them being the famous bronze horses taken from the

[1] " Sketches from Venetian History," *op. cit.*, vol. i. chap. iii.

Hippodrome of Constantinople.[1] They also rescued a number of gems, jewels, gold and silver cups, and other trophies, now to be seen at St. Mark's; where, likewise, many a carved column and goodly slab of marble and alabaster bear witness to the splendour which once adorned the now despoiled " Queen of Cities." The only order attempted by the conquerors was in regard of the distribution of the booty. Strict injunctions were issued that it should all be brought to three churches set apart to receive it, and there apportioned to those whose claims entitled them to its possession. By this means, though much was embezzled and stolen, the sum of 1,125,000 marks of silver remained in the hands of the Crusaders, who discharged to the Venetians their standing debt of 50,000 marks, and gave them beside their allotted share of 450,000 marks.

The allies then proceeded to nominate an emperor, when Dandolo, as chief organiser and director of the

[1] The exact origin of these four horses is uncertain. Some writers ascribe them to the Roman schools, others to a far earlier period, that of the Greeks of Chio. They are said to have been brought to Rome by Augustus, and to have ornamented his triumphal arch, and afterwards those of Nero, Domitian, Trajan, and Constantine. When Constantine made Byzantium the capital of his empire, he removed the four horses there, and set them up over the Hippodrome. When brought to Venice they were first set up at the Arsenal, and afterwards erected over the west front of St. Mark's, where they remained till Napoleon the Great carried them to Paris, and placed them on L'Arc de Triomphe. From here they were restored to Venice, and put back in the original place in the presence of Francis II., Emperor of Austria, and a vast concourse of people, on December 13, 1815. It is said that they suffered less than other art treasures in their journey back to Venice, owing to the excellent way in which they had been packed by English hands.

enterprise, and to whom its fulfilment and success were mainly owing, was first chosen ; but the suggestion was quickly vetoed by his countrymen, who pointed out the incompatibility of uniting in one the dignities of Doge of Venice and Emperor of the East, and the incongruity of the head of a republic occupying at the same time the imperial throne of Constantinople. The choice then fell on Baldwin, Count of Flanders and Hainault, a choice that met with universal approbation, and was ratified by his coronation in Sta. Sophia on May 23, 1204.

The portion claimed by the Venetians was a quarter and half a quarter of the Empire ; they were also allotted the Ionian Isles ; most of the islands in the Ægean Sea ; the larger number of the harbours on the coasts of Greece and Albania ; and as many other ports and sea towns as they judged advantageous for their commerce. The Doge assumed the title of " Doge of Venice, Dalmatia, and Croatia, Lord of one-fourth and one-eighth of the Roman Empire ; " [1] a title which his successors bore till the year 1356 ; the Emperor also conferred on him the title of Despot (a rank only one degree below that of Emperor) ; he was absolved from doing homage for his fiefs, and was allowed, in Greek fashion, to assume marks of recognised sovereignty by wearing purple-dyed buskins.

The portion of lands and towns that fell to the share of the Venetian Republic was treated in that spirit of concentration and centralisation which for

---

[1] "Dominus quartæ partis et dimidiæ totius imperii Romaniæ."

so many centuries upheld that republic in so wonderful a way. Venice then recognised that the sea was her kingdom, that outlying provinces and possessions only sapped the vitality and energy of her home-life and weakened her power of unity. She therefore wisely allowed the more powerful among her patricians to hold most of the newly acquired lands in fief;[1] and while she retained and exercised a protectorate over towns and islands owned by her subjects, and which did but swell the list of her dependencies, she herself was free from all other charges on their account. The islands apportioned to her remained under her rule for no less than four centuries, among them being Crete or Candia, which had been first assigned to the Marquis of Montferrat. This island, eventually to prove one of Venice's most important acquisitions, Boniface ceded to the Republic in exchange for some lands situate nearer his capital. Of her other gains Venice gleaned no special advantages, while time was to show the harm consequent on her triumphs in Constantinople, for the East was now weakened and laid open to Turkish hordes and invasions ; and two centuries hence Venice was to see in the fall and sack of Constantinople the ruin and destruction of a town whose existence had helped to form her own, and to whose level she had been raised by friendly trade and intercourse. She was then to realise the criminal part she had played, though for the moment that part was veiled in glories

---

[1] It is in consequence of this that the family of Sanudo became princes of Naxos ; the Navagero, grand-dukes of Lemnos ; the Dandolo, lords of Andros ; and so on.

and victories which hid out the future, and cast only a halo of renown and prestige over the present.

These glories were, however, now over-shadowed by misfortune and disaster, that only Dandolo's sagacity and foresight could mitigate to some extent, and that clouded the last scenes of this great undertaking with discomfiture and sadness. The efforts made by the Emperor Baldwin to establish and consolidate his empire met only with failure ; and the arms of the Crusaders sustained a crushing defeat under the walls of Adrianople from Joannice or Calo-John, King of Bulgaria, at the head of vast tribes of Bulgarians, Tartars, and Comans. Baldwin was taken prisoner, and had it not been for the valour and promptness of Dandolo, who organised an able retreat for his defeated followers, it is probable the whole army would have been cut to pieces. Boniface, Marquis of Montferrat, died soon after from wounds received warring against the Bulgarians ; and even the resolute and indomitable spirit of Dandolo was weighed down and broken by the loss, either through imprisonment or death, of all his old comrades-in-arms. He breathed his last in Constantinople on the 14th of June, 1205, in the ninety-sixth year of his life, and the thirteenth of his reign, and was buried with pomp in the Church of Sta. Sophia.

The glory that attaches to his name and deeds wipes out to a large extent the accusations of obstinacy and ambition laid to his charge. The vigour and energy of mind and body displayed by so old and infirm a man cannot but excite admiration, and the reproach both of obstinacy and ambition pales before

the reflection that those very faults were always
employed for the welfare and aggrandisement of
his country; for the safety and prosperity of that
country's friends; or for the defeat and destruction
of her foes. But the seed sown by Venice and
Dandolo in the action of the Fourth Crusade took
root, and poisoned the soil from which so much that
was fair and beautiful had sprung, and was yet to
spring. The altered condition of Constantinople—a
condition brought about almost entirely by Venice—
was to prove the undoing of this latter; and though
for the moment she gained great wealth and glory,
the day of retribution was looming ahead, when long
and disastrous wars were to prove the consequences
of her error, and to act as elements of wrath in the
work of her ruin and decay.

GONDOLA IN USE IN THE YEAR 1600.
From Franco, op. cit.)

VII.

LAWS AND LEGISLATION IN VENICE.

(1205–1297.)

ON the death of Enrico Dandolo, the agitation and excitement that for so long had absorbed the thoughts of all concerned in these stirring events continued for a while. In Venice, Pietro Ziani was appointed Doge, while in Constantinople the Venetians resident there had lost no time in appointing a *Bailo* or *Podestà* to watch over their welfare and interests, and to guard against any infringement of the rights and privileges enjoyed by them so largely in the East. The first Bailo named was Marin Zeno, who immediately assumed royal titles, proclaiming himself: "Nos Marinus Zeno Dei gratia Venetorum potestas in Romania ejusdemque imperii, quartae partis et dimidiae dominator." He also donned the insignia of royalty by wearing a red silk stocking on the right foot, and a white one on the left, assumptions of prerogatives which, though granted to the late Doge and worn by him, caused no small anxiety to the existing powers in Venice. But they deemed it prudent for the present to approve the choice of Zeno, and leave him in office,

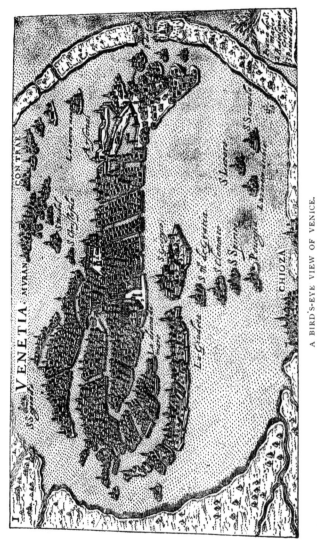

A BIRD'S-EYE VIEW OF VENICE.

(From "Viaggio da Venetia a Costantinopoli." Venice, 1600.)

though declaring that for the future the Bailo should be sent from Venice.

The fruits of the overthrow of the Greek Empire were already beginning to show themselves, and to demonstrate to Venice the blunder she had committed by sharing in that exploit. Her increased trade and opulence aroused afresh the jealousy of Genoa, who encouraged her pirates and corsairs to molest the Venetians whenever the occasion offered. The Doge despatched a fleet against the marauders who were infesting the waters around the Ionian Isles, and the success of the Venetian arms enabled the Republic to send on her forces to Candia, and suppress the efforts made there by the inhabitants to throw off the Venetian yoke. Again the Venetians succeeded in their enterprise ; Candia was reduced to obedience ; a ruler was appointed with the title of Duke of Crete, the island was colonised by Venetian nobles, and a regular form of government instituted.

Taken as a whole Ziani's reign may be considered as peaceful, and a contrast in every way to the brilliant stirring one of his predecessor. The Doge himself was chiefly remarkable for an extraordinary memory, and a piety as genuine as it was fervid. He abdicated in 1229, when Jacopo Tiepolo was elected in his stead.

His election was conducted according to the rules instituted in 1177 : the Forty met to appoint the new Doge, but for a long time were unable to come to any conclusion, twenty votes being for Tiepolo, twenty for Marino Dandolo. For two months this uncertainty continued, when it was decided to draw lots, and the lot fell upon Tiepolo. To prevent the re-currence of a similar dilemma, it was determined to add another member to the Forty, and from now till the close of the Republic this election was known as the XLI. (*Quarantuno*) instead of the XL. (*Quaranta*) as heretofore. Fresh regulations were also effected in regard of the *Promissione ducale ;* and a new council was formed, namely, that of the *Inquisitori del Doge defunto.*[1] They were three in number, and were to examine into the rule and administration of the late Doge, to see whether he had lived up to the promises made by him in his *Promissione ;* and if in any case they found him wanting, they could call upon his heirs to atone as far as possible for the shortcomings laid against him.

The alterations wrought in respect of the *Promissione* were carried on by persons chosen on purpose and known as " Correctors " (*Correttori*), their office being to inquire on what points the late Doge had failed, and to alter the new *Promissione* so as his successor should avoid the same errors. These Correctors or Revisors consisted of five members, always chosen from among the leading patricians, and they remained in office only till their work was done. This work had an importance beyond what may at first sight appear, since by it the power of the Doges became ever more limited, their authority more restricted ; till by degrees they were despoiled of the absolute sovereignty exercised by their prede-cessors, and degenerated into mere figure-heads of the Republic. It may be well to give some of the chief

[1] An institution similar to this existed of old among the Egyptians.

rules of the *Promissione* drawn up for Tiepolo, since
this served as the basis for those of his successors, and
will show how tightly the Doge and his family were
bound by the laws and regulations to which on their
nomination they had to subscribe. The Doge had
to swear to administer right and justice to whoever
appealed to him ; at debates in Council he was to
side with those who could show most right and
reason ; he might not send or receive letters to or
from the Pope or any other prince without the
knowledge and sanction of his council ; he might
decide nothing in regard of notaries, &c., without the
consent of that same council ; he was to watch
jealously over the just issue of the coin of the realm,
and punish any corrupters of the same. He might
receive no presents or gifts from any one, except
offerings of rose-water, leaves, flowers and sweet
herbs ; or in the event of a marriage he might accept
gifts, though only then of the nature of victuals, and
he had also to exact an oath from the Dogaressa and
all his children to observe this rule strictly. He was
to be bound by whatever laws and regulations were
passed by his own or by the Great Council ; he might
not seek for more power than that accorded him by
law ; he was to endeavour to keep good will and
harmony between the Great and Lesser Councils ;
keep strict watch over the prisons ; and every Friday
give audience without respect of persons. His salary
was fixed at two thousand eight hundred *lire*[1] of
Venetian money a year, paid every three months,
with a gift of over two hundred *lire* more from the

[1] The Venetian *lira* was valued then at about half a franc.

community of Veglia. The annual offering of cloth of gold sent by the lords of Negropont was to be divided between the Church of St. Mark and the Doge, who was also bound to present three silver trumpets and a cloth of gold to St. Mark's ; and see to the repairs of the ducal palace. His staff of servants, including the cooks, was to consist of twenty. Such were some of the regulations to which Doge Tiepolo subscribed ; and henceforward each new election was marked by the deduction of some privilege, or the abridgment of some prerogative, till no real liberty was left to the Doges, and no freedom of action allowed to those who filled one of the proudest posts in Europe.

The dukedom of Tiepolo was occupied by several wars, in most of which Venice was to be found fighting for different allies ; at one time supporting the Emperor of Constantinople, and at another taking part in the second Lombard League, when one of the Doge's sons was killed in battle against the Emperor Frederick II. She had also some struggles on her own account against her rebellious subjects at Zara and Candia ; when against Candia especially she was entirely successful. But this reign is chiefly noted for the civil changes enacted as to the laws and fiscal administration of Venice. A written code of laws was drawn up entitled " Novelli Statuti Veneziani," consisting of five books (a sixth was added in Doge Andrea Dandolo's reign in 1343), and relating in turn to all the social, legal and religious questions of the day, and entering minutely into the commercial, criminal and other laws, both for Venice and for her colonies. There was a stern law too against the sale of such drinks as were intoxicating or over exciting, and which punished such practices with the loss of a hand or an eye, or by branding. Besides these there was a code of "nautical statutes" (*Statuti nautici*), that entered minutely into the construction of vessels, with regulations as to ballast, anchorage, cabling, and so on ; as well as directions as to the service of ships' crews, dispositions as to shipwrecks and salvage ; the loading and unloading of merchant vessels ; with a host of injunctions and minutes in connection of shipping matters. Treaties were also signed with Eastern princes as to trading and settling in their lands, especially with the Soldan of Aleppo, with Abdel-Malek, Despot of Egypt, with Armenia, and with Barbary.

Besides his reputation as a statesman and law-giver, Doge Tiepolo has left no less a one as to piety ; a proof of it being found in his gift to the Dominicans of the ground on which they built their Church and Monastery of SS. Giovanni e Paolo. The following legend is related as to this gift : Doge Jacopo Tiepolo saw in a dream the oratory and small square of St. Daniel full of flowers ; and some white doves, carrying on their heads crosses of gold, hovered over and about the flowers, while two angels descended from heaven carrying incense burners of gold with which they spread sweet odours around, and a voice was heard saying : "This is the spot that I have chosen for my preachers." So this piece of ground was given for the purpose, and according to his desire Doge Jacopo was buried here, and his

CANAL OF STA. MARINA LEADING TO SS. GIOVANNI E PAOLO.
(*From " Calli e Canali," op. cit.*).

tomb in the façade of the church is to seen with that of his son Lorenzo (who eventually became Doge), having on the corners of the tombs the doves with their crosses, and the angels with their censers. The Doge resigned his office on May 20, 1249, having earned the gratitude and admiration of his country for the laws and codes he had so wisely compiled and instituted, and was succeeded by Marino Morosini.

The fact of most interest in the three years' reign of this Doge is the admission of the Inquisition into Venice. Till now the city had resisted the introduction of this tribunal into its midst, and even when it did creep in, it did so almost under protest, and in a crippled, restricted form, curbed by much civil authority, and by no means the free, unfettered agent it was in other places. The Government reserved to itself the right to search out the heretics, and also the right to pass sentence after the clergy had examined the accused. This arrangement did not satisfy the Pope, but it remained unaltered till 1289 when the Holy Office was admitted more fully into Venice, although still in a manner to leave much power and judgment in the hands of the home Government. It was then that the *Savii all' Eresia* were instituted, and formed a court to guard all Venetians against false accusations, and to prevent the officers of the Inquisition taking too much upon themselves where any Venetian was concerned. And in this state affairs remained till 1551, when Rome and Venice were more irritated against each other, and had to settle with some asperity their controversies and exactions respecting this question.

It was also in this dukedom that the *Signori di notte* were appointed to watch over the safety of the town by night, and keep guard and vigil against the secret murders and assassinations occurring frequently after nightfall.

Marino Morosini died in 1253, when Renier Zeno was chosen to succeed him. The fifteen years of his dukedom were engrossed by perpetual wars ; the first being one in which the Venetians joined a league against the horrors and cruelties perpetrated by Ezzelino da Romano and his brother. The inhumanities committed by these monsters are too well known to be enlarged on here, suffice it to say that the Venetians contributed largely to the overthrow and death, first, of Ezzelino, and afterwards at Treviso of his brother Alberico.[1]

The next war that occupied Venetian arms was in the Levant against the Genoese. The hatred and jealousy between these two powers had grown stronger and bitterer ever since the conquest of Constantinople, when whatever favour was accorded to one nation was regarded by the other as an outrage and insult, to be atoned for sooner or later. A small cause was sufficient to bring matters to a climax, and involve the two nations in a long and bloody struggle. The Church of S. Saba in the town of Acre was claimed alike by Genoese and Venetians, the Pope supporting the latter, while the Genoese

---

[1] Ezzelino was successively lord of Verona, Vicenza, Padua, Feltre, and Belluno. His enormities and excesses were so cruel and inhuman that Pope Alexander IV. preached a crusade against him, which led to his overthrow and death. His brother Alberico was lord of Treviso.

asserted their right by taking possession of the church. Each side flew to arms, and in two desperate battles the Venetians under the command of Lorenzo Tiepolo, son of Doge Jacopo, remained conquerors. Several trophies accrued to them from these successes; one being the porphyry pillar, standing at the corner of St. Mark's, facing the Piazzetta, and known as the *Pietra del Bando* or Stone of Proclamation, as from it were proclaimed the laws of the Republic, it having served a similar purpose at Acre. Other spoils were the two square marble columns, adorned with strange lettering and flowery scrolls and patterns which stand on the south side of St. Mark's, and were erected in 1256. At the same time the four porphyry figures grouped together were brought from Acre and set up at the south-east angle of the church, close to the Porta della Carta. They are supposed to represent the four Cæsars who reigned jointly at Byzantium in the eleventh century—Romanus IV., Michael Ducas and his brothers, Andronicus and Constantine.

After their victories the Venetians entered into an alliance with Manfred of Sicily, a natural son of Frederick II., and also with the Pisans; while the Genoese strengthened their cause by a league with Michael Paleologus, the aspirant to the throne of Constantinople, and the fierce enemy and opposer of the Latin Emperor Baldwin. Fortified by this increase of allies, the Venetians were well able to respond to the appeal made to them by Baldwin for help to maintain his Eastern Empire. The greater part of the Latin Emperor's life had been spent wandering from court to court to collect forces to avert the ruin threatening his state, and make head against the usurpations of Michael Paleologus. He had pawned his son Philip to the Venetian Republic, and had raised a loan on the crown of Thorns from the banking house of Querini in Venice,[1] hoping with the money obtained in this way to arm his troops and rid himself of his foe. Michael Paleologus however was not to be disposed of easily ; he had been scheming for some time to deliver Constantinople from the Latins, and proclaim himself Emperor of the East. Availing himself of a moment when the fleet sent by Doge Zeno to the assistance of Baldwin had sailed on a further expedition to the Black Sea, he ordered an attack on the city, and remained master of the situation. The Venetian fleet only returned in time to shelter the luckless Baldwin, and the other refugees who fled for protection to the galleys, and with this flight and desertion of Baldwin the Latin Empire in Constantinople was swept away for ever.

Michael Paleologus was now acknowledged and crowned as Emperor, but seeing the wisdom of encouraging foreign settlers in his state, he granted to the Venetians and Pisans rights and privileges in Constantinople such as they had enjoyed of old. They were allowed to dwell in their own quarter, their Podestà or " Bailo" was permitted to exercise his powers as formerly, and they were still entitled to

[1] This crown of Thorns, reputed to have been worn by our Lord, was bought by St. Louis of France from the house of Querini to whom Baldwin had pledged it, and was taken by him to Paris, where he built the "Sainte Chapelle " to contain it.

appeal to and be judged by their laws and magistrates. To his allies, the Genoese, more numerous advantages still were conceded. The Emperor gave them the palace of the Pandocrater, where the Venetian Bailo had always lived ; an action looked upon by the Venetians as a direct insult, for the palace was in a different part of the town to that where the Genoese had their quarter ; and the insult did but gather force when the Genoese demolished the house and sent the stones to Genoa, where they were built up in the Church of S. Giorgio. Fresh disputes and quarrels resulted from this and other real or imagined offences ; for eight years the struggle lasted, and during that time five great battles were fought, the Venetians each time remaining victors. These victories however were unsatisfactory ; they led to no decisive conclusion ; they sapped the resources and wealth of the countries ; and heightened the animosity between the two nations so greatly that not till all Christendom intervened to persuade them did they yield with a bad grace to sign a truce for five years.

Many new institutions were inaugurated in this reign in connection with the manufactures and industries of Venice. The office of High Chancellor (*Cancelliere Grande*) was also established, an office that ranked only below that of the Procurators of St. Mark. The Chancellor retained his office for life, and had a princely salary ; to him was entrusted the great seal of the Republic ; his dress was gorgeous and costly, and his funeral was celebrated with a pomp equal only to that of the Doge.

Renier Zeno died on July 17, 1268, and was buried in the Church of SS. Giovanni and Paolo. He was the first Doge who added a circlet of gold to the ducal cap, an addition adopted in turn by all his successors. After his death the mode of electing the Doges underwent considerable change, and became so involved and intricate, that one can but wonder how any conclusion was reached, or how from so complicated a labyrinth any disentanglement could ever be attained. It was decided that after the death and funeral of the Doge, and after the Revisors and Inquisitors had examined into his life and actions, the Great Council should be convened, into which no member was to be admitted under the age of thirty. These members then placed in an urn a number of balls according to the number of members present ; thirty balls being of gold, the rest silver. The youngest member together with the head of the "Quaranta" after this descended to St. Mark's, and taking the first child they met, led him back to the ducal palace, where he was made to draw the balls ; each golden ball drawn proclaiming the member whose name was on it an elector.[1] Upon this the father, brothers, uncles, or other relations whom the new member might reckon among the assembly withdrew, while all those whose names were on the silver balls had equally to retire. Afterwards began the process of sifting in all its complications, when perhaps the following form of relation may make it easier to understand. Of the members of the Great

---

[1] Hence the proverb so frequent in Venice : " toccar," or " cavar bala (palla) d'Oro," to denote one on whom fortune smiled.

Council, who were over thirty years of age, thirty were chosen by ballot.

I. The 30 were reduced by ballot to 9.

II. The 9 by plurality of votes, or suffrage, elected 40. Each having at least 7 votes.

III. The 40 were reduced by ballot to 12.

IV. The 12 elected 25. Each having at least 9 votes.

V. The 25 were reduced by ballot to 9.

VI. The 9 elected 45. Each having at least 7 votes.

VII. The 45 were reduced by ballot to 11.

VIII. The 11 elected 41. Each having at least 9 votes ; and each of whom must be confirmed by a majority in the Great Council.

IX. The 41 elected the Doge by not less than 25 votes.

These last 41, who were recognised as "the Electors" were guarded with the strictest privacy when they sat to appoint the Doge ; all communication with the outer world was forbidden them ; they might not leave the room where they were assembled, and where the very windows were barred. At the same time they were entertained sumptuously at the expense of the state ; their every wish was gratified, provided it in no way affected their political bias, while any attempt to curry favour with one elector sooner than with another was strictly forbidden. Indeed, so scrupulously was this law observed that, on one occasion, when a pious elector expressed a desire for a rosary, forty-one rosaries were immediately supplied to the Assembly ; and when again, after printing had been introduced, and one elector demanded a copy of Æsop's fables, the town was ransacked to supply the whole party with the literature demanded by one.

The first Doge elected under the new regulation was Lorenzo, a son of Doge Jacopo Tiepolo, who had distinguished himself fighting for his country against Genoa, and whose nomination caused universal joy and satisfaction. Space is wanting to dwell on the pageants and festivities that celebrated his appointment, or to describe the processions of the different guilds of arts and trades that paraded the town, and displayed at once the enormous wealth and prosperity reigning at that period in Venice, and the revels in which all joined as one vast, united family. The account of this prosperity is almost sarcastic when we read that it was followed by an awful famine and scarcity of food in Venice. The distress and mortality were intense, and the efforts made to buy provisions and grain from neighbouring states, especially from Lombardy where the harvest had been more than usually abundant, failed altogether. Venice however succeeded after a time in replenishing her garners from Dalmatia, and then turned to avenge the cruelty and inhumanity shown by her neighbours in her hour of need. She placed large embargoes on all the goods and merchandise coming from these countries, and instituted a fresh office in the person of the Captain of the Gulf to investigate into all the boats and vessels arriving from the Adriatic and from the rivers trading with the Republic. She revenged herself also by forbidding the export of salt, and so bitter was the animosity between Bologna and herself on this head, that Pope Gregory X. had to arbitrate to bring about a reconciliation between them.

Lorenzo Tiepolo died in 1275 ; when Jacopo Contarini was appointed in his stead, an old man of over eighty years of age and at whose accession fresh alterations were again introduced in the ducal *Promissione.* The Doge and his sons were now forbidden to hold fiefs or lands outside the Venetian realm ; they were not permitted to contract marriages with foreign wives without the sanction of the Council ; [1] whatever they bought must be paid for within eight days ; and the Dogaressa and her children were all forbidden to send presents to any of the citizens. Another clause was also inserted as to prisoners, pronouncing that they were not to stay in prison a month without being brought to trial ; and other rules were also passed for the swift and right administration of justice.

The greater part of Contarini's reign was occupied by wars against Ancona, a town with which Venice was constantly at variance ; and in these wars she was terribly worsted. The chief interest relating to this struggle is the unconcern again manifested by the Republic as to the wishes and orders of the Holy See. The Pope had taken the city of Ancona under his protection, and ordered the Venetians to desist from

---

[1] Doge Lorenzo Tiepolo had married a princess of Servia, and his son a princess of Slavonia, and this law was passed to prevent the Doges having interests, or in case of necessity help and allies, outside the kingdom.

a war discountenanced by him. But his orders were totally disregarded by the Republic, who, as will be often seen in the course of her history, never sacrificed her aims and interests to those of Rome ; and treated with absolute indifference the threats or rewards before which other nations trembled or rejoiced.

In 1280 Doge Contarini, either voluntarily or forcibly, renounced the dukedom, and Giovanni Dandolo was named in his room. His first act was to sign a treaty of peace with the town of Ancona. Soon afterwards he concluded a long and weary war waged by Venice against Istria, where the Patriarch of Aquileja

FIRST GOLD DUCAT OR ZECHIN COINED IN 1280 UNDER
DOGE GIOVANNI DANDOLO.

had fomented the dissensions, and done his utmost to continue a struggle now brought happily to a peaceful issue ; and Venice remained mistress and suzerain of the rebellious province and Patriarchate. Under this Doge Dandolo the first Venetian zechin or ducat was coined, and was now in vogue for over five hundred years. The purity, ductility, and colour of its gold caused it to be a coin immensely sought after, while for later times it possesses great interest as indicating the dress of the Doge and the fashion of the ducal cap.

Giovanni Dandolo died in 1289, and on the occa-

sion of his funeral the populace clamoured to appoint
Jacopo Tiepolo, son of Doge Lorenzo, to the dukedom.   The people were beginning too late to realise
that their voice in the nomination of the Doge was
being taken from them, and that all share claimed
by them in his election was being removed from
their grasp.   Such was indeed the case, for the
Venetian nobles who had increased in wealth
and power were now advancing with energy to
concentrate in their own hands all sovereign rights ;
while they aimed also at suppressing all dynastic
tendency in regard of their rulers, and in checking
the flow of extraneous aspirants who sought admission into the Great Council.   These nobles were
strongly opposed to Tiepolo's election, and chose
instead Pietro Gradenigo, a man imbued with all the
prejudices and opinions of his surroundings and with
a will and courage to support those characteristics in
the face of all opposition.   The feeling against the
dynastic tendency that was called into play by
Tiepolo's appointment was brought forward to urge
him, as a good citizen, to withdraw from the contest, and to this appeal Tiepolo was not deaf.   He
left the field free to Gradenigo, who was named
Doge, notwithstanding the vexation and dislike of
the people, among whom he was extremely unpopular.

Two years after his accession important events
to Europe, and especially to Venice, occurred in the
close of the Crusades, and the collapse of the Latin
Kingdom in Palestine.   This was in 1291, when at the
siege of Acre, or Ptolemais, the Christian forces were

entirely routed by the Saracens, and the fall of the city utterly and for ever quenched the spirit of Crusading chivalry. Such events cannot be passed by without glancing at the effect produced by them, and particularly by the Crusades, on Venice ; for it was an effect differing in many ways from that exercised on most other towns and countries, and one far from advantageous or profitable to the Venetian state. For the rest of Europe the Crusades opened out the East and enlarged trade and business to an enormous extent ; but to Venice this was a fact of some centuries' standing, and the wider commerce now offered to other nations was a loss to her of a monopoly enjoyed for many and many a year. Henceforward the Eastern traffic was no longer to be her exclusive prerogative ; she was to share and divide where she had absorbed and amassed, and that too with rivals in the shape of Pisa, Genoa, and Flanders, who were determined to prove the force of their rivalry and the fearful odds against which she would have to contend. Genoa was the first to commence operations. Her thirst for war had been aroused by the fall of Acre ; the truce concluded with Venice had expired, and she was keen to assert her superiority and consolidate her possessions in the East. She was mistress of Scio, and of several towns on the Black Sea ; she governed in Caffa, a town of great importance as commanding the entrance to the Sea of Azof ; and she was in possession of Pera, the well-known suburb of Constantinople. From the vantage ground assured her by such a position, her object was to dispossess Venice of her Levantine trade, and establish herself in the place too long occupied by the "Ocean's Queen." But Venice was not disposed to cede without a struggle, and a large fleet, manned by all capable of bearing arms, sailed from S. Nicolò del Lido on October 7, 1294, only to encounter a severe defeat in the Black Sea. Undismayed by this disaster, the Venetians under Andrea Dandolo repaired their losses and again met the Genoese, commanded by Lamba Doria, in the waters of the Adriatic off the island of Curzola. But Fortune again frowned on Venice, and she experienced one of the most overwhelming defeats that had ever befallen her: sixty-five of her ships were burned and eighteen were captured with seven thousand prisoners. Among these was Marco Polo, the great traveller, who beguiled the four years of his imprisonment at Genoa by writing the story of his travels and adventures, which created such admiration among his captors that it is said to have led to his release. A less happy fate was in store for Andrea Dandolo, the Venetian admiral, who was also made prisoner and chained to the mast of a Genoese ship, that he might be led to Genoa to swell the triumph of his victors. But he was able to save himself from such ignominy, and dashed his brains out against the mast, escaping in this way a disgrace far worse than death.

The next year the Venetians were again defeated off Gallipoli, but the reverse was not so crushing as that of Curzola, and some brilliant skirmishes gained over the Genoese by a Venetian pirate, named Domenico Schiavo, wiped out to a slight extent the disgraces brought on their arms. But neither

Republic would consent to peace, and it was not till Matteo Visconti, lord of Milan, had employed all his powers of persuasion that a treaty was signed between the belligerents, favourable on the whole to Venice, but forbidding her to send armed ships into the Black Sea or along the Syrian coast for thirteen years.

WINGED LION OF ST. MARK FROM A SILVER DUCAT
OF THE YEAR 1500.

VIII.

THE COUNCIL OF TEN.

(1297–1311.)

AN epoch had now arrived in Venetian history when a silent revolution in her very midst was to effect changes in her government of a nature to alter the constitution of the state, and to disturb, if not violate, the traditions of her old nobility. This was the famous measure known as the " Closing of the Great Council" (*Serrata del Maggior Consiglio*), and was brought about in February, 1297. Before enumerating the different items contained in this act, it may be well to recount the reasons which called it forth, and explain at the same time against whom the doors of the Great Council were now to be closed. Ever since its regular foundation in 1172, it had been shaking off bit by bit the " slight control of annual election ; " and its twelve electors, always chosen from the same families,[1] and reserving to themselves the right of re-election, ended by making the Great Council in semblance permanent or hereditary. But, in fact, it was not so, and there was no citizen of

[1] In 1293 there were 18 Contarini, 10 Foscari, 11 Morosini, &c., in the Great Council.

however low an origin or humble a condition, who might not hope some day to be included in the governing body of his country. Such hopes were now to be done away for ever.

The time had come when the opinions and ideas floating through the minds of the aristocracy were to take form and reality in the foundation of a more solid basis to the governing power, and establish more firmly the Great Council of Venice. The aristocratic party had increased in wealth, in power and in importance so gradually but so surely, that they were able to frame laws to their liking, and execute them in their fashion. They were now resolved to admit into the Great Council only those whose father or grandfather had been a member of that Council. As for the rest who could not claim such a prerogative, they were occasionally admitted by favour, or as it were on suffrance, but by degrees even this concession dwindled away. The powers of the Doges were again to be reduced, and as has been said, the people were to be completely dispossessed of the share they had had in the choice of their Doge. This too had been accomplished, and it only remained for the aristocracy to assume the authority and rule for which they had striven and worked so long. It has been seen how the people endeavoured on the death of Doge Giovanni Dandolo to reestablish their old right to choose their duke, and had clamoured for Jacopo Tiepolo, a man who belonged to the old-fashioned nobility, and was linked by name and tradition to the old order of things. But Tiepolo was devoid of ambition ; he lacked too the power to rule at such a moment; and the more advanced nobles, seeing to what a crisis things had arrived, had resolved to exalt one of their own partisans, who in his capacity as Doge could help them to accomplish their aims. This man they had found in the person of Gradenigo, and seven years after his nomination to the dukedom he brought forward the measure known as the "Closing of the Great Council," establishing the absolute oligarchy of Venice, and containing the following regulations:

I. All those who for the last four years had sat in the Great Council and obtained a suffrage of at least twelve votes from the XL.,[1] should be members of the Great Council for a year, dating from St. Michael's Day.

II. If any member, owing to his sojourning in a foreign land, has lost his seat in the Great Council, he shall on his return apply to the heads of the XL. for re-admission.

III. That three electors be created beside the annual ones, who, on a hint from the Doge and his Council, shall elect as members those not heretofore named. These must, however, equally obtain twelve suffrages from the XL.

IV. That these three electors be members of the Great Council.

V. That these laws be not repealed, except by five

---

[1] Under the name of the "Quarantia," or XL., were known the three supreme councils or tribunals, which judged all civil and criminal cases. They were the "XL. al criminale;" the "XL. civil vecchio," and the "XL. civil nuovo," and were each composed of forty judges.

out of the six Ducal Councillors, with twenty-five votes of the XL., and two-thirds of the Great Council, and this Council shall further decree that twenty-five days before the end of the year, they will move whether they confirm or abolish this statute; and what shall then be decreed shall remain henceforward.

VI. That at the beginning of each year the Ducal Councillors shall lay this law again before the Great Council; and no one shall be admitted into the Great Council who is excluded from other councils.

VII. That notice shall be publicly given by the heads of the XL. three days before the names are to be balloted for the Great Council. No name can be accepted unless supported by thirty out of the XL.

By these regulations the citizens found themselves divided into three categories: (1) Those who had never been nor had any ancestors in the Great Council; (2) those whose ancestors had belonged to it; (3) those who had been in, and whose ancestors also had belonged to it. The first were called " new men," and were only admitted by favour to the Council; the second were admitted now and again; the third had every right to be elected. In this way the famous Great Council was established on a basis of strictly aristocratic principles. The accomplishment of such a deed, though consummated as we have seen, was in reality the work of many years and of steady labour. By degrees the aristocratic party had shaped itself to hold the reins of office in so firm and well-organised a manner that it was able to maintain its form of government intact for centuries. The period of democracy which came to an end with the closing of the Great Council, and which was perhaps the grandest epoch in Venetian history, had lasted for well-nigh four centuries, and now gave way to the aristocratic Republic which entrusted all its high offices into no hands but those of nobles, and which was ruled and guided entirely by the patrician class. These statutes, however, took some time before they settled into becoming the regular law of the land, and many changes and additions took place before they were in the full swing of working order.

Before passing on to describe how the Great Council worked its way through revolution and opposition into the established governing power of the land, it may be well to see to what point the civilisation and industry of the town had arrived, and over what kind of men and manners the Council had now to watch and legislate. The conquest of Constantinople, though on one side it increased the wealth and added to the beauty and art of Venice, on the other hand corrupted the habits and customs of the people; and excited among the nobles a spirit of greed and ambition, that often carried them on to seek their own aggrandisement and advantage, forgetful of their country's welfare and gain. And doubtless the facility with which fortunes could be accumulated and wealth increased by travel, trade and adventure must have presented an alluring side to the Venetian of the thirteenth century. The rod of Venetian Empire stretched over the Black Sea from the Hellespont to the Sea of Azof. The towns where her merchants

collected, and where a small patch of Venetian territory afforded safety and equity to her subjects, included Laodicea, Bursa in Bithynia, Scutari, Sinope,
Nicæa, Nicomedia, Amiso, and Trebizond; while
further westward she traded with Apollonia, Silivrea,
Rodosto, and Gallipoli; with the Crimea, Turkey,
Armenia, Arabia, and even with Mongolia and Tar-
tary. The traffic she carried on in Asia with India,
China, and other countries of the East, was brisk
and active; while the story of Marco Polo and his
voyages, together with the experiences he underwent
at the Court of Genghis Khan and in China, are a
history in themselves. The account he gave of the
riches and luxuries to be amassed in those distant
climes stirred many of his countrymen to follow his
example of exploration and travel in the far East,
and to realise for themselves all the glories and
wonders of that fabulous land.

The laws in regard of trade were strict in Venice,
and though in a spirit to favour the traffic brought by
adventurous explorers to their native town, these laws
were not closely observed, and smuggling and contra-
band were largely in vogue. regardless of the efforts
made by the Government to suppress them, and to
conduct matters honestly and honourably. Every
year convoys of from eight to ten merchant vessels
sailed to the Black Sea and Roumania; from six to
eight sailed to the Crimea; the same number went to
Trebizond; others to Cyprus, to Armenia, Apulia,
and the coasts of Spain and Portugal; others again
to England, France, and Flanders, where at Bruges
and Antwerp the Republic had large emporiums.

The merchant ships generally sailed escorted by
men-of-war ; sometimes they had to provide for their
own safety, and protect as best they might the
merchandise committed to their charge. The laws
extant in relation to the vessels whether for trade or
war belonging to the Republic are infinite, and serve
to show the care and attention bestowed by Venice
on so important a branch of her service, equally with
the appreciation she attached to so vast a source of
her wealth and power.

The nations with whom the Republic had most
intercourse and dealing had their special warehouses
allotted them in Venice. The two most important,
the Fondaco de' Tedeschi and the Fondaco de' Turchi,
remain to this day, the latter being now the well-
known Museo Civico, or Correr ; while the Fondaco
de' Tedeschi, standing close to the Rialto, still bears
on one of its outer topmost edges faint traces of a
fresco by Giorgione, the only record of a blaze of
colour and decoration once painted by him and by
Titian on these walls.

The Fondaco de' Tedeschi is described by a
modern writer, who, speaking of it in connection of
Venice, says : " This factory . . . was very differently
constituted from that of other cities. The [Hansa]
League never obtained a monopoly or special
privileges in Venice. The Fontego at Venice was
merely the warehouse or dwelling-house of the
German traders, without any internal jurisdiction or
president.

" They were permitted to sojourn with their wares
at stated times in Venice, received on their arrival the

keys of the fifty-six rooms of the building, which on their departure they had to re-deliver to the Venetian authorities. . . . Three Venetian citizens under the title of Visdomini de' Tedeschi, and native secretaries, and a 'fontegaro,' always inhabited the building and kept strict watch over the traders, whose commerce was subjected to all manner of tedious restrictions. The house, as we have said, was only open to them at stated times of the year. They were only permitted to sell to and buy from Venetians; all wares exported or imported had to be weighed in the public balances, and only this weight was accepted as just."[1] There follows much of interest as to these trading relations, but space forbids a longer quotation, and we must return to the affairs and operations of the Great Council.

The closing of this Council had been effected with quiet and seeming acquiescence, but two revolutions had to be met and put down, before the measure was accepted in Venice. The first of these protests against the usurpation of their privileges was uttered by the people in 1299, when Marino Bocconio conceived the idea of entering the Great Council by main force with a band of armed retainers, and once there to massacre the Doge with most of the nobles, and restore to the people the right of belonging to the Council. But his plot failed. News of his intention reached the Doge in time, and he ordered every member of the Council to come armed; consequently when Bocconio and his followers arrived and asked for admission, they were let in, overpowered im-

[1] The Story of the Nations, "The Hansa Towns." Period II., No. vi. p. 175, &c., by Helen Zimmern.

mediately by superior numbers, and all executed that same night. The rest of their adherents on learning their fate sought safety in flight or submission, and the plot died away in the silence of the scaffold or the oblivion of a watery grave.

Soon after this rebellion was over, the Venetians found themselves entangled with the affairs of Ferrara, where domestic broils in the house of Este had divided the town into two parties. Azzo, Marquis of Este, had just died, when his throne was claimed by his brother Francesco, and by his natural son, Fresco. The latter, driven out of Ferrara by the people, appealed to Venice for help. This was at once granted, while the Pope, Clement V., espoused the cause of Francesco. The Venetians sent a large fleet to the support of their ally, which entered Ferrara and disputed with the Papal troops the possession of the town. Clement, judging that his temporal arms were weaker than those of his foes, determined to resort to his spiritual weapons, and in October, 1308, uttered a sentence of excommunication against the Doge, the Signory, the town and the people of Venice. This sentence was discussed in the Great Council, when Gradenigo pleaded eloquently that they should still support their ally, and continue to defend Ferrara against all and every assailant. The resistance offered by Venice enraged the Pope, who resolved to make the Republic feel the weight of his displeasure. He renewed the sentence of interdict and excommunication ; he deprived the Republic of all former concessions and privileges granted by the Holy See ; he freed the Doge's subjects, in whatever country they resided,

from their oath of allegiance ; all property belonging
to Venetians was declared confiscate, and a crusade
was preached against them all over Christendom.
This sentence was most faithfully executed. Whether
from a desire to obey the commands of their spiritual
father, or from a wish to humble the pride and wealth
of a state more prosperous than themselves, the
Christians in Europe lost no time in carrying out
Clement's decree. In France, in England, in Spain,
in Italy, the Venetians were pillaged, their goods
seized, their lives even taken ; they met with a cruel
defeat by sea from the Papal fleet, and the whole land
groaned and suffered under a cessation of all sacra-
ments and the privation of the comforts and supports
of religion.

The Doge had never been popular, and his reign,
marked by one misfortune after another, was to
endure yet another revolution destined to shake the
government to its very foundations. That shock
however was to invest it with fresh powers, and its
forces were presently to be augmented by the dread
mystery of the Council of Ten, which now sprang
into being, and which ruled Venice with a rod of
iron. Mention has been made of the failure of the
first revolt consequent on the "Closing of the Great
Council," a revolt undertaken by the people without
the co-operation or countenance of the nobility. It
was now to be shown how the second revolt, the
work of the older nobility, supported by many of the
lower classes, was to meet with a failure greater even
than that of Bocconio, and to bring in its train consequences of a more tragic and lasting nature.

The organisers of this plot were the heads of the great families of Querini and Tiepolo, but the chief leader and the one who has given his name to the conspiracy, was Bajamonte Tiepolo, son of that Giacomo Tiepolo whom the people had desired as Doge when Gradenigo was named to the post, and grandson of Doge Lorenzo Tiepolo. He was son-in-law of Marco Querini, the head of that powerful house, and extremely popular with the people, among whom he was known as " il gran cavaliere." Querini was a man of vast ambition, and possessed with the idea that some services he had rendered his country during the war with Ferrara had met with insufficient return. His son-in-law was also irritated by an act of fancied injustice on the part of the Government, so that both men were imbued with all the antagonism and opposition born of party feeling and fed by disappointment. Their animosity too against Doge Gradenigo ran high and strong. How could any true patriot, they argued, give allegiance to such a chief ? By what right had he closed the Great Council to so many worthy citizens ? On what ground had he insisted on continuing the terrible and losing strife against the Pope at Ferrara ? Why had the excommunication fallen on so many innocent victims, but owing to him ? The time had now come to put an end to such calamities, and the way to compass that end was by the death of the Doge. For the first time in Venetian history the watchwords of Guelph and Ghibelline re-echoed through the town ; these cries of party faction which had rung throughout the rest of the peninsula had never till that moment penetrated to the heart of the lagunes ; but now the Doge was denounced as Ghibelline, for the sole reason that he had opposed the Pope, and his opponents classed themselves as Guelph and clamoured for his death.

The morning of June 14, 1310, was the day fixed for the execution of the design, when it was settled that two bands of armed men, one led by Marco Querini and his sons, the other under the command of Bajamonte, should come by different ways to St. Mark's Square, and from there carry out their plan. Querini's force was to advance by the present bridge *del Lovo*, the *Calle dei Fabbri*, across what was then the bridge *del mal passo*, now that *dei Dai*, on to the Piazza ; while Bajamonte was to lead his band through the *Merceria*, from whence they were to emerge under the clock tower on to the square. Another ally, Badoero Badoer, had in the meanwhile gone to Padua to raise more adherents to swell the insurgent ranks, and his return to Venice was timed to fit in with the decisive blow that Querini and Tiepolo meant to deal on this 14th of June.

But Fortune did not smile on the conspirators. An awful storm of wind and rain that broke out at the very moment of their operations retarded their movements and hindered their advance. And besides this the Doge was aware of their intentions. Among the many to whom the plot had been confided in all secrecy was one Donà, who turned traitor and revealed the conspiracy to Gradenigo. With an energy and promptness worthy of his character the Doge prepared to meet the danger without loss of time. He gathered around him his

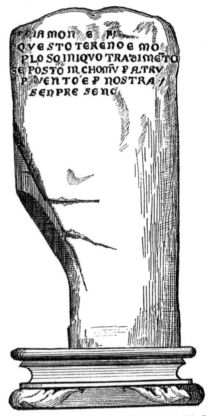

COLUMN OF INFAMY ERECTED ON THE SITE OF BAJAMONTE TIEPOLO'S HOUSE. (*From a drawing at the Museo Correr.*)

councillors, the *Avogadori*, the heads of the XL., the *Signori di notte*, with all whom he knew attached to his cause and on whom he could depend, and armed for action. When Querini and his sons marched into the square, they were confronted and put to flight by the Doge's troops. Querini and his son Benedetto were slain in the encounter, while Bajamonte, ignorant of their fate, was fighting his way to join them through the crowded narrow streets of the *Merceria*. The inhabitants sided against him, and the fight raged hotly from the windows overhead as well as in the compressed space below. Bajamonte's standard-bearer was dashed dead to the ground by a stone mortar, which a woman hurled on him from above, and the fall of the banner whereon the word " Liberty" was engraved in large letters was the signal for the overthrow and flight of Tiepolo and his followers. Bajamonte fled to Rialto, where he crossed the bridge with those of his retainers who still clung to his cause, and, once on the other side, he determined again to try the fortune of war. Had Badoer arrived then from Padua, things might have gone differently, but Gradenigo's powers exceeded those of the insurgents, and Tiepolo's men were discomfited at every turn. The Doge, not willing to push his successes too far, offered to pardon all who would lay down their arms, but it was some time before Tiepolo would be induced to believe his cause hopeless, or accept any overture. Seeing at last the failure of his undertaking, he accepted the mediation of some Milanese merchants in the city, who volunteered to negotiate between him and the Doge. Bajamonte himself was exiled, several of his followers beheaded, and an order given to raze his palace at Sant' Agostino, and to erect on the site a column of infamy.[1] Querini's palace was converted into the public shambles, and preserves to this day the name of the Butcher's Square ; while an order was given to erase and cancel all the arms and badges of the two families of Querini and Tiepolo. And so ended the famous Querini-Tiepolo conspiracy, famous as having established the power of the younger aristocracy, which now guided the destinies and fortunes of Venice, and specially famous in bringing about the formation of that dreaded tribunal of the Council of Ten, around whose name and doings such a flood of mystery and misconception has arisen.

These ten magistrates were first named as criminal judges, and were appointed to inquire into the Tiepolo conspiracy, and disentangle the complications contained in it. Their duration was but for a few days ; it then was extended to five months, from that to five years, till in 1325 it was declared permanent. Its powers were supreme, and consisted in a " plenary, inquisitorial authority, with entire sovereignty over every individual in the State, and with freedom from all responsibility and appeal." [2] A popular Venetian rhyme has fixed the date of its first foundation in 1310, and describes how " Bajamonte, at the middle of the month of cherries, passed over the bridge

---

[1] A few years after it was erected this column was split by a hot-headed follower and admirer of Tiepolo, who paid for his zeal by having his hand cut off and his eyes put out. The column then remained in a broken, half-buried condition till 1785, when the Venetian patriot, Angelo Querini, was allowed to remove it to his villa at Altichiero. From here it was bought by an antiquary, and ultimately sold to the Duke Francesco Melzi, who has placed it in his lovely villa on the Lake of Como.

[2] " Sketches from Venetian History," vol. i. chap. v.

(Rialto), and for this was formed the Council of Ten." [1]

These Ten were chosen from the noblest and most respected of the citizens of Venice, and not more than one out of any family, or even bearing the same name, might rank among its members at the same time; they were chosen annually at four different assemblies of the Great Council, and remained only a year in office; they received no pay, and might assume no other magistracy; no member might sit in judgment when any of his relatives were brought before "the Ten" for trial; and to accept presents or gifts was a capital offence. Their year of office ended, they returned to the grade they formerly occupied, and were no more exempt from the judgments of the tribunal to which they had belonged than if they had never sat amongst its dreaded ranks. And the dread that it inspired was no vain fancy. The mystery that encircled it and the secrecy of its actions have cast over it a veil, that has flung more opprobrium than is perhaps deserved, though at the same time it cannot be denied that it ruled as a tyrant over Venice, and a tyrant whom no dagger could reach, no threats intimidate, no bribes seduce. A modern writer says of it: "It was no concrete despotism, but the very essence of tyranny. To seek its overthrow was vain. . . . Evasive and persuasive, this dark, inscrutable body ruled Venice with a rod

---

[1] " Del mille tresento e diese
A mezo el mese delle ciriese
Bajamonte ha passà el ponte
E per esso fu fato el consegio de diese."

of iron. For good or for bad the Council of Ten was the very child of the new aristocracy, which had won its battle against both the people and the old nobility."[1]

And yet it is strange to reflect that this Council lasted for a period of five centuries, gaining in strength,

DOORWAY IN DUCAL PALACE LEADING TO THE ROOMS OF THE COUNCIL OF TEN. (*From Yriarte's " Venise," op. cit.*)

in mystery, in despotism from year to year, dictating to nobles and Doges, and sparing neither the one nor the other in its onward march to power and pre-eminence, when a single action of the Great Council might have annihilated it for ever. Had the Great

[1] " Venetian Studies," by Horatio F. Brown, London, 1887.

Council, on whom after all it weighed more heavily than any other institution, chosen to discontinue the four elections which annually formed the Council of Ten, it would have gone out of existence in the simplest of ways; and that this remedy was never exercised, still less ever suggested, is proof enough that a belief was extant as to the need and necessity of such a magistracy, till habit had established it as a law not to be gainsaid or overthrown. This Council, though always spoken of as "the Ten," in reality consisted of seventeen members, as the Doge and his six councillors were present at every meeting and debate of the Council; and when any question of extra gravity and importance arose these members were again increased by an addition (*giunta*, or, in Venetian, *zonta*) of occasionally twenty or more, who, chosen from the best and noblest of the citizens, helped by their wisdom and advice to guide the vessel of State safe through the quicksands and shoals of peril or intrigue. The Lion's mouth (*Bocca de Leone*), which poets and novelists have invested with a romantic horror and interest, was one of the adjuncts of this Council, and might, but for the commonplace sound of it, be called the Council's letter-box. In it were placed accusations, denunciations, petitions, disputes between different parties; but the laws in regard of these papers were very strict; no paper was accepted without a signature, and even then many minute regulations were in force as to whether it should be brought under discussion or no. In fact, the Ceremonial (*Rito*) alone of this Council is in itself a study, and a proof of the wonderful amount of rules, restrictions, forms and statutes enveloping this body. The punishments it reserved in its own hands were many and varied, and beginning with fines, exile, torture, imprisonment, and the galleys, passed on to mutilation, death by hanging, and by strangling or drowning, either openly or in secret.

CAMEO OF THE DOGE PIETRO GRADENIGO.
(*From an engraving in the Museo Correr.*)

IX.

WARS IN ITALY AND IN THE EAST.

(1311–1381.)

DOGE PIETRO GRADENIGO died in 1311, leaving the realm in a state of disturbance and agitation. Tiepolo, though banished, was still making efforts to stir his countrymen up to rebellion ; the excommunication pronounced by Pope Clement V. lay heavy on the land, trade languished, and Zara was again in open rebellion. Gradenigo's death passed almost unobserved by his people ; he was laid to rest first in St. Mark's, and afterwards in St. Cyprian at Murano, with no funeral honours, or token of lamentation or mourning, and no sign or word denotes the resting-place of a Doge who certainly left his mark on the Government of Venice, and whose reign had been fraught with such remarkable events.

An old chronicle (that attributed to Daniele Barbaro) speaks of Gradenigo as a man of much wisdom and cunning, and one bent on carrying out his ideas by craft and dissimulation rather than by force. He was prompt and ready in speech, it says, resolute of purpose, and " muchly did he attend to

his friends, to whom he was generous and true above
every other ; while to his foes he was implacable,
and a cruel persecutor, never satisfied unless he
worked them harm, damage, and death." This
verdict is hardly borne out by facts, for his conduct
in regard of the Tiepolo-Querini conspiracy was
neither vindictive nor revengeful, and the benefits
he wrought for his country might have softened the
old chronicler's judgment. It was by Gradenigo's
exertions that the Arsenal was greatly enlarged and
many new laws and reforms were introduced relating
to it. Much was done to reanimate trade, treaties being
formed with the Saracens and with the Egyptians,
as well as with Leo the Armenian, and the island of
Cyprus for this purpose. There were rejoicings, too,
in Venice in 1304, when Pietro, son of the King of
Portugal, visited the town, and when the Doge and
his people held high revelry in honour of their
princely guest.

Gradenigo was succeeded by Marino Zorzi, and he
again, after a reign of ten months, by Giovanni
Soranzo in 1312. This Doge was a man of power
and talent, and his dukedom was a bright epoch in
Venetian story. He was successful in bringing the
war with Zara to a happy termination, and also in
obtaining from the Pope the removal of the excommunication laid upon Venice at the time of the
Ferrarese war. Soranzo despatched several ambassadors to Avignon to treat with Clement, and
Francesco Dandolo, the chief of these envoys, is said
by his submission to the Pontiff's demands, and by
undertaking that the Republic should pay a fine of

100,000 ducats of gold, to have compassed the desired end.

The peace and quiet that prevailed during the reign of Doge Soranzo were of immense advantage and gain to Venice, and enabled her to recover the vigour and dignity of her government, which had been so severely shaken and interrupted by the Tiepolo-Querini conspiracy. A great impetus had been given to trade by this tranquillity in matters spiritual as well as temporal, and the friendly relations entertained by the Doge with many foreign powers added largely to the prosperity of his country. The Emperor Frederick sent to apprise him of his victory over the Guelphs at Mühldorf (1322); amicable negotiations were established with Frederick II., King of Sicily, whose successor, Alfonso, apologised for insults offered by his subjects to some Venetian vessels; and treaties of commerce were signed with Matteo Visconti, lord of Milan, as well as with the towns of Bologna, Brescia, Como, and Recanati. The Count of Gorizia swore fealty to Venice, and King Charles of Hungary offered her terms most advantageous for her commerce ; while with England and Flanders a brisk trade was carried on, and a document exists to show how Venice supplied the London market with sugar, and how in return she received wholesale bales of wool. These were converted by Flemish looms into cloth ; from Flanders they were conveyed to Venice, and from Venice again to Dalmatia and the Levant. Other treaties of the same nature with Andronico, Emperor of Constantinople, with the Sultan of Tunis, and with Trebizond, prove how widespread and universal Venetian traffic was, and the riches accumulated by these means raised Venice to giddy heights of wealth and celebrity. In the town itself manufactories began to increase; some exiles from Lucca fled for refuge to Venice, bringing with them the art of silk weaving; looking-glasses were now made in an abundance, requiring more hands and larger factories; Murano enlarged its glass fabrics, and the chronicles of the time are loud in their praises of a Doge under whose sway the well-being of the town was so wonderfully enhanced, and who neglected no means to add to the beauty of his city and the prosperity of his people.

It was during this dukedom that the embassy from Ravenna to Venice took place, when Dante was one of the ambassadors from Guido Novello da Polenta, lord of Ravenna, to the Republic; but the special object for which he came is lost in the archives burnt in one of those numerous fires that robbed Venice of so many of her treasures; and it is only surmised that the embassy was one of those connected with some question of trade or navigation.

Soranzo died on the 31st of December, 1328, and four days after he was succeeded by Francesco Dandolo. This choice gave universal satisfaction; Dandolo had been the successful ambassador to Avignon, when it is said (though the story is not well authenticated), that he gained the surname of *Cane* (dog) for having crawled under the Pope's feet to obtain the removal of the excommunication, and this act of degradation undergone for his country's sake had endeared him to the hearts of all.

It was soon after his accession that the Venetians were engaged for the first time with foes afterwards to become such bitter antagonists to Europe as well as to Venice, and who in the persons of the Turks were now to assume so important a position in the world's history. In these naval fights the Venetians, commanded by Pietro Zeno, were encountered by the Ottoman Turks, and the Eastern invaders had well-nigh been completely overthrown by the Venetians, when these latter were recalled by a danger threatening them nearer home. This was the war between the Carraresi, lords of Padua, and the Scaligeri, lords of Verona, who both referred their quarrel to Venice, and forced the Republic to take a part, and that an important one, in their disputes.

Can Grande della Scala aimed at adding Padua to his own possessions, and for this purpose made war against the reigning seigneur, Jacopo da Carrara, till 1328, when the marriage of Taddea,[1] Jacopo's only child and heiress, with Mastino della Scala, the nephew and heir of Can Grande, assured the lordship of Padua to the house of della Scala. But no sooner was Can Grande's ambition satisfied in regard of Padua than he coveted to possess himself of Treviso, to which he at once laid siege. His arms were successful, but he died a few days after his triumphal entry into the town. His death was the signal for disputes and

---

[1] Her mother was Anna, only daughter of Doge Pietro Gradenigo, and when, in 1318, her (Anna's) husband was made lord of Padua, her wisdom and tact did much to assure his new position to him. She died in 1321, three years before Jacopo, and on the death of her parents Taddea withdrew to Venice, where in 1328 her marriage with Mastino della Scala took place with great pomp at S. Giorgio.

wranglings among the three houses of della Scala, da Carrara, and da Camino (these latter had been lords of Treviso before Can Grande's conquest), who all claimed some of his vast heritage. Mastino della Scala, consumed with ambition, was determined to add to his uncle's possessions, and not content with the lordship of nine towns,[1] he aimed at becoming master of all Italy, and, but for the opposition offered him by Florence and Venice, it is possible that he might have attained his project.

Mastino had wrested Lucca from Florence at a moment when its possession was specially necessary to her, and the Tuscan Republic was bent not only on vengeance, but on regaining the dominion of her vassal city. Towards Venice Mastino's offence, though of a different nature, was equally grave. He had erected a factory between Padua and Chioggia for the manufacture of salt, and levied duties and taxes on Venetian vessels coming down the rivers of North Italy. To such an infringement of her most sacred rights Venice was not going to submit, and as an embassy sent by Dandolo to remonstrate with Mastino met with no redress, the Doge willingly listened to overtures from Florence to join with her against the lord of Verona. The treaty between them was signed on the 21st of June, 1336, when Pietro de' Rossi[2] was appointed commander-in-chief

[1] These were: Verona, Padua, Vicenza, Treviso, Brescia, Feltre, Belluno, Parma, Lucca.

[2] Pietro was the younge t of six brothers of the house of de' Rossi, lords of Parma, from which rank they had just been despoiled by Mastino. Pietro was looked upon as the most perfect model of a knight and a gentleman in all Italy, and the nobility and chivalry of his character

of the allied forces, and in October of this same year was solemnly invested by the Doge at St. Mark's with the standard of the Republic. The armies of the allies were victorious on several occasions, but their cause was greatly furthered by a league formed in a strange unexpected way between Marsilio of Carrara and Doge Dandolo. Mastino had appointed his brother Alberto governor of Padua, warning him at the same time to beware of Marsilio and Ubertino of Carrara, whom he knew were plotting to regain their former lordship of the town. Alberto della Scala, Mastino's elder brother, had neither the talents nor ambition of his brother, and lived for pleasure only. He had insulted the wife of Ubertino, Marsilio's cousin, and since he himself had forgotten the outrage, he imagined that the husband was equally oblivious. But Ubertino only bided his time, and the blind confidence placed in him and in Marsilio by Alberto helped the cousins to mature their plans, and execute their vengeance.

Marsilio had been entrusted by Mastino with an embassy to Venice, never thinking that his trusted envoy would set his own interests before those of his suzerain lord. The story goes that at a banquet, Marsilio sitting next to Dandolo, said: "I wish to speak to you." Upon this the Doge dropped his napkin, and both stooped to pick it up. "What reward would you give to him who placed Padua in your hands?" was Marsilio's question. "The lord-

were only equalled by the grace and beauty of his person. His soldiery were devoted to him, and his generosity and ability as a leader made him in every way worthy of their devotion.

ship thereof," was the Doge's reply, and when the heads reappeared above the table the bargain had been struck and the league formed which led eventually to Mastino's overthrow.

Marsilio returned to Padua, where soon after Mastino's suspicions were aroused afresh against the Carraresi, and he wrote again and again to his brother urging on him greater caution. Then, as his fears increased, he bade him distrust them entirely, and finally he wrote ordering their apprehension and execution. This letter was to be given into no hands but Alberto's, but he, absorbed in a game of chess, handed it to Marsilio, who was standing watching the game, and told him to read it. Marsilio calmly perused the instructions and provisions made for his and his cousin's deaths, then telling Alberto that Mastino had written for some falcons that he wanted, he left the room, and lost no time in preparing for his and Ubertino's safety and escape. He despatched a messenger to the allied forces, telling Rossi that a certain gate would be open to admit him and his troops if he would advance next morning upon Padua. Rossi instantly did so, and the armies of the league entered and took possession of the town. Alberto was made prisoner and sent to Venice, where he remained three years in confinement; Marsilio, according to the compact made with Dandolo, was proclaimed lord of Padua, and Mastino's power received a vital shock. Soon after the loss of Padua he had to surrender Brescia and Bergamo to the Visconti, and Feltre and Belluno to the King of Bohemia. Most of his other domains were taken from him one by one, and in December, 1388, he was glad to make peace with Venice and her allies, when he remained lord of only Verona, Vicenza, and Parma, while the town of Treviso was granted to

PUBLIC WELL IN THE COURTYARD OF CÀ BATTAGIA AT S. CANCIANO;
NOW DRIED UP AND UNUSED.
(*From " Raccolte delle Vere da Pozzo," op. cit.*)

Venice. This was the first time since she had become a power that Venice owned any territory on the mainland of Italy; for more than nine centuries she had ruled and reigned over her watery kingdom with ever increasing success and stability.

Now however the beginning was laid of that fatal policy which carried her thoughts and ambitions on to the mainland of Italy, and drew away her power from the sea, that element whereon her true strength and vitality lay. The first Podestà sent by Venice to govern at Treviso was Marino Falier, who was afterwards to attain such notoriety as Doge. Shortly after his appointment Francesco Dandolo died, and Bartolomeo Gradenigo was named Doge in his stead.

In Gradenigo's short reign of three years the quaint legend is told of how St. Mark visited and saved the town of Venice, a legend that has procured for us such a beautiful record in the picture of the Fisherman and the Ring, immortalised by Paris Bordone's brush and now on the walls of the Accademia. The story goes that in February, 1340, an awful storm of wind and rain visited the town, threatening to sweep all before it and submerge Venice. On the night of the 15th of February, this tempest raged with even extra fury, and the surprise of an old boatman sheltering on the Riva degli Schiavoni can be imagined, when an unknown individual accosted him, and ordered him, regardless of the storm, to row him across to the island of S. Giorgio. The stranger was a man not to be gainsaid or withstood, and to S. Giorgio they accordingly rowed. Here the stranger alighted, went to the Church of the monastery, and before long returned with a companion. The two entered the boat, and ordered the boatman to row to S. Nicolò del Lido. Here the passengers again alighted, went on shore, and soon returned with a third friend, when all three got into the boat, and directed that they should be rowed towards the sea. The little bark floated safely through the raging ocean, and when well out to sea they encountered a boat laden with infernal spirits, which the three friends ordered to disappear, and the boat with its demoniacal crew sank from sight. This done they rowed back to Venice, each passenger alighting where he had embarked, till, arrived at the Piazzetta, the fisherman was alone with the stranger who had first accosted him. He told him he was St. Mark, his two companions were St. George and St. Nicholas; that they three had saved Venice from the overthrow threatened her by demons and evil spirits, and that he was to go to the Doge and relate to him and the Procuratori the incidents of the night. The fisherman objected that his story would meet with no credence unless he could produce some proof wherewith to convince his hearers. Thereupon St. Mark drew a ring from his finger, telling him to present it to the Doge and say that it was his, St. Mark's, own ring, taken by him from the treasury, where they would find it to be missing ; and that he now restored it as a sign of his manifest presence, and of his guardianship and watchfulness over the town which owned him as its patron saint. Whatever doubts may be cast over the story of St. Mark's appearing, there can be none as to the inundations and storms which took place at this epoch, and worked great harm and devastation, besides requiring extensive and costly works to repair the mischief done and guard against its recurrence in the future.

It was in this year (1340) that Edward III. of

England applied to the Doge for a loan of ships and money to help him in his wars with France. He added that, should Venice be unable to furnish him with the required supplies, he trusted the Venetians would observe a strict neutrality, and that they would write also to the authorities in Genoa asking the same of them. In return for these services Edward would grant special privileges as to trade, &c., and also should the Doge be minded to send two, or at least one, of his sons to visit his court he should be treated with all honour. To this offer the Doge replied lamenting the strife between the kings of England and France, as well as his inability to supply the needed vessels, but owing to the increasing inroads and advances of the Turks, the Republic required all her ships and men to guard against a danger about to become universal. He did not deem it suitable to write to Genoa ; but for the rest he was grateful to his Majesty for the privileges that might have been conferred, and for the courtesy held out to his sons.

On the 28th of December, 1342, Doge Gradenigo died, and early in the following year Andrea Dandolo was chosen to succeed him. Andrea had refused on a former occasion the dignity now conferred on him, probably to pursue the studies he loved so passionately, and for which his name has become so famous. He was one of the earliest among the Venetian patricians to take a doctor's degree at the University of Padua, where for some time he had also been professor of law, and he was too the author of that learned history or chronicle of Venice " to which we owe half

of what we know of her former fortunes." [1]   One of
the first acts of his reign was to sign a treaty between
the Emperor of Constantinople, the Pope Clement VI.,
the Kings of France and of Cyprus, the Grand Master
of the Knights of Rhodes, and Venice, against the
Turks.   Smyrna was taken by the allies, but the
campaign was a succession of victories and defeats
on both sides, and closed without any conclusive step
being attained.

A few years after Venice was at war for the seventh
time with her rebellious vassal, the town of Zara.
This revolt against her suzerain was supported by
Louis, King of Hungary, and Beltrando, Patriarch of
Aquileja, and was only put down after a struggle
which lasted sixteen months, and ended finally in the
complete supremacy of Venice.

The following year (1348) saw that awful outbreak
of the plague over all Europe, described so graphic-
ally by Boccaccio.   It fell with severity upon Venice,
but before it declared itself virulently, the town was
shaken by an earthquake which lasted several days,
and was so severe that many houses and belfrys fell,
many canals were dried up, and the terror, widespread
among the citizens, was a bad preparation for the
pestilence now stealing upon them and requiring
courage and nerve to meet it.   No effort though was
spared to grapple with the evil—every possible
measure was taken to avoid the spread of the infection, and to lessen the sufferings and agonies of the
sick and dying.   But all was in vain, and the only
thing that seemed of use was to provide for the burial

[1] Ruskin, "Stones of Venice," vol. ii. chap. iv. p. 68.

of the dead. "It was necessary," says Sanudo, "to
send and bury the bodies at S. Giorgio L'Alega, at
S. Marco Boccalame, at S. Lionardo di Fossaruola,
and at S. Erasmo ; such was the number of the dead
who were buried one above another in the cemeteries,
and hardly covered. . . . And many died without
penitence and without being seen. And all who
remained hid for fear one of another. And it was

THE ISLAND OF S. GIORGIO IN ALGA.
(*Vignette from an engraving of " Christ and the Woman of Samaria,"
by Giulio Campagnola.*)

provided to send round to each *sestieri* [division] of
the town 'piatte' [*peate*, or large flat boats] crying,
'Dead bodies!' and those who had any dead in the
house had to throw them in the boats under punishment of heavy fines." It is calculated that three-
fifths of the population perished, and fifty noble
families became extinct ; so to repair such losses the
rights of citizenship and of nobility were offered to
" foreign settlers after two years' residence."

A fierce war broke out in 1350 between the Republics of Genoa and Venice; their rivalries and jealousies in the East had but increased as the trade and prosperity of one or the other gained the ascendant, and nothing but war could satisfy the anger and passion raging between them.[1]   The first encounter of the forces was favourable to Venice, and in the Bay of Caristo, in Negropont, she gained a slight victory over the Genoese, who were commanded by Paganino Doria.   The Venetian fleet, under Nicolò Pisani, one of Venice's greatest admirals, was inferior in numbers and strength to that of the Genoese, and to compensate for this inequality the Venetians sought and obtained the alliance of Peter IV. of Aragon, and of John Cantacuzenus, Emperor of Constantinople, whose wrath against the Genoese for the insults and contempt they had heaped upon him at Pera, induced him to support their rivals.   Early in 1352 the allies met their foes in the waters of the Bosphorus; the Genoese were outnumbered by their adversaries, but their ships were larger and more powerful, and the desertion of the Greeks, who at the outset of the action fled in a cowardly way and abandoned their allies, secured the victory to Doria.   The fight began towards evening, when a storm was also threatening; the darkness of the night was so dense that no one could distin-

---

[1] It is difficult to trace with precision and exactness the accounts of this war, and Sismondi, speaking of the confusion existing among historians in regard to this period, says: "Not only are different historians at variance as to the order and chronology of events, but beside that, each one relates several contradictory versions, and seems embarrassed how to choose between them."

guish friend from foe, and the fury of the elements combined with the enmity and strife of two deadly adversaries, presented a ghastly scene of havoc, bloodshed and confusion. The allies had to withdraw; but the losses on both sides were so heavy as to leave the victors scarcely more triumphant than the conquered. These latter had also to mourn the death of the Aragonese admiral, Ponsio di Santa Paz, who died a few days after from chagrin and despair at the discomfiture of his fleet.

The unnaturalness of this war excited the regret of all Europe; the Pope interposed to make peace between the rival powers, urging them to turn their arms against the infidels, whose approach upon Constantinople created consternation to all minds sufficiently clear-sighted to grasp the on-coming danger. A more famous mediator still, the poet Petrarch, also endeavoured to arbitrate between them, and used most flowery language to induce the two nations to dwell at peace as brethren.[1] A strong friendship, based on their literary tastes, existed between Petrarch and Doge Andrea Dandolo, and the poet hoped that his eloquence and learning would prevail with his friend to make him advocate the desired peace. But Dandolo turned a deaf ear to all the poetry and rhetoric which Petrarch lavishly poured forth, and in reply dwelt only on the hatred entertained by Venice for Genoa, and on the impossibility of making peace "with the most pestilent of nature's works." With increased forces and animosity the war was renewed in 1353, when the Genoese, this

[1] See Sismondi, "Histoire des Rép. Ital.," vol. iii. ch. xiii. p. 315.

time commanded by Grimaldi, sustained a crushing defeat at Loiera in Sardinia. Thirty-two of their galleys were captured by the Venetians, who stained the glory of their victory by throwing all their prisoners—said to number no less than four thousand —into the sea. The despair into which this defeat threw the Genoese was so great they considered the grandeur of their Republic as at an end for ever; and thirsting for revenge sooner than for the maintenance of their liberty, they offered to sell themselves to Giovanni Visconti, Lord Archbishop of Milan, in return for men and forces wherewith to continue the war with Venice.

Visconti had long been desirous to add Genoa to his other dominions; but he saw what disasters this continued war between the two great naval powers of Italy could not fail to bring upon the land, and strove as others had done before him to persuade the combatants to lay down their arms. He likewise availed himself of the services of Petrarch, and despatched him as ambassador to Venice to plead with the Doge for mercy and peace; but the mission was in vain, Venice refused to listen to any overtures, and war was again resolved on. The Genoese were this time under the command of their former admiral, Paganino Doria, and the Venetian fleet, with their Aragonese allies, awaited him off the island of Sardinia; but he gave them the slip, entered the Adriatic Gulf, and boldly sailed up it to the attack of the town of Venice itself. The peril that threatened the city was great; Paolo Loredan, the captain-general of the town, was called on to provide for its safety and defence, and a great iron chain was drawn across the port of the Lido. While preparations were making on all sides for assault and resistance, Doge Andrea Dandolo sank under the accumulation of cares and anxieties, and died on September 7, 1354, at the early age of forty-six.

He left behind him a renown for learning and wisdom, to which his splendid chronicle bears ample testimony ; his character is that of a man of irreproachable life and habits ; and the judgment passed on him by Petrarch pronounces him to have been "just, upright, full of zeal and of love for his country, and at the same time erudite, of rare eloquence, wise, affable, and humane."[1] Besides the history which he left of his native town—a history drawn from old chronicles and authentic records, and one of the most reliable fountain-heads for the story of Venice—he also revived the old code of laws drawn up by Jacopo Tiepolo: and compiled a new one as well, known as the "Sixth Book of the Venetian Institute," where all matters relating to civil, maritime, and criminal laws were specified and put in order. He was the last Doge who was buried in St. Mark's,[2] and four days after his death his successor was named in the person of Marino Falier.

The fatal renown that encircles the name and story of this Doge render him a more conspicuous character than most of his predecessors or successors on

---

[1] Variarum, epist. xix.

[2] See the beautiful description of his tomb in Ruskin's "Stones of Venice," vol. ii. ch. iv. p. 61. It seems that Petrarch had written an epitaph for his friend's monument, which comprised a biography of the Doge, but for some unknown reason it was not adopted.

the ducal throne. Possessed of one of those strong individualities that too surely stamp their mark either for good or for evil on the history of the time, Falier has left a celebrity more suitable apparently for poetry and fiction than for history and reality ; and the writer of his story must occasionally forego the halo created around him by romance and compassion in order to rebuild the tale with the more abiding stones of truth.

Marino Falier, descended from one of Venice's most old and noble families, was at Avignon at the moment of his election in the capacity of ambassador to the Pope. He was already seventy-six years of age at the date of his nomination, and had served his country frequently in both civil and military employments before being named to the highest dignity. His reign opened disastrously for Venice, for though Doria had found it expedient to withdraw his fleet from the Adriatic, the war with Genoa still continued, and a terrible engagement between the foes at Sapienza off the Morea on the 4th of November, 1354, ended in the complete defeat and overthrow of the Venetians ; Doria returned to Genoa in triumph with over five thousand prisoners, among them being the Venetian admiral Pisani. The woe and mourning in Venice were universal, for there was not a family that had not to weep over some member dead or imprisoned. The misery and lamentation incurred by the disaster at Sapienza were, however, well-nigh effaced by the peril now threatening the life and existence of Venice. For insurrection and dissatisfaction were surging in the heart of the government, and all thoughts were concentrated on the danger existing in the midst of the capital. This plot was the work of the Doge himself, but doubt and uncertainty surround the motive of his action, and different causes are ascribed for the origin of a deed which has branded Falier as a traitor. The character of the man helped no doubt to fan the flame unfortunately kindled by circumstances, and the hot, ungovernable and ambitious temper he possessed came into contact with all that tended most to irritate and unbalance him. Fresh restrictions had been put upon the Doge's power before his appointment ; and probably not till he was actually in office did he grasp what a prisoner of state he was, surrounded and overlooked by spies, and with watchers and officers on every hand eager to suppress any movement towards liberty and independence, that a fiery proud spirit would but too probably manifest.

One story goes that a young courtier, Michele Steno, had paid his addresses to a maid of honour of the Dogaressa in an impertinent and forward manner in the ducal palace, and the Doge, annoyed at such insolence, forbade the young fellow to enter the palace, and ordered him then and there to be expelled. Steno resolved to be avenged for what he considered an unjust injury, and wrote the following insulting lines on the Doge's throne :

> " Marin Falier
> Dalla bella muger
> I altri la galde
> E lu la mantien."

Falier's weakness in regard of his wife, the young and beautiful Lodovica Gradenigo, was a well-known fact. He had married her as his second wife late in life, and his sensitiveness in all that related to his bride was no secret. His anger at Steno's behaviour was unbounded ; he hoped that the judgment passed on him would be nothing short of death, and was furious when he learnt that a short term of imprisonment was the sentence pronounced on the young noble. From that moment Falier was a changed man, and plotted for the overthrow of a state and nobility from whom he considered he had received neither justice nor consideration.

Another story relates that the Doge was insulted by some young noblemen, that he could not obtain the redress he desired, and determined to take the law into his own hands. An occasion presented itself almost immediately when Stefano Gisello, Admiral of the Arsenal, appealed to him for justice against a noble, who had insulted him and some others at the Arsenal, and had refused to give him satisfaction. Falier asked him what hope he could have of justice, seeing that to him, the Doge, none had been dealt ? Gisello replied, " But one binds wild beasts, and if one cannot bind them, one kills them." This answer suggested to the Doge the nature of the man with whom he had to deal, and he lost no time in propounding to him the plot teeming in his brain, and which suggested nothing less than the murder of almost all the nobles and the proclamation of himself as Prince. To this Gisello readily gave in his adhesion, and the conspiracy thickened apace. The Doge and his nephew, Bertuccio Falier, were the ringleaders, their ranks being joined by Gisello, Filippo Calendario (one of the reputed architects of the ducal palace), and numerous workmen and sailors from the Arsenal. February 15th was the day determined on for the execution of the plot, when the signal for the commencement of action was to be a false alarm that the Genoese fleet was advancing upon the town and attempting an entrance into the harbour.   The conspirators felt sure that, when the citizens heard this, and heard too the great bell of St. Mark's (only rung in moments of special peril and danger) peal out the alarm, they would all flock to the square.   There the nobles would be overpowered and cut down, and amid the shouts of " Long live Prince Falier ! " the people would join in the cry, and Venice, like the other cities of Italy, would fall under the rule and dominion of one lord and tyrant.

And Venice but narrowly escaped this fate.   The secrecy with which the plot had been carried on escaped even the vigilance of the Council of Ten, and it was only through the anxiety of one of the conspirators to save a patrician and friend, and who warned this friend to keep next day within doors, that the whole thing was discovered.   This nobleman's suspicions were alarmed, he questioned and inquired, and, seeing cause for alarm, communicated what he knew to the heads of the different offices, and all was discovered.   Sentence was quickly passed on all the conspirators ; some were exiled, some were hanged in couples from the arches of the outer gallery of the ducal palace, beginning with that arch supported by two red columns ;[1] and some few were set at liberty. The fate of the Doge is well known. The Council of Ten summoned for the first time since their creation an addition of twenty extra nobles, known as the *Zonta*, or *Giunta*, who were called in on any great emergency or when the occasion was so important as to require more opinions than those of the Council alone, to pass judgment on the head of the Republic. The judgment passed was a condemnation of death. Falier acknowledged his crime, confessed the conspiracy and the share which he had in it, and owned that he deserved the doom passed on him. His sentence was soon carried out. On April 17, 1355, Marino Falier was led to the stone terrace of the ducal palace by the stairs,[2] from which the Doges were wont to proclaim their oath to observe their *Promissione*, despoiled of all his ducal insignia, and at one stroke his head was severed from his body. The corpse of the Doge was placed in a stone coffin, no attendants or mourners following to do him honour, and buried in the cloisters of the now suppressed chapel of Sta. Maria della Pace.[3]

---

[1] These two columns of red marble in the loggia looking on to the Piazzetta, and facing the royal palace, mark the spot from where the Doge assisted at any public festival. In later times all criminal sentences passed by the Austrians were proclaimed from that spot.

[2] Not the Giant Stairs, as has been so often thought and believed, for they were only built 130 years later than the period now under discussion.

[3] This chapel stood to the right of the Scuola di S. Marco (now part of the Hospital of Venice at SS. Giovanni e Paolo), and a few years ago a stone coffin was discovered near the entrance of the chapel. On being opened it was found to contain a body with the head between its

Doge Falier's sentence is not recorded in the annals of the Council of Ten. It may be that a sense of shame forbade their recording so fearful a judgment on the chief of their government, and adding his name to those of more ordinary criminals ; but the space where it should have been entered is left void, and the sole words, *non scribatur*, mark more forcibly than any lengthy inscription the solemnity of the blank, and the meaning of such an omission. A few years later the Council of Ten decreed that Marino Falier's condemnation should never be revoked ; in 1366 his effigy was removed from among the other Doges, and now a black curtain veils the spot where his picture should have hung among those of the Doges in the Hall of the Great Council, and on it are the words : " Hic est locus Marini Falethri decapitati pro criminibus."

The next Doge appointed was Giovanni Gradenigo, whose first care was to effect peace between his country and Genoa. This peace was signed June 1st of this year (1355), and for the rest of his reign Gradenigo was occupied in opposing Louis, King of Hungary, who stirred up the town of Zara to fresh revolt, and who, when defeated in this quarter, turned his arms against the Republic nearer home. He was joined in this war by the Patriarch of Aquileja, the Count of Gorizia, and Francesco of Carrara, the supposed ally and friend of Venice, and

knees, a proof that this head had been cut off by the sword of justice. It was the corpse of the unhappy Doge Marino Falier, whose bones have been dispersed, while the tomb, after having the inscriptions erased, was converted into a water trough. Only lately has it been rescued from this usage, and taken to the Museo Civico.

operations had commenced by the siege of Treviso when Doge Gradenigo died.

The man chosen to succeed him was Giovanni Dolfin, at that moment "Provveditore" of Treviso, and shut up in the besieged town. A safe conduct was demanded of King Louis to allow Dolfin to pass out and take possession of his new dignity, but this was refused, and Treviso, encouraged by the presence of the Doge within her walls, made so vigorous a defence that Louis, discouraged by the opposition, retired to Hungary. Dolfin was then able to accom-plish his journey to Venice, where he arrived in state on August 25, 1356.

His dukedom is marked by the surrender to the King of Hungary of Croatia and Dalmatia, and henceforward the Doges no longer added the titles of these duchies to that of Venice. The surrender of these lands and titles was a blow and humiliation to Venice and the Venetians ; but the motive that prompted the action was a wise one, and one that now and again guided the policy of the Republic. The need of giving up provinces and territories whose possession only sapped and drained her resources was of use in that it strengthened for the present the powers of Venice, and also left her free to regain what she now resigned should the occa-sion for so doing present itself; as eventually proved the case in regard of Dalmatia. This treaty was signed February 18, 1358, and three years later Doge Dolfin died, and Lorenzo Celsi reigned in his stead.

One of the peculiarities dwelt on in regard of Doge Celsi by his biographers is the passion he had for horses. The taste may at first seem strange in a Venetian, but it must be borne in mind that they were a people much given to the science and pursuit of equitation, and their breed of horses on the mainland was one of the most famous in Italy. In earlier times riding and tournaments were much in vogue in Venice, when the bridges were sloped up and down with gentle inclines so as to allow of horses crossing them with ease and safety, instead of the steps familiar to us nowadays.

It is said that Doge Celsi introduced on to the ducal cap a small cross, out of consideration for his aged father, whose dignity was offended at bowing to his son, but who, saluting the sacred sign, saved his parental sensitiveness by reverencing the cross and not his son, who he declared to be by nature inferior to him.

Celsi's reign was engrossed by a war with Candia. This war, when the Candiotes were supported by many of the Venetian residents in the island, was long and bloody ; but after many vicissitudes it resulted in the ascendency of the Venetian arms. Petrarch, who was at Venice at the time, relates the joy that spread through the city when the galley bearing the glad news from Candia hove in sight, and with its festive decorations and the captive banners trailing at the stern, announced the triumph of Venetian arms. The poet's house [1] was on the Riva degli Schiavoni, and he describes how from his win-

---

[1] This house, still known as " Casa Petrarca," was formerly one of the palaces of the Molin family, and used to be called " the house of the two towers," from two small towers which flanked it on either side. It was given to Petrarch in acknowledgment of the gift made by him to the Republic of his library.

dows overlooking the wide expanse of lagune and island he watched the crowd below, and listened to the shouts and cries of rejoicing and victory. From that he goes on to speak of the tournament held in the Square of St. Mark to celebrate this retaking of Candia. "No sex, no age, no condition was wanting," he writes. "The Doge with a numerous retinue sat in front of the church above the vestibule, and from that marble balcony saw all in movement below him. It was actually the site where stand the four horses of gilt bronze, a work of antique craft, and of a cunning artificer, whoever he was; and they seem on their heights to excel even living steeds, as they raise and stamp and paw the air with their hoofs. In order that the sun should not molest our sight with the splendour of his setting rays, curtains and stuffs of different colours had been hung, and I was seated at the Doge's right hand, invited there by him; an act of condescension frequently shown by him to me wards. The great square, the church itself, the tower, the roofs, the porticoes, the windows, all were—I will not say full—but crammed, packed with people. On one side of the church was erected a splendid stand for the Venetian matrons, who, numbering at least four hundred, rendered the festival still gayer. There were also present many English, relations of the king, who were then in Venice, where for several days joy reigned supreme, and every foreigner remained transfixed at the sight of such magnificence."[1] The victories in Candia were, however, followed by fresh insurrections, and the rebels, headed

[1] Letters to Pietro Bolognese.

by the brothers Calergi, involved Venice in constant struggles and difficulties. They were finally overcome in 1366, and from that time forward the island was governed by stricter rules, and kept under with more vigorous laws and measures.

Apart from this war Doge Celsi's reign was rendered famous by the gift made to Venice by Petrarch of his library. He intended he said to make " the blessed St. Mark heir of his books and manuscripts," of which he had been a great collector, on condition that they should not be sold or dispersed, but kept in a building secure against fire and damp, and serve " for the amusement and benefit of noble and literate persons in the city." He hoped at the same time that others would follow his example. This gift was made on September 4, 1362, and was accepted with words of gratitude by the Government, who provided a house for the poet, but did not show the care and regard required for such a bequest. His books and manuscripts were housed under the roof of St. Mark's, where they lay for many years neglected, almost forgotten, and many of them have perished. To Petrarch, however, must be ascribed the honour of having been the first to conceive the idea of a public library in Venice, an idea however which only came into being many years afterwards.

The dukedom of Marco Corner, who in 1365 succeeded Lorenzo Celsi as Doge, was on the whole peaceable and quiet, and gave, as it were, a breathing time wherein to prepare for the calamities and disturbances now about to darken the reign of Andrea Contarini, who became Doge in 1368.

It was no easy matter to induce Contarini to accept the honour conferred on him. He retired to Padua to escape from notice while the electors were sitting, as it had been rumoured that he would be appointed to the vacant post, and even when the news reached him that the choice had fallen upon him, he refused the office, and not till he was threatened with all the penalties consequent on those who prove traitors to their country did he consent to sacrifice his own wishes to those of his fellow citizens. It is said that a prophecy once made to him by a dervish in Syria, that under his rule his country would suffer great calamities, made him reluctant to become Doge, but it is perhaps more probable that the fresh restrictions made in the two last ducal *Promissioni* weighed still more with him, and made him unwilling to renounce his liberty and independence for chains even so gilded and gorgeous as those Venice wove round her nominal rulers.

These restrictions required that neither the Doge, his wife, his sons, nor his grandsons or nephews should possess or hold any fief or estate in the dukedom,[1] and if at the time of their election they owned any, they had to sell it. The *Avogadori* were instructed to examine, with a scrupulousness both galling and insulting to a prince, into his money matters, and see that his bills were discharged monthly : if this were not done, the sum owing was kept back from the public revenue. The Doge was

---

[1] The "Dogado," or dukedom, comprised only the town of Venice, the islands of Malamocco, Chioggia, and Brondolo, and the slip of coast between the mouths of the Adige and the Musone.

COURTYARD OF THE PALAZZO CONTARINI DEGLI SCRIGNI.
(*From " Calli e Canali," op. cit.*)

ordered to provide himself with a coat of cloth-of-gold ; and when at the councils the *Avogadori* expressed their views and intentions, the Doge was bound to agree with them.

There can be small wonder that a position so exalted, and at the same time so fettered, so jealously watched, and so constantly and offensively rebuffed, should have offered few charms to a bold, free and generous nature, and many a noble spirit must have chafed at being appointed to a post so full of humiliation and repression.

The beginning of Contarini's dukedom was occupied with a war with Trieste, in which Leopold, Duke of Austria, sided with the Triestines. Venice finally conquered, and had then to turn her arms and thoughts to a more serious undertaking in the struggle between herself and Francesco da Carrara —a struggle destined to end so fatally for the descendants and race of the Carraresi.

Francesco had repaid his debt of gratitude to the state which had restored to him and his family the lordship of Padua, by a course of policy so treacherous and cold-blooded it is little wonder that Venice determined to be revenged, and though she had to bide her time, she meted out the measure of her vengeance to the very end. Da Carrara had proved a most faithless ally and friend, when, at the moment of the Republic's war with King Louis of Hungary (1356), he had supplied this monarch with provisions for his army at the siege of Treviso, and all the entreaties of Venice to desist from so doing availed nothing. He now erected two forts, one at Castellaro on the Brenta, the other at Oriago on the Bacchiglione, and set up some salt works at the latter—a privilege exercised in that quarter only by Venice, who was by no means minded to watch with indifference one of her most important and lucrative branches of commerce passing to other hands. Deputations were sent to Padua to expostulate with Francesco, and request him to withdraw from a business and trade wherein he had neither part nor parcel, and his friends and allies [1] besought him to submit to the lawful remonstrances of the Venetians. But Francesco maintained that he was in the right. He refused to yield as to the monopoly of the salt trade, and on seeing how serious a turn matters were taking determined to further his cause by treason and intrigue. He despatched spies and emissaries to Venice to gain over to his faction all who he thought disaffected towards the Government, and among these some names of men in places of trust were found when the plot came to light, and justice was administered by the prompt action of the Council of Ten. An attempt was also made, it is said, on the part of Francesco to poison the wells, and the animosity ran so high on both sides that war broke out between them.

Hostilities began by the Venetians destroying the works erected by da Carrara towards the lagunes, and several engagements took place, the Venetians being defeated at Narvesa—when their general, Taddeo

---

[1] These were the Cardinal legate of Bologna, the Archbishop of Ravenna, the Marquis of Este, Louis of Hungary, and the Communes of Florence and Pisa.

Giustinian, was taken prisoner, and the flags of the Republic were captured and hung with pride in the Church of St. Antonio at Padua—and at Fossanuova. They wiped out these disgraces, however, by a brilliant victory, when the Vaivode of Transylvania, nephew of the King of Hungary, who commanded the joint forces of Austrians, Hungarians, and Paduans, was taken prisoner. This victory bore yet more important fruit in encouraging Marsilio and Nicolò, brothers of Franceso of Carrara, to join a secret conspiracy in Venice against the life and authority of their brother. The plot however failed, and Marsilio fled for safety to Venice, while Nicolò was taken and imprisoned in the fortress of Monselice, where he ended his days. Peace was at last concluded between the belligerents, owing to the entreaties of the Pope, and of the King of Hungary, whose anxiety as to his nephew's safety and liberty was great, and on September 21, 1373, terms were agreed on. Da Carrara then consented to the following stipulations :—To pay a large sum to Venice ; to come in person, or depute his son, to kneel and implore pardon of the Doge ; the forts were all to be demolished ; free trade was to be allowed to Venetian merchants ; his supply of salt was to be drawn exclusively from Venetian works ; with other details, all tending to the advantage of Venice. Da Carrara's son, Francesco Novello, spared his old father the indignity of kneeling at the Doge's feet, and came in person to fulfil the humiliating compact, accompanied by Petrarch, who recited a long oration extolling the glories and benefits of peace. This was the last public appearance of the poet ; he retired afterwards to his mountain house in Arquà, where he died the following year (1374) on the 18th of July.

The peace signed by Venice and Padua was too unfavourable to the latter to be long regarded by her, and da Carrara urged the Duke of Austria to invade the Venetian territory and harass the towns under the protection of the Signory, and all appeals sent by Venice to Francesco to adhere to the promises made by him were utterly futile. It was in these wars, brought about by the treachery and at the instigation of da Carrara, that the Venetians for the first time made use of cannon, then but just invented, and employed by them against the small town of Quer or Guero. An old chronicler describes these cannon as being " huge iron weapons, bored throughout their entire length, and having large mouths. Within them is placed a round stone on black powder composed of sulphur, charcoal, and saltpetre. This powder is ignited at a hole, and the stone is discharged with such violence no wall can resist it. One would think that God were thundering." [1]

Francesco of Carrara meantime was seeking on all sides for allies to help him in his strife against Venice, and he turned to the Genoese, whose rivalry with the Venetians made them accept with readiness an opportunity to molest the Republic, whom they were always longing to humble and surpass. The quarrel into which Francesco involved these two great maritime powers was to develop into the war of Chioggia—a war that shook both republics to their very founda-

[1] Radusio di Quero, " Cronaca di Treviso."

tions, and left them, weakened and exhausted, to the inroads of the Turks, who knew well how to profit by such an opportunity. The position of the republics of Venice and Genoa had in different ways a degree of similarity that made them alike under certain aspects, and gave them too a character distinct from other Italian states. Genoa, surrounded by her Ligurian mountains, and Venice, by her lagunes, were equally shut off from the rest of Italy, and both of them often acted as though they had neither knowledge of nor interest in that country. Their commerce and riches were alike drawn almost exclusively from the East, and it was here that their differences were always arising, and from whence their disputes almost invariably sprang. The incident which brought about the war fostered by Francesco of Carrara originated in Cyprus on the occasion of the coronation of Peter of Lusignan, when a question arose as to the precedence of the Venetian and Genoese representatives. It was settled in favour of the Venetian, and the Genoese were so embittered at the preference shown to their rivals that they stirred up their Government to declare war immediately. A fleet was accordingly armed and sent to besiege Famagosta, and the King of Cyprus, who had favoured the Venetians, applied to them for aid ; but beyond despatching many embassies to Genoa to remonstrate against this invasion of the island and against the insult offered to their Bailo, the Venetians forbore for awhile to arm. But war was only delayed, not given up, and an occasion soon occurred which gave both powers full scope for their animosity and fighting tendencies, and plunged them both in a long and bloody war.

As has been said, the quarrels between Venice and Genoa originated nearly always in the East, and this case was no exception to the general rule. Affairs in Constantinople must be touched on for a moment to show how matters reached this pass, and explain how the flame lighted between the two powers in Italy was fanned into full height in the Eastern capital. The Emperors of Byzantium had committed the irreparable error of calling to their assistance the Turks, who had gradually dispossessed Andronicus the Elder of the whole of Asia Minor and all the Greek possessions beyond the Bosphorus and the Hellespont. John Cantacuzenus again summoned them to help him maintain his usurped throne ; and his successor, John Paleologus, who had been both his pupil and rival, lost during his reign, which lasted from 1355 to 1391, the provinces hitherto owned by the empire in Europe. All passed into the power of Amurath I., whose son and successor, Murad, said to Paleologus : " Close the gates of your town and reign within the circuit of your walls, for all without that circle is mine." The Greek Emperor, sunk in debauch, sought to forget his losses by every dishonourable pleasure. He was roused, however, by an insurrection headed by his son Andronicus, and Sauzes the son of Murad. This plot, organised to dethrone both the Emperor and the Sultan, was discovered by Murad, who punished his own son with death, and ordered the Emperor to do likewise. But Paleologus preferred his own mode of vengeance, and caused his son and innocent grandson to be blinded and imprisoned in the tower of Anema. The Genoese determined to make capital out of the misfortunes of the blind princes. They offered to assist them to escape and to place them on the throne, if in return for such services they would hand over to Genoa the island of Tenedos. This was agreed to by Andronicus; the treaty was signed in August, 1376, and the Genoese lost no time in attacking Constantinople, where, with the help of the Emperor's discontented subjects, they succeeded in dethroning him, and placed Andronicus on the throne. The gift of the island of Tenedos to Genoa roused the anger of Venice: the island was nominally under her sway, having been ceded to her by John Paleologus in pawn for a debt incurred by him to the Republic, when, finding himself in Venice and destitute of money, he had raised a large loan to pay for his homeward journey and other debts. The situation too of the island made it one of special value and importance for all trading purposes, and both to Venice and to Genoa the possession thereof was one ardently and eagerly desired. Venice sent a fleet under Donato Tron to assist the inhabitants, who had refused to acknowledge any sovereign but their dethroned monarch Paleologus; but their attention was soon called off from Tenedos to Cyprus, where fresh disputes had again arisen between the rival powers. Venice was supported by Barnabò Visconti, lord of Milan, whose daughter Valentina had married the young King of Cyprus; while the Genoese gained to their side the King of Hungary, the Patriarch of Aquileja, the lords of Verona and Padua, the community of Ancona, the Queen of Naples, and the Duke of Austria. Against so formidable a league Venice made every preparation for a vigorous and steady war; every citizen capable of bearing arms was called on to prepare for the defence of his country; Vettor Pisani was entrusted with the command of the forces, and Carlo Zeno[1] was sent to Negropont to watch over Venetian interests in that quarter. Though the quarrel had originated in the East it was nearer home that the first engagement took place, and on May 30, 1378, the Venetians gained a brilliant victory off Antium, when Luigi Fiesco, the Genoese admiral, was taken prisoner. But this defeat was speedily avenged. In the following year the Genoese fleet under Luciano Doria sailed up the Adriatic Gulf, and in May, 1379, gained a great victory off Pola over the Venetians. This reverse was a terrible one for Venice, and dismay reigned through the city: Carlo Zeno with his ships was far away, the enemy were at hand, and to crown all the Council of Ten passed sentence of imprisonment on Vettor Pisani, the only man capable of saving them. He was unjustly accused of having caused the overthrow at Pola; and besides a captivity of six months he was deprived of all state appointments.

The Genoese meanwhile followed up their victory,

---

[1] Space does not allow of my enlarging here on the history of Carlo Zeno. A son of one of Venice's oldest and noblest families, the story of his life reads like a romance, and his adventures in the East, where he engaged in a most perilous enterprise for the liberation of the Emperor Paleologus, abound with incident and peril, and prove him to have been a true knight-errant of the Middle Ages, with a keen love of risk and danger, and ever on the look-out for adventure.

and sailed under the command of Pietro Doria into the very port of the Lido. But the Venetians had made preparation for this danger, and by linking several large ships, called " cocche," together with strong chains, had formed a kind of floating barrier, through which it was impossible to pass. Zeno was ordered back to Venice, where his services were so urgently needed, and efforts were made, though in vain, to detach the King of Hungary from his allies. The enemy had now taken possession of a suburb of Chioggia, known as " Chioggia Minore," and proceeded to besiege Chioggia itself, while on the mainland the Hungarian and Paduan troops attacked all the towns dependent on Venice. Never yet had the Republic been in so perilous a strait; and to add to her danger and distress, in August of this same year (1379) Chioggia fell, and the banners of the King of Hungary, of the lord of Padua, and of Genoa floated proudly where St. Mark's lion had waved for centuries.

The news of the loss of Chioggia spread despair and terror throughout Venice; six thousand Venetians were said to have perished in the siege, and three thousand five hundred were prisoners; the canal leading right up to Venice, and the fortified town which guarded its entrance were in the hands of deadly foes; and it might be said of her as of Dunedin of old—

> " All without is flight and terror,
> All within is woe and fear—
> God protect thee, maiden city !
> For thy latest hour is near." [1]

---

[1] Aytoun, " Lays of the Scottish Cavaliers."

And as in the Scotch capital, so too in the midst of the lagunes every heart seemed beaten down with dread and dejection, and no one seemed capable of courage or resistance, till the Doge, who showed a presence of mind and firmness beyond that of his subjects, roused them to action by calling on all who could bear arms to prepare to defend their city; he also endeavoured to treat with the victors, and appealed to them for mercy. Francesco of Carrara, to whom (according to agreement) the town of Chioggia was ceded, was willing to treat with Venice; but the Genoese, who, had they but advanced then and there upon Venice, could have possessed themselves absolutely of the town, were bent on the complete overthrow and annihilation of their rival by force of arms. They would listen to no overtures, but sent a haughty message to Contarini, declaring that they would only speak of peace when they had bitted the horses of St. Mark. "By God, Venetian senators," so ran Doria's message, "you shall never have peace with the lord of Padua, or with our Republic, till we have ourselves bridled the bronze horses which stand in your square of St. Mark. When we have the reins in our hands, we shall know how to keep them quiet." Together with this insulting answer came news of the surrender of all the forts along the coasts, as with one exception (that of the Castello delle Saline, which defended itself gallantly until the conclusion of the war) all looked upon the cause of Venice as hopeless, and gave themselves up to the enemy. In this state of abject misery and despair all minds turned to the one man in whom the soldiers and citizens had confidence, and in whose skill and courage lay the only hopes of rescue and safety. The name of Vettor Pisani was in every mouth, and his release from an unjust captivity was clamoured for in a way that admitted of no refusal. The modesty and magnanimity of his behaviour when restored to liberty and to office show what a really great man he was, and his conduct all through the war proved clearly to his countrymen how worthy he was of their love and confidence. His first care was to provide for the security of the town by outworks and fortifications along the Lido, and to raise ships and galleys to form a new fleet. His efforts were nobly supported ; each individual and each family in Venice strained every nerve by gifts of money, jewels, clothes, personal labour, or whatever lay in their power to contribute towards the safety and defence of the Fatherland. To encourage still more the zeal of the citizens, it was decreed that when peace was concluded thirty families, chosen from those who by their fortune or by personal aid had most helped their country in her present emergency, should be admitted into the Great Council and enrolled as nobles. Others were to be advanced to all the privileges of citizenship, others again provided with pensions from the Government, and no measures were neglected to encourage a patriotism, which certainly on this occasion was not wanting. The short time in which Pisani was able to collect a few ships, and provide for some fortifications on the Lido, shows how energetically and ably his countrymen seconded him ; and when the little fleet put to sea on the 22nd of December, 1379, the

Doge himself, although an old man of seventy-two, accompanied it, declaring that he would not return till peace had been obtained. The whole expedition, organised under Pisani's directions, was so well carried out that in a short while the Venetians had succeeded in closing all the canals and approaches leading into Chioggia, and blocked the Genoese in the town. The siege began again, though this time the besiegers of a few months ago were turned into the besieged.

The position though of the Venetians was one of extreme peril: at any moment a contrary wind might scatter their ships, destroy their dykes and bastions, and set Doria free. The trials and privations to which they were exposed had also raised a spirit of discontent and subordination among the men ; Carlo Zeno's fleet so eagerly expected delayed its appearance, and Pisani was driven to such a strait as to promise that if in two days Zeno did not arrive, he would raise the siege. It was a tremendous hazard, on which he had staked not only fame, honour, glory, but the very life and existence of the Republic, and no greater proof exists of the despair and dejection that reigned in every Venetian mind than this condition of Pisani. We can almost see the straining eyes that hour after hour were turned eastward, looking for the sails that would bring salvation ; and when on the morning of the 1st of January, 1380, a distant shimmer of boats was seen on the horizon, the agitation in every breast must have been agonising. For the question now arose: Was it friend or foe ? Was it Zeno with his fleet ? or succour from Genoa to the besieged? The anxiety for some hours was intense, but when the eager watchers could at last distinguish the pennon of St. Mark no words are needed to describe the courage and joy that sprang to every heart, and that nerved every arm with hope and confidence. Zeno brought with him not only fresh supplies of men, arms, and food, but also news of victories obtained over the Genoese in the East, and on the coast of Liguria ; and with strength and confidence renewed by this addition both of practical help and of triumph, the Venetians set again to their task with redoubled vigour and prowess. In an attack upon the fort of Fossone, the Genoese admiral, Pietro Doria, and his nephew were killed by the discharge of one of the huge clumsy pieces of artillery used in those days, consisting of a sort of cannon, loaded with stones of enormous size and weight. These machines were often discharged but once a day, and when they did succeed in hitting their mark (a matter of perfect chance, and as often as not a failure) they carried death and destruction with them. Doria was inspecting some of the works near the canal of Brondolo, when one of these immense balls fell on a wall close by, and buried him and his nephew in its ruins. He was succeeded in the command by Napoleone Grimaldi, who strove to cut a passage through the canals blocked by the Venetians, but a combined attack by land [1] and sea routed his attempt, and the Genoese

---

[1] The great English "condottiere," John Hawkwood (who had been one of Edward III.'s generals), was to have commanded the Venetian

were repulsed with fearful loss. These latter, shut up closely in the town of Chioggia, were reduced to terrible privations, provisions were scarce, and their sufferings well-nigh past endurance. They still however held out, while the Venetians clamoured to be led to the assault of the town ; a measure strongly opposed by Pisani and by Zeno, who, not willing to risk in a fight what they foresaw time and famine would more surely effect, had to endure accusations of cowardice and indifference from their impatient comrades in arms. Their endurance however met with its full reward. On June 24th the town surrendered at discretion, after having been occupied by the Genoese for ten months, and after a gallant resistance of seven. The Doge made a triumphant entry back to Venice, but the war dragged on for yet another year, the Genoese still endeavouring to harass and molest their foes ; and in April of the following year Vettor Pisani, who had been sent to oppose them on the Dalmatian coast, died from wounds received in battle. His body, brought back to Venice, was buried in state ; the Doge, the Senate, and all the leading men of the city being present to render the last act of reverence and respect to one of the noblest of Venice's sons. Carlo Zeno was appointed to succeed him as commander of the forces, but the injustice that had so often fallen on Pisani fell too on him, for the Government, displeased at some of his actions off the Dal-

---

land forces on this occasion, but he threw over the appointment for one of greater gain, and Carlo Zeno became general of his country's troops, and proved as great a commander on land as on sea matian coast, summoned him home to answer accusations prompted no doubt by the jealousy often entertained by Venice towards her greatest men. Zeno refused to obey till he had provided for the safety of his fleet. He then returned to Venice, where he was treated by the Great Council in a way that reflects small credit on that body, and not till the populace had insisted (with thundering applause at Zeno's noble conduct) that he should be reinstated with full powers in his office, did he return again to the fleet. This however was but for a short time ; war had exhausted the resources and strength of both Republics, and the offices of Amedeo II., surnamed "Il Conte Verde," Count of Savoy, were accepted to make peace between them. On the 8th of August, 1381, the treaty was signed at Turin, when the chief points regarding Venice were that she should cede Treviso to the Duke of Austria, that she should evacuate Tenedos, and demolish all its forts. On the other side, Francesco of Carrara agreed to destroy all the new forts he had made, and content himself with the former limits of his dominion ; the King of Hungary was to remain in possession of the whole of Dalmatia, where however he was to suppress the corsairs ; all the prisoners taken on both sides were to be set free without ransom. Thus terminated a war of over six years' duration, that had brought the two Republics down to the very ground, and reduced them to a state of feebleness and exhaustion, from which Genoa never fully recovered, while Venice only lifted up her head after a long and difficult effort.

X.

VENICE AND THE CARRARESI.

(1382–1441.)

IN June, 1382, Doge Andrea Contarini died. He had never recovered the fatigues and agitation of the Chioggian war, and soon after his return became so ill that a vice-Doge was named till his death, when Michele Morosini was appointed to succeed him. Before this however the thirty families which had been promised admittance into the ranks of the nobles and a seat in the Great Council for services rendered during the war were confirmed in these rights, and were often spoken of by the honourable title of "Nobles of the War."

The election of Morosini was combated by a faction who strove to appoint Carlo Zeno to the dukedom, but, though it was pleaded that he could ill be spared from the command of the forces, it is more probable that the electors were opposed to him ; or again, that he himself was of far too free and independent a nature to accept or wish for a post of bondage and supervision. Morosini's reign had lasted but four months when a fearful pestilence broke out and swept away the Doge himself and 20,000 of his subjects.

He was succeeded in October of the same year by Antonio Venier, under whose administration the ill effects produced by the Chioggian war were largely removed, for the prosperity of the town began again to flourish, and commerce, which for several years had been almost at a standstill, revived with unwonted energy and industry. The Republic too again took a foremost position in the affairs occupying the north of Italy, and bore an important share in their transaction. At the close of the war with Chioggia she had ceded the town and territory of Treviso to the Duke of Austria sooner than see it fall into the hands of Francesco of Carrara. But Francesco now bought it from Austria, an offence and injury which Venice refused to tolerate, and she accordingly appealed to Antonio della Scala, lord of Verona, to attack da Carrara, promising him her support if he would do so. Antonio willingly accepted the proposal, and engaged several times with the Paduan forces. He was generally worsted in these engagements, but reimbursed with money and supplies from Venice, he was able to make head against da Carrara, when a new actor appeared on the scene and considerably altered the aspect of affairs.

This was Gian Galeazzo Visconti, lord of Milan, a man who had attained to that position by treachery, and who intended by treachery to sweep away all the smaller states around him, and erect for himself a kingdom out of their ruins. With this intent he watched with interest the strife between da Carrara and Della Scala, while to further his cause he thought it politic to offer them both his alliance, determining when the moment came to turn that alliance to his own advantage. In regard to Della Scala, his plan soon succeeded; the reign of the Scaligeri, after lasting one hundred and twenty-eight years, came to an end, and Verona acknowledged Visconti as her lord and master. Gian Galeazzo then formed a fresh league with da Carrara, which led eventually to the overthrow of the Carraresi. Before matters came to such a pass Venice had formed a treaty with Visconti, and Francesco of Carrara immediately aided and abetted Philip of Alençon, who, to the annoyance of the Republic and of the Patriarchate, had been appointed Patriarch of Aquileja. Francesco also protested against the Venetian-Milanese alliance; he represented to Visconti that he was his ally, and at the same time he warned the Republic against trusting a man who had gained over the lord of Verona only to work his overthrow, who he was sure was but biding his time to play the same game at Padua, and who then would use Padua as a stepping-stone to Venice. But the hatred felt by the Republic to Francesco made her blind to other considerations, and the desire to be revenged on him overruled the danger of a league with Visconti. The treaty was signed on March 29, 1388, when it was settled that Treviso, Ceneda, and some other fortresses, should be delivered to Venice, while the town and province of Padua should be allotted to Milan. Francesco of Carrara, seeing himself cut off from all his former friends and allies, and knowing that his unpopularity at home left him exposed to every foe, decided to abdicate in favour of his son Francesco Novello, to whom he handed over the government in June, 1388, and retired to the town of Treviso, which was still in his hands. But the change of rulers did not work, as da Carrara had hoped it would, a change of feeling in Venice. The animosity against the man, who had acted so constantly and persistently as their enemy, was continued towards his son ; they remarked that "sons of cats are fond of mice," and sent a defiance to him the day after his succession. This was accompanied with one from the lord of Milan, and immediately after the allies, under the command of Jacopo dal Verme, marched to action. The fate of Francesco Novello and his heroic wife, Taddea d'Este, who accompanied her husband in his flight to elude Visconti, and in his wanderings from one court to another for aid and protection against Gian Galeazzo, belong more to the page of romance than to that of history. The gallant noble bearing of the fugitive young husband and wife must enlist all sympathies, and a feeling akin to relief is evoked on their behalf, when Venice finally afforded them the help they so sorely needed, and, seeing the danger of supporting Visconti, entered into alliance with Francesco Novello.

And well might Venice open her eyes to the schemes and ambitions of the lord of Milan, and throw the weight of her arms and influence against the progress of a man, who aimed at the subjugation of all Italy, and whose ever-increasing power made him the most formioable ruler at that time in Europe. In Germany the Empire was under the feeble rule of Wenceslaus, King of Bohemia ; France was divided by a state of anarchy utterly beyond the control of her imbecile monarch, Charles VI. ; England, under Richard II., was witnessing the commencement of the Wars of the Roses ; in Aragon Peter IV. relegated to his wife the affairs of the kingdom ; in Hungary all was confusion and disorder ; and in Italy the discord and rivalry throughout the land made Visconti's scheme a feasible and possible one, and one too of which an ambitious unscrupulous prince would not be slow to take advantage. The oppressions of Visconti had however wearied and disgusted the Paduans, and when, after endless obstacles and displaying undaunted courage and energy, Francesco Novello presented himself once more under the walls of Padua, his subjects rose against the Milanese and re-established their former master in the city of his ancestors. He quickly apprized the Signory of his good fortune, obtained the promise of their support, and a general league was formed between Florence, Bologna, Padua, and Venice, against Visconti. On August 28, 1397, an engagement took place at Governolo, when the Milanese were entirely routed, and eight months later a treaty of peace was signed for ten years, and confirmed anew two years after.

Shortly before this Venice had again been warring in the East. John Paleologus had been succeeded by his son Manuel, under whose feeble sway Sultan Bajazet Ilderim (" Lightning ") had made inroads and conquests of so alarming a nature, that the Christian powers of Hungary, Genoa, and Venice, entered into a league against the Turk, more perhaps in regard of their own interests and commerce than from zeal on behalf of Manuel, and endeavoured to persuade other states to help them. Venice despatched Carlo Zeno to France and England to induce those countries to contribute men and money to repel the Turk. He gained but slight success, though the supplies he collected enabled a Venetian fleet to sail to the mouth of the Danube. Here its chief exploit was to bring off in safety the scattered remnant of its allies, who had sustained an overwhelming defeat from Bajazet's forces at the battle of Nicopolis (1395).

In the year 1400 Doge Antonio Venier died, having restored his country to a flourishing, prosperous condition, very different to that wherein he found her on his accession, when worn and enfeebled by the Chioggian war, her commerce had been reduced to a very low ebb, and her resources and finances crippled by that long arduous struggle. Doge Venier left too a character for justice and equity, of which the following story is a strong proof. His son Luigi, a youth of wild and wanton manners, had one night, in company with some of his friends, affixed some insulting words on the house door of a noble, derogatory to the honour of the nobleman's wife, and sister, and mother-in-law. The youth was condemned to pay a fine and be imprisoned for two months. In prison he fell ill and implored to be released ; but the Doge, who had striven hard to repress the bad habits and fashions prevalent among the young nobles, and scrupulous as to the execution of a just sentence on however high-born an offender, refused to grant his petition, and the unfortunate Luigi died in prison.

The commencement of the century just entered upon may be regarded as about the most flourishing moment of Venetian commerce and traffic. The extraordinary national wealth was supported and augmented by the business and trade in which many of the nobles were employed,[1] so that the public revenues were supported by enormous private means, while both the state and individual families traded in all the then known parts of the world. In the East [2] and West [3] Venetian ships were to be met carrying cloth, velvet, wrought silver, cord, rope, serge, canvas, glass, beads, iron, metal, &c., &c., and received in exchange, drugs, spices, indigo, precious stones, furs, silks, cotton, &c., &c., which they again put into other markets, and multiplied their trade and their riches a hundred-fold.

The laws too framed for the administration of Venetian subjects are such as to excite admiration : the care extended to widows, orphans, and the destitute, and the good feeling that existed between the nobles and their retainers, show what a protecting, fostering, wise government that of Venice was on the whole. This is no plea for asserting that the government was

[1] The following names are given just to mention some of the chief Venetian families engaged in commerce : Giacomo and Nicolò da Pesaro, Marcello, Soranzo, Dolfin, Morosini (three branches), Corner (two branches), Giustinian, Barbarigo, Bon, Trevisan, Emo. Bembo, Capello, Bragadin, Loredan, Duodo, Contarini, Da Canal, Querini, Gradenigo, Dandolo.

[2] There are documents that prove that in 1390, the Venetians traded with India, and had their Consul at Siam.

[3] The first embassy to England was in 1318 1325.

faultless, nor in all things to be admired, for such is far from being the case; but, on the other hand, the amount of obloquy and reproach heaped upon Venice and her councils is often unjust; the character ascribed to her of guilt, treachery, and cruelty is often exaggerated; while the difficulty of the age, and of the natures with which she had to deal, is often not sufficiently weighed against the sentences passed in moments of peril to the very life and existence of the Republic.

Michele Steno was appointed to succeed Doge Venier in 1400, and three years after the Venetians and Genoese were again at war, the cause of their quarrel originating as of old in the East. Carlo Zeno, though a " Procuratore " of St. Mark (an official who except in great emergencies rarely left the town), was named general of the forces, while the enemy were commanded by the Maréchal de Boucicault, who had been appointed governor of Genoa by the King of France, under whose protection the Republic had placed herself. Owing to the skill and bravery of Zeno a brilliant victory was gained by the Venetians, and, had his orders and wishes been properly carried out, there is little doubt that the whole Genoese fleet would have been utterly destroyed.

Hardly was this war ended when Venice had to turn her attention again to Padua. In 1402, Gian Galeazzo had died at Marignano of the plague, leaving three sons of tender age, and the different states of Italy, relieved from the pressure of his schemes and ambition, returned for the most part to the allegiance of their lords. Da Carrara, who had been a staunch ally of Venice so long as Visconti lived, had been gained over to the party of the Regent Duchess of Milan. He was now desirous to possess himself of Vicenza, and not content with Belluno and Feltre, bestowed on him by the Duchess, he besieged Vicenza. Meanwhile the Milanese councillors of the Regent, who hated da Carrara, persuaded her to break with him and join forces with Venice. This was accordingly done, and the Duchess applied to the Venetians to defend Vicenza against da Carrara. Venice, who had viewed with indifference the ever-spreading conquests of Gian Galeazzo pretended to be alarmed at the ambition of da Carrara ; an army was despatched against Francesco Terzo, Francesco Novello's son, who was conducting the siege of Vicenza, and the Republic remained in possession of the town. The relation of the wars and skirmishes which took place between the forces of Venice and Padua is long and intricate ; and the conclusion is one veiled in such reproach to Venice, and in such sadness as regards the Carraresi, that one would fain leave the tale untold. The gallant behaviour of Francesco Novello must make a hero of him in every age ; and his generosity and courage were inherited by his sons Francesco Terzo and Giacomo, who seconded their father nobly in his efforts to defend Padua against the force sent by Venice under Carlo Zeno to attack it in 1405. The siege was a fierce one, accompanied by all the horrors of famine, pestilence and want of water ; and the Carraresi only surrendered when all hope was over, and when a safe conduct from Venice made them believe that their lives at least were safe. From such a belief they were to be cruelly undeceived : and the sentence passed on them by the Council of Ten with the *Zonta* condemned them to be strangled in their prisons. This judgment was put into effect on January 20, 1406, when first Francesco and then his two sons were murdered in ghastly fashion, and the only comment made in Venice when their deaths were announced was : " Uomo morto non fa guerra " (" A dead man makes no war ").

This story of the massacre of the house of Carrara reflects on the one hand lasting dishonour upon Venice, but against it must be set the reasons which the Republic had, and they were many and valid, for distrusting and disliking the lords of Padua. The many wrongs done by them to Venice during the Chioggian war were still fresh in the memory of the citizens ; the designs of Francesco Novello upon Verona and Vicenza were such as to excite suspicion and alarm in so near a neighbour ; and one must not allow one's imagination to be carried away by the romance which surrounds the whole story of Francesco and his family, nor let one's judgment as to the tragedy enacted in the Venetian prisons be unhinged by the sympathy that cannot but be felt for the actors in so touching a scene. It must be remembered also that the Council of Ten did not pass sentence hurriedly, or without much debate and deliberation. Their numbers were swelled by the *Zonta* (that extra body only called in on momentous occasions), who were summoned on the discovery of certain papers belonging to the Carraresi, said to have contained matters of grave import and even of danger to the Republic. Besides it must be borne in mind, that during the siege of Padua Venice had frequently offered terms, and those not strict or harsh ones, but the hopes of succour from Florence had, unluckily for himself, always induced Francesco of Carrara to decline them. All these facts should be present when the temptation is to cry shame on Venice for her action in this matter ; and should make us feel there may have been reasons which made such action necessary, and rendered no other course possible, notwithstanding the odium she invoked on herself, and the horror excited by so stern a sentence and so bloody an execution.

An unpleasant page in Venetian story has also to be written as to the arrest and judgment of Carlo Zeno. This noble high-minded patriot was now cited before the Council of Ten to answer a charge laid against him of having accepted a bribe from Francesco of Carrara. Among the papers of this latter was found a memorandum of four hundred ducats paid to Zeno. In vain he stated that the sum was only a loan made by him to Carrara when he was in want, and repaid afterwards by Francesco ; he was not believed, and the mention of these few paltry ducats was considered sufficient evidence to establish the guilt of a man who had often expended more than double that sum for his country's need, and who was now condemned to the loss of all his appointments, with imprisonment for a year. On his release from prison he returned to his life of adventure and wandering in the East, and when he died in 1418, his countrymen finally awoke to the recognition of the hero who had passed from among them. They accorded him a public funeral, when all the sailors who had served under him insisted on bearing the remains of their loved commander to his last resting-place.[1]

In January, 1406, a great festival and tournament was held in St. Mark's Square, when the city of Padua formally gave itself over to Venice, and the privileges and ancient government of the town were confirmed to her with only slight modifications by her new masters. Other rights were also regained by Venice over some of her old possessions in Dalmatia, and were obtained in the following way : Sigismond, King of Hungary, had exhausted the endurance of his subjects by his tyrannies and oppressions, and they resolved to offer the realm to Ladislas, King of Naples. This monarch accepted the offer, but, more occupied with affairs in Naples than with his new possessions and being in urgent want of money, he readily consented to hand over the towns of Zara, Vrana, Spalato, Trau, Sebenico, and others, to the Signory on payment of a hundred thousand florins. This transaction, though restoring much of her traffic and commerce to Venice, involved her also in a war with Sigismond, who on the death of Ladislas resolved to regain possession of his empire ; and for two years he waged war with the Republic. This war exhausted the exchequers of both parties alike, without producing any other result, and the relief to the two countries

---

[1] He was buried in the Church of Sta. Maria della Celestia, a church suppressed in 1810, and now used as a school for young naval engineers.

was great, when in April, 1413, a treaty for five years was signed between them at Trieste.

In December, 1413, Doge Steno died, and fresh restrictions again circumscribed the ducal *Promissione* of his successor. The title of Monsignore, till then accorded to the Doges, had been altered on Steno's appointment to " Messer il Doge," and now the Doges were forbidden to exhibit their coats of arms outside the ducal palace, while other more narrowing rules were laid down as to their liberty of action with their council, the *Avogadori*, and so on. In spite of these restraints a truly great man was now found to fill the ducal chair in the person of Tomaso Mocenigo, who became Doge on January 7, 1414.

Two years after his accession Venice was again obliged to arm for the defence of her trade in the East. Though a truce had been signed with Mahomet, the son and successor of Sultan Bajazet, the terms thereof had not been faithfully kept, and Venice despatched a fleet under Pietro Loredan to protect both Venetian subjects and interests in case of danger. Loredan strove hard to preserve peace, but when this proved impossible, he prepared for war, and on May 29, 1416, the battle of Gallipoli was fought, and a great victory secured to Venice.

The external policy of Venice underwent a gradual change about this epoch : her possessions both in Italy and in Dalmatia demanded a less concentrated, self-absorbed form of government than that which had marked her course hitherto, and this change led by subtle degrees to the undermining of her strength and the dispersion of her forces and energies in ever wide-spreading directions. Instead of the centred power husbanding such vigour and strength in the heart of the lagunes, and flourishing with such life and prosperity, her ambition was about to drain that power away into weakening outlying channels, sapping the energy of the home government, and bringing in no fresh supplies to replenish and renew the wasting stores. In Italy Venice's possessions consisted of Padua, Verona, Vicenza on the west ; Treviso, Feltre, Belluno, Friuli on the east ; Rovigo and the Polesine had been ceded to her by the Marquis of Ferrara in 1405 ; she owned Istria and the Cadore, and was absolute mistress of the Adriatic. She now took occasion to confirm by right of conquest the towns on the Dalmatian coast lately bought by her from Ladislas, King of Naples, and while the Emperor Sigismond was engrossed with Turks on one hand and Hussites on the other, she despatched a fleet under Pietro Loredan to re-establish her sway over the towns of Zara, Trau, and other Dalmatian towns. The expedition was eminently successful, Venice remained mistress of these towns, as well as of Corinth and the island of Corfu.

The character of Doge Mocenigo was of too strong and marked an individuality not to have much influence and weight on his country's politics. His craving for peace and for restricting the conquests of Venice on the mainland forms the ruling feature of his reign, and proves how clearly he had grasped the situation of where the real strength of Venice lay, and what foresight and prudence dictated every measure of his dukedom. It was owing to his advice and

PORTRAIT OF THE DOGE TOMASO MOCENIGO, FROM A PAINTING
OF CARPACCIO, NOW LOST.

(*From an engraving at the Museo Correr.*)

insistence that the Venetian Government refused to join the Florentines in a league against Filippo Visconti, lord of Milan. Opposed to this peace policy was a strong party in Venice headed by Francesco Foscari, whose council for war had been eloquent and determined, and that Mocenigo was able to carry his audience with him, and gain a majority over Foscari and his followers, shows how firm a hold he had over the minds and judgments of his hearers.

Another great work due to Mocenigo is the erection of the ducal palace as it now stands. A decree had been passed in the preceding century, when the exchequer of the Republic had been drained by the Genoese wars, and when no funds were forthcoming for extra expenses, forbidding any one to speak even of repairs or embellishments in the palace under a fine of one thousand ducats. "But," says Ruskin, "they had rated their own enthusiasm too low ; there was a man among them whom the loss of a thousand ducats could not deter from proposing what he believed to be for the good of the state." This man was the Doge Tomaso Mocenigo, who, on September 27, 1422, appeared before the Senate bearing the fine in his hand, and having thus secured to himself the right to speak on the matter, he urged that the moment had come for re-building the palace. His proposal was accepted ; the thousand ducats were unanimously devoted to the expenses of the work, and the restoration and re-building were commenced straightway. But Mocenigo was not destined to see much of his suggestion carried out ; his noble life was almost over, and in April, 1423, he breathed his last, warning the electors as to their choice of his successor, and bidding them above all things beware of appointing Foscari, whose ambition and thirst for war and conquest, he knew well would work woe and ruin to his country.

There can be no doubt that the death of Mocenigo closes an epoch in Venetian history, and that epoch one which marks the zenith of her greatness. She had reached the topmost height of her glory and magnificence: her fleets traded in every part, and commanded all the commerce of the known world; her trade with Milan and Florence alone brought in a capital of ten millions of zechins; her mercantile navy numbered three thousand three hundred private ships; forty-five public galleys aided and protected the merchant vessels; and the number of her sailors was thirty-six thousand. And this state of things Venice owed in a great measure to Mocenigo. His clear-sightedness as to her true interests had ever been employed in urging the Venetian Government to abstain from strifes and contests which could bear but hollow rewards, while he had never refrained from war when the honour or advantage of his country demanded it. The anxiety of Mocenigo on his deathbed as to his successor and the policy that would be adopted over the land which he loved so well and had raised to such a height of glory, is keenly portrayed in the speech made then by him, wherein he pleaded against the election of Foscari, whose proclivities for war were well known, and whose whole line of action would be so opposed to that so successfully followed by the dying Doge.

Mocenigo died ; and many and hot were the discussions that raged as to his successor. The warning so pathetically uttered by the dying duke rang in the electors' ears, but the influence, not unbacked by the gold, of Foscari, proved too strong for the XLI., and on April 15, 1423, he was named Doge.

The first event after Foscari's nomination marked a great and important alteration as to all future elections, when the harangue (*arengo*) or appeal to the people as to their approbation or dissatisfaction as to their new Prince was entirely swept away. Till then it had been customary on the appointment of a Doge to present him to the people with the words : "We have chosen such an one to be Doge, if this be your pleasure." This final clause was now omitted ; for the dread that it might not be the pleasure of the multitude was paramount in all minds, and to avoid such a risk it was judged wiser to leave out the words that raised the question. From henceforth this became law ; and all share or voice hitherto enjoyed by the lower classes in their ruler's nomination was abolished, while the exclusive powers and prerogatives of the aristocracy were increased and consolidated.

Foscari's reign commenced under favourable auspices. The magnificent Great Hall, built for the sittings of the Great Council, was finished, and opened with much pomp and solemnity in this year in the presence of the Marquis of Ferrara and nine hundred Venetian nobles. In the East the power of Venice was increased by the possession of the town of Salonica. The town was offered to Venice by the

Emperor, John Paleologus, whose position daily becoming weaker and more unstable, he determined to dismember his kingdom among his Christian neighbours sooner than see it fall into the hands of his enemy, Sultan Amurath II. The Signory accepted the offer and despatched troops to occupy this new possession, to the indignation of Amurath who was about to invest the city, and who was little minded to let it escape him. His preparations for defence assumed such proportions that the Senate thought it wise to attempt negotiations, and come, if possible, to an understanding. For this intent Nicolò Zorzi was sent as ambassador to the Sultan, whose anger against Venice was so great that he not only refused to receive Zorzi, but caused him to be arrested. This conduct naturally enough roused Venice to action, war was declared against Amurath, and Pietro Loredan was sent to defend Salonica. Though Venice was generally successful in this campaign she was unable to obtain peace till April, 1426, when a treaty was signed and her claims to the town were confirmed.

One result of this intercourse with the East was the scourge of the plague, now of frequent occurrence in Venice. It broke out at this period with such virulence that fifteen thousand three hundred persons died in three months ; when to provide against so great an evil the island of Sta. Maria di Nazaret was set apart for the treatment and cure of all smitten by this fearful malady. This was the first institution of the kind started in Europe ; and from the island being called " Lazaret," the name " Lazzeretto " became synonymous with this sort of establishment ;

or, again, the name may be derived from St. Lazarus, the patron saint of lepers and of hospitals.

In the meantime the Florentines again appealed to Venice to join with them against Visconti, as, regardless of a treaty lately signed with him, Florence and Milan were warring again. But in spite of the accusations always levelled against Foscari as to engaging in war, it must be observed that on this occasion at least he dissuaded his countrymen from joining in their neighbours' quarrels, and the Florentine envoys left Venice without obtaining the desired help. Later on though they succeeded in gaining over the Venetians to their cause, and in December, 1425, a league was formed between Florence and Venice, together with the King of Aragon, the lords of Mantua and Ferrara, and the Count of Savoy against the Duke of Milan, and in the following month war was declared. The general of the Venetian forces was the famous Francesco Bussone, known from the name of his birthplace as Carmagnola, who had commanded the Milanese armies so frequently and successfully, and who had been raised by Filippo Maria from the rank of a private soldier to the supreme command, together with every mark of favour. His rise had created jealousy and hatred among Visconti's followers, who plotted his downfall, and who rejoiced when Carmagnola, unable to have access to the duke to answer the charges laid against him, retired in disgust and offered his services to Venice. This offer was accepted ; he was appointed to the post of Captain-General with all solemnity, and signalised his zeal and talents by the

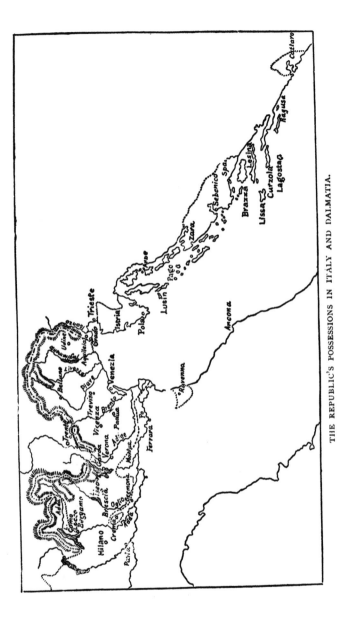

THE REPUBLIC'S POSSESSIONS IN ITALY AND DALMATIA.

conquest of Brescia. The success of the Venetian
naval forces under the command of Francesco Bembo
on the Po at the same time alarmed Visconti, and
made him suggest terms of peace to the Republic ;
but the conditions proved so distasteful to both
parties that no conclusion was attained, and the war
continued. The conduct of their general began to
cause suspicion ere long in the minds of the Venetian
Government : Carmagnola was always applying for
leave of absence from his command, and on the plea
of ill-health and the necessity to take the baths for
the healing of some old wounds, absented himself
often at critical moments and when the troops were
in special need of the presence of their leader. The
loss of the town of Casalmaggiore in April, 1427,
increased these suspicions ; but a brilliant victory
gained over the Milanese in October of this year at
Maclodio, calmed for awhile their fears, and earned
for their general fresh favours and rewards. This
defeat made Filippo again desirous for peace, and
through the intervention of Pope Martin V. a treaty
was signed between Milan and Venice, when the
latter remained in possession of Bergamo and nine
provinces in the north of Italy. But Filippo would
not abide by the conditions, and war began again.
The Venetians were not successful in this campaign.
They were defeated at Soncino, where Carmagnola
was compelled to fly and owed his safety to the swift-
ness of his horse ; and in June, 1431, they met with
one of the most severe reverses they had ever
encountered on the banks of the Po above Cremona.
The fleet was commanded by Nicolò Trevisan, and a

large force was at hand on *terra ferma* under Carmagnola, but for reasons best known to himself the general looked on at the complete overthrow of the Venetian navy without moving to the relief of his brother officer. It was a victory for Milan that more than wiped out the disgrace of Maclodio, and the satisfaction of the duke and the rage of the Senate were equal in their respective measures. A victory under Pietro Loredan over the Genoese two months after at Portofino served to atone in a slight degree for the disaster at Cremona, but served in no way to quiet the uneasiness now become general as to the loyalty or capacity of the man entrusted with the command. His conduct at Cremona was still more unaccountable when it was known that in November of that year a Venetian captain, Cavalcabò, supported by the great condottiere Bartolommeo Colleoni, by a stroke of daring and bravery got into Cremona and applied to Carmagnola for reinforcements to secure their conquest. Carmagnola sent neither forces nor supplies, and the town so well-nigh secured to the Venetians was lost to them by the strange apathy or indifference of their general. This seems to have been the last touch wanting to complete their suspicions, and sealed the doom which it may almost be said Carmagnola wove for himself in so unconscious but compact a manner. It was therefore decreed that Carmagnola should be summoned to Venice as though to confer with him over new conquests to be gained for the Republic and new honours to be conferred upon himself. The unhappy man in entire ignorance of his fate came to Venice, and once there was imprisoned in the cells of the Council of Ten. This body called in the *Zonta*, finding the case one that required extra advice and judgment, and though Doge Foscari pleaded eloquently for the prisoner's life, sentence of death was passed on him by a large majority. That sentence was carried out on May 5, 1432, when dressed in gala dress, with scarlet leggings, a cap "alla Carmagnola," a crimson jerkin and scarlet vest, and a gag in his mouth, he was beheaded between the two columns.

The question as to Venice's treatment of Carmagnola is one that has brought much opprobrium upon her, and is another case where she has been accused of cruelty and treachery. But the charge is unfair if the matter be considered from a broad point of view; for there can be no doubt as to the ineffectual way in which Carmagnola fulfilled his duties towards the Republic, and that in so flagrant and frequent a manner, that it seems almost strange the retribution did not fall sooner. The way wherein he was inveigled to Venice was nothing less than mean and underhand, but the same cannot be said of his sentence. The documents and proofs proclaiming his guilt are still extant, and from these his judges found him guilty and pronounced his doom.

The war with Milan dragged on with weary monotony for a year after Carmagnola's execution, when Gian Francesco Gonzaga, lord of Mantua, commanded the Venetian arms. Visconti made peace now and again only to break it the moment it suited his purpose; but in 1433 a permanent treaty was signed, and peace seemed really established to the relief of all parties, who were tired of a war unsatisfactory both as to action and result. Shortly before this a conspiracy had been discovered in which the young nobles of Venice had banded together to put down the ever-growing power of the Council of Ten. It was another of those efforts made by the older nobility to protest against a force that grew and increased from year to year, but the strength of the old party was gone, their vitality was sapped, and they had henceforward to bow to a power that crushed and annihilated them.

In 1433 the revolution of the *Ottimati* drove Cosimo de' Medici out of Florence. "With his unfailing astuteness he chose Venice as his place of exile; was welcomed there like a prince; with princely munificence ordered Michelozzo to build the library of the Benedictine monks of St. George ;[1] and led a life of ostentatious culture in the midst of humanists and scholars."[2]

The intrigues and manœuvres of Filippo Maria Visconti were all this time surging and bubbling on every side, and the treaty signed only so short a time previously went the way of other treaties, and war again broke out between him and Venice. The Republic was joined by Florence, whose armies were commanded by Nicolò da Tolentino, while Gattamelata was the

---

[1] It does not appear that Cosimo founded the library of S. Giorgio; he added to the volumes already there, and ordered Michelozzo to design the bookcases. The library was demolished in 1614, when the books were dispersed, though some few were saved and transferred to the Marciana library.

[2] The Story of the Nations, "The Tuscan Republics," by Bella Duffy, chap. xxi.

Venetian general.[1] In order to annoy Venice by every means in his power Visconti stirred up the last of the Carraresi to fling off the Venetian yoke, and restore the rule of the Carrara family in Padua. The attempt proved a failure ; Marsilio da Carrara was seized, brought to Venice, examined by the Council of Ten, and condemned to death. His head was cut off between the two columns, and with him ended the house of Carrara, while Padua was secured for ever to Venice.

In 1437 the Emperor Sigismond died, but before his death an interesting document had been signed between him and Marco Dandolo, then Venetian ambassador at his Court, when the Emperor invested the Doge with the lands belonging to the Signory on the mainland, and in exchange for this investiture Dandolo swore fealty in the name of the Doge and Signory of Venice. This document was signed at Prague on July 20, 1437, in the presence of a large and brilliant assembly, and it was also decreed that an annual offering was to be sent by Venice of a piece of cloth of gold of the value of one thousand zechins, or some equivalent according to his Majesty's good pleasure, in sign of reverence and recognition. It does not appear that either the right of investiture or the offering of cloth of gold were renewed after this one occasion, though Venice seems at a later date to

[1] The real name of this condottiere was Erasmo da Narni, whose extraordinary march across the mountains to the north of the Lake of Garda in the depth of winter when all the passes were closed has made his name famous. His equestrian statue outside the Church of Sant' Antonio at Padua is the work of Donatello, and only second in renown to that in Venice of Colleoni ascribed to Verrocchio.

have appealed to Germany in consequence of this act to espouse her cause and assist her feudal rights against French usurpations.

Ecclesiastical matters were at this moment occupying men's minds not a little, and Pope Eugenius IV., a Venetian of the family of Condulmer, summoned a Council to meet at Ferrara and discuss the possibility of cementing the union of the Eastern and Western Churches. The Council of Basle, which had met for that purpose, had offended the Pope in several ways; so to mark his displeasure he annulled it by a Papal Bull, and invoked one in its place at Ferrara. To this he invited the Emperor John Paleologus, and Venice sent nine galleys to escort him to Italy. The Emperor's position in Constantinople was beset with difficulties and distresses; he was reduced to such straits by the Turks, his power was almost *nil*, and he determined to come to Italy to implore aid from the monarchs of the West against the on-coming danger. He professed his readiness to merge the differences of his Church with those of Rome if, on the other hand, he could obtain supplies to drive back the Ottoman hordes. The description of the reception given to him, to his brother Demetrius, Despot of the Morea, and to the Pope, forms a bright page in the picturesque history of Venice, and shows what a pageant-loving people the Venetians were, as well as what glories and pomps the city could put forth in olden days for the honour of guests whom she delighted to receive. The following account from Gibbon describes the journey and reception of John Paleologus : " After a tedious and troublesome navigation of seventy-seven days, this religious squadron cast anchor before Venice ; and their reception proclaimed the joy and magnificence of that powerful Republic. In the command of the world the modest Augustus had never claimed such honours from his subjects as were paid to his feeble successor by an independent state. Seated on the poop, on a lofty throne, he received the visit, or, in Greek style, the *adoration*, of the Doge and Senators. They sailed in the *Bucentaur*, which was accompanied by twelve stately galleys : the sea was overspread with innumerable gondolas of pomp and pleasure ; the air resounded with music and acclamations ; the mariners, and even the vessels, were dressed in silk and gold ; and in all the emblems and pageants the Roman eagles were blended with the lions of St. Mark. The triumphal procession, ascending the Grand Canal, passed under the bridge of the Rialto ; and the Eastern strangers gazed with admiration on the palaces, the churches, and the populousness of a city that seems to float on the bosom of the waves. They sighed to behold the spoils and trophies with which it had been decorated after the sack of Constantinople. After a hospitable entertainment of fifteen days Paleologus pursued his journey by land and water from Venice to Ferrara."

In spite of merry-makings and festivities war was still hovering around, and the Duke of Milan was as usual seeking occasion for fresh strife with Venice. He now resolved to possess himself of Brescia, and sent a strong force under his general, Piccinino, to besiege the town. The Venetians were commanded by Gattamelata, while the Governor of Brescia, Francesco Barbaro, famed for his high literary attainments, animated the citizens by his courage and fortitude to endure all the trials and privations which fell on the devoted city. Venice too did all that lay in her power to succour the garrison, and having succeeded, after many futile attempts, to engage the services of Francesco Sforza for her general, she despatched him to the relief of Brescia. After countless difficulties, consisting of marches and manœuvres, that made the campaign a most remarkable and interesting one from a military point of view, Sforza outwitted Piccinino; Brescia was delivered, and the territory both of Verona and Vicenza saved to Venice. Sforza was enrolled among the Venetian nobles, and soon after Filippo Maria made peace with his great general, giving him at last the often-promised hand of his daughter Blanche in marriage. Filippo Maria also signed peace with Venice (1441), where processions and rejoicings of every kind proclaimed the universal satisfaction at the conclusion of this long and wearisome war ; and Sforza's arrival soon after in Venice with his bride was the occasion of renewed feastings, and served to cement the harmony once again established between Venice and Milan.

One consequence of this treaty was the acquisition to Venice of the town of Ravenna. Since 1275 this town had owned the sway of the family Da Polenta, but, when in 1413 dissensions had arisen beyond the power of Obizzo da Polenta to control, he had applied to Doge Tomaso Mocenigo for help. Mocenigo had sent a Podestà, and order being restored, the town had remained under the joint rule of Venice and the da Polenta. After Obizzo's death in 1430 his son, Ostasio, anxious to shake off the Venetian yoke, entered into a secret league with Visconti. This however soon came to light, and Venice sent Antonio Marcello to assert her power, and to rule as Podestà. When peace was signed with Visconti, da Polenta was handed over to Venice, who exiled him and his family to Candia, where this last of the seigneurs of Ravenna died, and his city was enrolled among the Venetian dependencies.

TOMB IN THE CHURCH OF SS. GIOVANNI E PAOLO, OF MARCO GIUSTINIAN, AMBASSADOR FROM THE REPUBLIC TO THE SCALIGERI IN 1336.

(From an engraving in the Museo Correr.)

XI.

THE FOSCARI.

(1441–1471.)

FOR the only time almost in Venetian history the family affairs of the Doge come forward in striking evidence, and assume an importance and interest heightened only by their historical import. The story of Jacopo, Doge Foscari's only son, has been related by poet and novelist till it has acquired an outline of romance and fiction not altogether consonant with the facts of reality and truth. The occasion on which Jacopo first comes before us is in 1441, when his marriage with Lucrezia Contarini was celebrated with a ceremonial and magnificence never equalled or surpassed. But four years after (February 17, 1445) the brilliancy and pomp of these nuptials were clouded over by an accusation made against Jacopo of receiving gifts of jewels and money. This was a State offence, for, as has been said, a decree existed forbidding the Doge and every member of his family to accept gifts, of whatever kind they might be, from any one. This decree of a most binding nature was renewed by each Doge in his *Promissione*, and to it Foscari had subscribed in his turn. Jacopo, it was said, had violated this law, and what made his guilt still more heinous was the assumption that he had accepted gifts from Filippo Maria Visconti, Duke of Milan, his country's deadliest foe. The Council of Ten summoned him to appear and answer these accusations, and the case was considered one of such importance that a *Zonta* of twenty extra members was called in, who found Jacopo guilty, and sentenced him to perpetual exile at Nauplia in the Morea. Instead of answering the summons and appearing to defend his cause, Jacopo, from a sense either of fear or of guilt, fled from Venice, and his father was appealed to in order to induce his son to present himself for trial, and submit to the sentence passed on him. The legend that Foscari on this or any other occasion sat in judgment on his son is utterly untrue. He was forbidden by the law of the land to do so, as no questions relating to the Doge or his family could ever be discussed in his presence. It was the Council of Ten that in every one of the trials of Jacopo Foscari sat in judgment upon him, and passed a sentence wherein his father had neither voice nor influence, but to which father and son had equally to bow. The sentence however was not carried out in all its severity; Jacopo Foscari remained for some months at Trieste, where he had fled for safety, when (Trieste being considered unhealthy) he was removed to Treviso. From there, at the urgent entreaties of his old father, who begged that this, his only son, might be given back to him, he was allowed to return to Venice.

While these matters had been taking place the wars with Milan had dragged on in wearisome continuance.

Filippo had been striving to retain the services of his son-in-law, Sforza, as general of his forces, and the Venetians had been equally keen to secure him for themselves in the same capacity. But these negotiations came to an end on August 13, 1447, when Filippo Maria, the last of the house of Visconti, died, and Venice was released from one of her deadliest foes. On his death Bartolommeo Colleoni, one of his generals whom he had imprisoned at Monza, escaped from captivity and came to Venice, where he was enrolled in the service of the Republic.

To revert again to Jacopo Foscari. It appears that after his return to Venice he lived in retirement and quiet, and no mention of him occurs till 1450, when the last events leading up to the final catastrophe of his story began once more to engross public attention. On the evening of the 5th of November in this year Ermolao Donato, who had been one of the heads of the Council of Ten in 1445 when Jacopo Foscari had been exiled, was murdered. No trace of the murderer was forthcoming, and not till the following January did any evidence prove conclusive, when early in that month Jacopo Foscari was denounced to the Council. The reason that attached suspicion to his name was of the very slightest, and no convincing proof could be gleaned either by torture or by bribe to show that he was the culprit, but nevertheless he was condemned to perpetual exile at Canea, in the island of Candia ; no appeal was to be made to alter or revoke this sentence, and should Jacopo attempt to escape he was immediately to be put to death. The arguments for and against Jacopo's innocence are

many, and too lengthy to be discussed here ; suffice
it to say he was banished to Candia, from whence
he was only to return for the last act in his tragic
story, when the cup of sorrow and suffering was to be
drunk to its very dregs by him and his aged father.

A more public catastrophe was now to be enacted
in the fall of Constantinople, and the establishment
of the Ottoman Empire on the throne of the Cæsars.
The Emperor John Paleologus had died in 1448,
leaving no issue, and his throne was claimed by his two
brothers, Constantine and Demetrius. The question
as to their right of inheritance had been referred to
Sultan Amurath, who decided in favour of Constantine. In 1451 Amurath died, and was succeeded by
his son, Mahomet II., who determined to conquer
Constantinople for himself, and plant his empire and
dynasty there. Mahomet knew well that the chances
for such a step were all in his favour. He knew to
what a state of weakness the Emperor was reduced ;
he knew too the apathy of the Christian rulers
towards the Empire of the East, and that from the
West, at all events he was not likely to meet with
molestation or interference. He collected the whole
of his army, amounting to three hundred thousand
men, and planned the attack and assault upon the
city in a way proclaiming him an undoubted general
and engineer. Against the Sultan's array Constantine could only muster an army of from nine to ten
thousand men, but he made an earnest appeal to all
Christendom, and especially to Venice and Genoa, to
come to his rescue. Both the Republics made an
effort to respond to Constantine's appeal, but for

Venice in particular it was no easy matter. Her exchequer was emptied by the long profitless war with Milan ; her resources were drained by her conquests and acquisitions on the mainland, and "the Safeguard of the West" was wanting when the hour came for her to make profession of her proud office and position. The divergence from the policy which Tomaso Mocenigo had striven so persistently to maintain, and for which with his dying breath he had contended so pathetically, was already bearing fruit. Venice had flattered herself that she could perform the impossible feat of burning the candle at both ends with impunity, and she never calculated the collapse that must inevitably ensue. The overthrow of Constantinople involved upon Venice the imperilling of her commerce and affluence ; and the blunder she committed in not straining every nerve for the preservation of a town whose interests were so interwoven with her own was fatal. Venice more than any other power had a stake in the welfare of Constantinople ; and no price should have been too great to pay for the maintenance of a city to whom she owed so much, and from whom so large a share of her wealth and prosperity were derived.

But Venice had neglected her navy and her sea defences. The ambition of Foscari and of his party had aimed at nothing less than the conquest of Lombardy ; that quiet building up of strength and power and concentration on the sea side that should have preserved her intact had been set aside for land victories and conquests, which had drained her exchequer, exhausted her resources, and left her powerless to help the Greek Emperor. For the defence of Constantinople Venice could only muster five galleys. These sailed under Jacopo Loredan, but, owing to numerous delays, they arrived too late. Constantine could do nothing against the fearful odds opposed to him, and after a gallant resistance he fell fighting for his crown and country, and all was lost. The Turks entered Constantinople in triumph after a siege of fifty-two days, and Europe received with consternation the news of a disaster that not one of her rulers or princes had striven in any way to avoid, for the feeble support sent by Venice and Genoa, by Alfonso of Naples and Pope Nicholas V., cannot be spoken of as help or assistance in the real sense of the word.

The dismay caused in Venice by the news of the fall of Constantinople did not, however, blind the Republic as to the course she considered best and wisest to pursue with the victorious Sultan. The crescent now waved where the cross had floated for so many an age ; and in the saying adopted by Venice in regard of her transactions with Mahomet, " We are Venetians, then Christians " (" Siamo Veneziani, poi Cristiani "), lies the key to her policy in the East. Religion was not to sway the aims and interests of commerce or diplomacy ; business must be carried on with Turk as well as with Christian ; and though regret and lamentation might weep for the last of Constantine's line, it was surely wiser to make treaties of peace and goodwill with his successor than to mourn over opportunities missed, and let trade be for ever interrupted. Bartolommeo Marcello was accordingly sent to make friends with Mahomet, and to offer terms and securities whereby the intercourse and traffic between the two countries might be continued without let or hindrance. A treaty to this effect was signed in April, 1454, when it was settled that an agent or Bailo should be sent by the Signory to watch over Venetian affairs and interests in Constantinople, and the first Bailo appointed was Marcello himself.

Two years after this, on January 8, 1456, S. Lorenzo Giustinian, the first Patriarch of Venice, died. He had been Bishop of Castello till 1451, when Nicholas V. united the Patriarchate of Grado (which had existed and flourished there for almost nine centuries) to the Bishopric of Castello, and afterwards merged them both in the Patriarchate of Venice—a dignity and office existing to this day.

In this same year, 1456, occurs the third and final act in the tragedy of the Foscari family. Six years had elapsed since Jacopo's banishment to Candia, and now he was to come back for the last time, though what actually occasioned his return seems lost in doubt and hypothesis. Some accounts say that Jacopo addressed a letter to the Duke of Milan in which he begged him to intercede to the Council of Ten on his behalf and obtain from them leave to return to Venice. This petition would be a crime on Jacopo's part, it being a State offence for any Venetian subject to appeal to a foreign potentate, and to address it to the Duke of Milan, Venice's most bitter enemy, would but render the offence doubly heinous. The letter, it is said, was left unsealed and carried before the Council, and Jacopo, summoned to Venice, confessed under torture to having written it, with the sole object of being recalled in order to see once more his native land, his father, his wife, and children. This poetical version is a very distorted one, and the arguments to disprove it are many and powerful. In the first place the dates and assertions of the different chronicles are more than usually confused and involved on this point ; secondly, Jacopo's letter was as likely as not never to reach its destination, when he would never receive a summons to answer inquiries over a letter which had never been delivered ; thirdly, it was by no means certain that coming to Venice as a criminal he would be allowed to see his family, for under such circumstances special leave had to be obtained from the Council of Ten ; and lastly, if his letter had the touching object ascribed to it, was it likely he would have waited till torn and tortured by the rack to reveal its aim and intention? The Ten always granted a safe conduct to exiles, who had some State secret to tell, and why—given that the story of the letter were true—Jacopo should not have applied for such a pass, must seem most unaccountable and irrational.

Another and more probable story appears to be as follows : Certain letters and papers were conveyed to Venice from the Governor of Candia relating to Jacopo Foscari, containing matter so urgent and serious that the Council of Ten demanded the *Zonta,* and sat in judgment on these papers, which were found to be of a nature to create " fresh scandals and disorders," [1] and to refer frequently to the Duke of Milan. In short, the contents of these documents were of so compromising a nature that Jacopo was brought to Venice and put to the torture. Under this pressure he confessed his guilt, and was then sentenced to return to Candia in perpetual banishment. The closing scene with his family is described by an old chronicler and eye-witness,[2] and presents as moving a spectacle as can be found in rhyme or fiction. " Leave was afterwards granted to his mother, his wife and children to go and see him in Torricella " (a prison in the ducal palace), " where they found him mutilated by thirty strokes of the lash which he had received in those days. He was then removed to the room ' delle oselle del cavalier,' where Messer the Doge, his father, went to see him with so resolute a voice, and so firm an aspect, it seemed as though he were not his son. And although he saw him so disfigured and tortured, and unshaven, yet was he not overcome. His son said : ' Father, I entreat you to obtain leave for me to go to my own home.' And Messer the Doge : ' Jacopo, go and obey the behests of your country, and seek no more.' And having taken leave of his father, he was placed on a galley and conveyed to Canea. Messer the Doge, his father, remained in the room after his son had gone, and in his grief threw himself into a chair, fainting and exclaiming in tears: 'Oh, pietà grande!' " Jacopo was banished to Candia on July 31, 1456, but the extent of his guilt cannot have been considered

---

[1] Nuovi scandali e disordini (Misti xv. 8 Giugno, p. 96).

[2] Cronaca Dolfin alla Marciana DCCXCIV. Classe vii. Ital.

so enormous, as soon after he left Venice a powerful plea was put forward by the Doge and several leading patricians for mercy on his behalf ; the boon was granted, and a message of pardon sent to the exile. But it arrived too late, for on January 12, 1457, the unfortunate Jacopo had " passed to where beyond these voices there is peace."

The sorrows and trials borne by Doge Foscari in private life, and the cares and anxieties consequent on a reign of thirty-four years told heavily on the old man. He was eighty-four years of age, and it cannot be matter for wonder that he no longer attended the meetings of the Senate or of the Ten, and was indifferent as to affairs of state. This apathy and indifference was highly displeasing to the Council of Ten, and they determined to remove Foscari from the head of affairs and depose him from the dukedom. There can be little doubt that private jealousy and intrigue had much to do with this resolution, though romance has heightened the actual point to which those promptings arrived. The powerful family of Loredan was foremost in animosity to the Doge ; the ill-will too was of long standing, and dated from the time of Foscari's election, when Pietro Loredan was a close competitor for the throne, and never forgave his rival for having defeated him. Constant aggravations and slights increased the enmity, and some accounts go so far as to say that Doge Foscari connived at, if he did not actually compass, the deaths of Pietro Loredan and his brother Marco. Had there been the slightest ground for such an accusation Foscari's enemies (and he had many) would not

have ignored such a charge, or failed to clamour for
the vengeance due for so criminal an offence. But
though the accusation was in all probability a most
unjust one, it has laid the basis for a legend that
survives to this day, and that tells how Jacopo
Loredan, Pietro's son, looking upon the Doge as
guilty of the deaths of his father and uncle, entered
Foscari's name on the debit page of his account-book,
leaving a blank on the credit page opposite, where,
after his vengeance had been consummated, and the
Doge had been deposed, he wrote : " He has paid
it " (" L'ha pagato "). There may be some authority
for this story which has become such a well-known
tradition in the family history of the two houses, but
no documents exist to prove it ; and if it be really
authentic, it is strange that Jacopo Loredan allowed
seven years to elapse between his father's death and
Foscari's deposition.

This step was now fully determined on by the
Council, who sat without intermission for several
nights and days, closeted with the *Zonta*, who had
been summoned on so momentous a question. The
conclusion they arrived at was that Foscari, being
unable to attend to affairs of state, should be released
from his vows, that a pension of one thousand
five hundred gold ducats (some say two thousand)
should be granted him annually, and that his answer
must be tendered in a few hours' time. This
conduct on the part of the Council of Ten is
most reprehensible. They were acting beyond their
powers in the first place, and their want of courtesy
and consideration towards a man bowed down with

years and sorrows is absolutely inexcusable. But
the Doge's spirit was not yet crushed. He refused
to accept the verdict of the Ten, and maintained
that it was impossible for him to violate the oaths
he had taken, and which forbade him to resign his
office. The Ten, alarmed lest he should summon the
Great Council and appeal to their decision to confirm
or annul the sentence passed on him, insisted on his
abdication in so compulsory and positive a manner,
that he had no choice but to obey.

It was evening when the order was brought to him
to quit the palace where for thirty-four years he had
ruled and suffered, and the poor old man was in bed
and asleep when the heads of the Council of Ten
came to announce to him the sentence of banishment.
The calmness and dignity of his bearing on receipt
of the message shows a grandeur of mind which must
have inspired the respect and admiration of those
around him : he observed that he had always striven
from the moment when he had been made Doge to
keep and enlarge the State, and above all to preserve
peace in the country, and goodwill and harmony
among men ; he would not alter his tactics now and
by throwing the city into confusion be the cause of
disturbance, but would submit cheerfully and abide
patiently by what was settled, leaving the justice of
his sentence in the hands of God. To prove his
willingness to obey, he drew the ducal ring off his
finger, which was broken in his presence ; the ducal
bonnet was handed to the Councillors, who removed
from off it the horn and the gold fringe, in sign of renunciation of all sovereign power, and Foscari promised

to leave the palace in two days, and go to his own house at S. Pantaleone. This was on October 21st, and the next day it was to be announced that the Doge, feeling incompetent by reason of his great age to continue in office, had renounced the dukedom, and the Great Council was to be called to elect his successor. They met with that intent on the 24th, and on the 27th Foscari left the ducal palace for ever. He was accompanied by his brother Marco and many patricians and friends, and his brother suggested to go by a hidden staircase in order to avoid the gaze of the crowd, but he refused to pass by any than the great stairs whereby he had ascended to power, and from whence when he gained the last step he exclaimed in a loud, clear voice : " The malice of others has driven me from that eminence whereunto my merits had raised me."   Then crossing the courtyard, he entered his gondola by the Ponte della Paglia, and went to his own house.

The Great Council had met in the meantime to appoint his successor, though the clamour and indignation raised by this deed of the Council of Ten was so great that a rebellion was feared among the lower classes, with whom Foscari had always been very popular. All allusions to the Doge's deposition were forbidden in the most arbitrary way, till the wrath and discussion provoked by so shameful a proceeding were stifled and silenced under the heavy hand of the law.

On Sunday, October 30th, the Great Council, who had sat with locked doors since the 24th, declared Pasquale Malipiero Doge in the room of Foscari, and the day following he assumed office. But twenty-four hours after on All Saints Day, November 1, 1457, Francesco Foscari died. The story that the sound of the bell pealing out his successor's nomination caused his death has been proved untrue. The new Doge had been elected and proclaimed on October 30th, and that this important fact remained a secret for so many hours is neither credible nor likely, nor too is the legend corroborated by any chronicles of the time. Most of them assert that Foscari died from the bursting of an internal tumour or cancer, and the Dolfin Chronicle tells how on that " same day (November 1st), the new Doge being in St. Mark's to hear mass, Messer Donato, son-in-law of the late Doge, came to announce the fact of Foscari's death. On hearing it all looked one at another, saying that, after all, they might have delayed ten days. To all it seemed a miracle he should have died so soon, and great displeasure was felt at the treatment he had received, and at the death of such a prince, whose like has never been seen on this earth, nor will ever be again." A decree was at once passed that a public funeral should be accorded to Foscari, a proposition strongly combated and opposed by his widow, Marina Nani. She refused to give up her husband's body, declaring that such honours were a poor and tardy apology for the injustice done to him, and that no one but herself should defray the funeral expenses, even should she have to spend her dower for the purpose. But the poor Dogaressa was forced to yield, for the Council of Ten sent to her, saying, should she decline to give up her husband's body willingly, it should be taken from her by force, and against such a mandate she was impotent. A solemn, gorgeous funeral was held when Foscari's remains were laid to rest in the Church of the Frari, and for the first and only time in Venetian story one Doge was seen assisting at the funeral of another, for Malipiero was present at the obsequies, dressed only in senator's robes, while all the insignia of the ducal office were exposed on the coffin of his predecessor.

Before passing on to other events, it may be well to glance at the effect produced on Venice by this long dukedom of Foscari. It has been said that from this date the ruin and decay of Venice commenced, that her age of greatness and glory began now to wane, and that henceforward it is the downward course of her story that has to be told. But till then her career had been a splendid one ; she had attained a degree of opulence, civilisation, and greatness unique at that period ; she had stood as a rampart to all Europe against the barbarians and infidels of the East; her title " Queen of the Sea " had in it a degree of actuality and reality rarely possessed by such sur-names ; and the position she held in regard of the arts and letters is one that deserves our undying admiration and gratitude.

The inroads made by the Turks in the Empire of the East, as step by step they pressed onward to the capital itself, drove many scholars and collectors of manuscripts out of the country, and induced them to settle in Italy, where safety, protection, and an honourable welcome awaited them on all sides. Even before the fall of Constantinople this spread of Greek students in Italy had borne fruit, and made the Greek language the fashion, so to speak, among all who affected letters. Foscarini [1] recounts the names of several Greeks who came and settled in Venice ; he speaks too of how several among the Venetian patricians patronised the new fashion, and it is a historical fact that one of the accusations laid against Jacopo Foscari was that of accepting some Greek codices as a gift—a proof that he was either following in the stream of learning, or wished to be considered literate and fashionable. The mania for Greek literature received too an impetus from the gift made to Venice by Cardinal Bessarion of his collection of manuscripts and codices in 1416. This Greek, a native of Trebizond and Patriarch of Constantinople, fixed his abode in Italy, where his services and adherence to the Church of Rome gained for him a cardinal's hat, and had almost at one moment procured him the triple crown. His donation to the Library of St. Mark formed the nucleus of that great collection which was soon to be enriched by the art of printing, when that art found a home and shelter in Venice, and developed so famously under the skill and guidance of Aldo Manuzio. The town itself also underwent numerous improvements and embellishments in this reign ; great additions were made to the ducal palace ; the erection of the Porta della Carta was completed, much of the palace was faced with slabs of marble, and many regulations as to insurance against fire, together with

[1] "Della Letteratura Veneziana," del Doge Marco Foscarini, Venezia, 1854, p. 74.

provision for lighting the town were introduced by Foscari.

Apart from this increase of lands, territory, luxury, and learning must be set the question as to whether Venice really was the gainer by these seeming acquisitions. The answer can only be in the negative ; for, as has been shown, her strength and power lay in concentrating all her energies and resources on the sea, and leaving the land to those who, by position and nature, were fitted to rule thereon ; while the fatal policy urged by Foscari led to the irreparable mistake of forsaking the element where Venice was born to rule, and which, once forsaken, never owned or acknowledged her sway again. She was also soon to rue the inability that had crippled her movements and helpfulness in regard of Constantinople. The feeble subsidy of six galleys, the utmost force Venice could contribute towards maintaining Constantine Paleologus on the throne, proved useless against the numbers and powers of the Turk, with whom for the next three generations she was at constant war. In these wars she lost one after another the rich lands and islands won for her by the skill and bravery of her early warriors, and was finally compelled to pay taxes and custom for the privilege of trading where of old she had dictated terms and exacted tribute.

In 1462 Cristoforo Moro followed Pasquale Malipiero as Doge   To English readers a special interest attaches round his name in connection with " Othello," and sufficient proof exists to show that this Doge served as the original for Shakespeare's " Moor of

Venice," though how far the appalling tragedy was enacted in Moro's real and private life is too elaborate a question to be considered here. His tomb in the Church of S. Giobbe is a lovely specimen of Pietro Lombardo's work ; and the scrolls and wreaths of stone "twined in many a freakish knot," with the mulberry leaf (the Doge's family badge) traced in each corner, give rise to a fantastic idea as to whether Shakespeare had that device in his mind when he speaks of " the handkerchief spotted with strawberry leaves," the first gift made by Othello to Desdemona !

An alteration of an important nature was effected in Doge Moro's *Promissione* when the words " Comune Venetiarum " were changed to " Dominium," or " Signoria," so as to efface even in word what had long been done in deed, *i.e.*, all share of the common people in the choice of their ruler. The Government of Venice had long intended to sweep away all option and voice of the people in public affairs ; and the way they carried through their purpose, no matter the years it took them to accomplish it, demonstrates the determination and persistency of their resolution. Examples of it exist in the closing of the Great Council, a measure that had been planned several years before it was carried into effect ; and again in the suppressions of Bocconio's and Marino Falier's conspiracies, when the last struggles were made to share the power between the upper and lower classes and prevent the absolute supremacy of the aristocracy. But all these strivings were in vain ; the people of Venice were condemned to be underlings, and even the word hinting of their participation in the government was no longer to be tolerated.

A long and weary war with the Ottoman Empire in 1462 occupied the Republic for many years. At the commencement of this war she was supported by Matthew Corvinus, King of Hungary, but that help was soon withdrawn, and for sixteen years she had to maintain alone and unaided a long and unequal contest. When at the end of that period, with failing means and powers, she made peace with Mahomet II., a cry of execration and indignation arose from the rest of Europe, mingled with accusations of egotism and self-interestedness to which her subsequent policy did not sufficiently give the lie. In November, 1463, Pope Pius II. preached a crusade against the Turks and urged on the Venetians and on the Doge the duty of sharing in the undertaking, in which he himself meant to take part. But Cristoforo Moro was old, and more bent on works of piety at home than on girding himself for action, and announced his intention to stay in Venice. Upon this Vettore Cappello, one of his councillors, hurled the following command at him : " Serene Prince, if your Excellency will not go willingly, we will make you go by force, for the honour of our country is dearer to us than your person ; " and Moro had to go. But the death of the Pope (1464) changed the whole prospect of affairs ; many withdrew from the expedition, and the Venetians who sailed to the coast of Istria had to retire to Negropont after a disastrous encounter with Mahomet's forces at Patras.

Fresh fightings began in 1469 at Negropont, when

the Venetians repulsed the Turks, and the slaughter
and massacre that followed form a sad and sickening
theme of horror and bloodthirstiness ; the more so as
they are only the beginnings of a long struggle waged
by the Republic against Mahomet and his successors
to maintain their rights and privileges in the East.
The following year the fearful siege of Negropont
took place, and the Venetians suffered a terrible repulse. Mahomet was bent on conquering the town,
and though the Venetians, women as well as men,
made a gallant and vigorous defence, they were outnumbered by the Turks and insufficiently supported
by their own ships under the Admiral da Canal. The
fleet had been sent to the relief of the besieged town,
but da Canal's courage failed him when the moment
presented itself for striking a blow ; he remained
passive when he should have fought for the deliverance of his country-people, and lost the town by
what can only be termed a cowardly prudence. The
carnage and butchery that followed the entrance of
the Turks into Negropont was horrid ; no respect
was shown to age, sex, or rank ; and it is said that
a huge pile was erected of the heads of only the
innocent victims massacred by the Turks. The loss
of Negropont and the defeat sustained by Venetian arms was a terrible revelation to the Republic
and to all Europe beside. Till then Venetian sailors
had been the first in the world both for skill and
valour ; their experience had rendered them superior
to others, while the degree of excellence to which
they had attained in their art was at that date unequalled. But now their ascendency was over ; the

Turks, whose maritime forces had been reckoned at a very low rate, and whose sailors had been looked down upon as far inferior to those of other nations, had defeated them, and forced them to acknowledge a supremacy over that element, where till now they had been judged omnipotent and invincible. This addition of power to the Ottoman nation could not but increase the dread already existing in regard of them, besides creating panic and dismay in every country open and contiguous to Turkish waters.

But to return to Canal. He was recalled to Venice, and condemned to perpetual exile, while Pietro Mocenigo was appointed admiral in his stead.[1] Under his command the Venetians in the following year (1471) gained a few advantages over the Turks, and the Doge who died in this year had the satisfaction of seeing the honour of his country's arms restored to some extent in the East.

But a greater honour still is connected with Doge Moro's reign, namely, the patronage then given in Venice to printing ; and this welcome and encouragement extended to an art about to gladden and enlighten the whole world is one of the proudest titles which Venice has to claim the praise and gratitude of all ages. Before enlarging on this important argument it may be well to glance at the conditions of Europe, and specially of Italy, which caused this invention to meet with such an eager reception ; together with the

---

[1] Canal was essentially a man of letters, and though he had often served as ambassador on his country's behalf, he was not fitted for war, or for the special talents called for in that service. He was banished to Portogruaro, where he died in 1470.

reasons why, in the peninsula more than elsewhere, the soil was so ready for the introduction and cultivation of the art. It should be remembered that the study of Greek had been preserved in Italy, when the rest of Europe was overrun with habits and customs far removed from culture and civilisation. The traffic existing between Venice, Genoa, and the East had kept alive some knowledge of the Greek tongue, and rekindled in the first half of the fourteenth century a desire to revive the learning and literature of Greece. It was from the South that the first movement towards this revival came, when Bernard Barlaam, a monk of Calabria, after a long residence in Constantinople, returned to Europe and imparted his love of Greek to Petrarch, who began under his tutelage to study the language. Another of his pupils was Leontius Pilatus, the friend and protégé of Petrarch and Boccaccio, and for whom this latter caused the first Greek chair founded in Florence to be established there in 1360. This move though was not very successful, and not till 1393, when Manuel Chrysoloras came to Italy, did this branch of learning flourish. Chrysoloras occupied the chair founded by Boccaccio for Pilatus, and also spent much of his time and energies in travelling from Florence to Milan, Venice, Padua, and Rome, teaching with unflagging zeal the language and letters of his native land. His Greek grammar, the first compiled in the West, was published at Venice in 1484. The instruction begun by him was carried on by Guarini of Verona, who taught in Venice from 1415 to 1422, and whose son Baptista Guarini taught

Greek to Aldo Manuzio. Another Greek scholar, Francesco Filelfo (Philelphus), was reputed the greatest light of his day, and after him came George of Trebizond, who accepted the invitation of the learned Venetian patrician Francesco Barbaro to replace Filelfo as Greek professor at Venice. Together with him flourished Theodore of Gaza, who with " Messer Giorgio " was much patronised by Nicholas V.

On the other hand the new taste met with serious opposition. The dearth of teachers, the scarcity of Greek books and manuscripts, the animosity of the Catholic Church against the " Schismatics," all tended to chill and repress the rising mania. This however was counteracted to a wide extent by the fall of Constantinople. The feeling of animosity, till then active and vigilant, was largely allayed by that catastrophe, and in its place a great wave of pity and compassion was evoked on behalf of the defeated, outcast Greeks, who were now welcomed with open arms, and whose poverty and misfortunes filled all hearts with softness and respect. These wanderers from the East " arrived with their hands filled with books, their minds more or less adorned with a literature for which Europe now began to evince a strong curiosity, chiefly due to the vivid exhortations of several men of heart and genius, such as Petrarch ; finally, they were, so to speak consecrated by sorrow, and this little band of exiles found themselves strong enough to contribute largely to one of the most fertile growths of the human mind, to the inauguration of a new era in the works of thought." [1]   Thus the Greeks

[1] Egger : " L'Hellénisme en France," Tom. I. p. 107.

became unconscious factors in that great movement about to develope in all minds, leading up to the Renaissance in letters ; and it was to Venice, as the most enlightened and most tolerant of Italian towns, that the specially learned Greeks took refuge. It was too this greed and avidity for Greek books that led Aldo Manuzio to devote his life and powers to the publication of these rare treasures, and induced him to fix upon Venice as the most commodious and suitable home from whence these publications and treasures should emanate.

But some writers (among them the German Voigt) [1] deem that the favour accorded by Venice to letters was slight, and almost accuse the Republic of not having granted an extensive official protection to the Humanism then spreading throughout Italy. And without casting any reproach upon Venice or her government, there is some truth in the observation. It is true that the development of learning took place later in Venice than elsewhere in the peninsula ; but in the second half of the fifteenth century many learned students and collectors of books—Venetians and foreigners alike—were to be found in the city of the lagunes. The conditions of Venice were widely different from those of other Italian states and towns, where principalities had been established under the rule of despotic seigneurs. These rulers in their capacity of *Mecænates* received at their courts scholars and writers, and found among their richer and more

---

[1] Georg Voigt, "Il Risorgimento dell' Antechità Classica, ovvero il Primo Secolo dell' Umanismo." Traduzione italiana del Prof. D. Valbusa, Sansoni, Firenze, 1890.

powerful subjects imitators ready to follow the
example they had set. At Florence, where the
Medicean supremacy was daily asserting its sway,
Lorenzo de' Medici gave to arts and letters in Tuscany
(the home and cradle of learning in Italy) a protection
at once liberal and efficacious. But in Venice it was
another thing altogether; and the exceptional conditions of the town claim special consideration and
judgment. Her rulers, an aristocratic body, had for
the supreme aim the political and commercial prosperity of the Republic, and patronised particularly
military and administrative capabilities. The nobles
in their capacity of rulers exercised no direct influence on Humanism; but there were many among
them who devoted themselves to letters and protected
learning. The state, although not playing the part
of a *Mecœnates*, readily availed itself of the services of
its most cultivated nobles, and drew from their ranks
all whose views and ambitions were in common with
its own, and who aimed at one object, *i.e.*, the good of
the state. The names which have become most famous
in letters are all of them patrician, and are as follows :
Francesco Barbaro, Giovanni Cornaro, Pietro Miani,
Lauro Querini, Marco Lippomano, Leonardo Giustinian, Fantin Dandolo, Zaccaria Trevisan, Daniele
Vetturi, Luigi Foscarini, Ermolao Donato, Ermolao
Barbaro. The luckless Jacobo Foscari was a scholar ;
Francesco Barbaro and Leonardo Giustinian delivered
an address in Greek to the Emperor John Paleologus ;
Carlo Zeno, the great general, was a keen student of
the classics ; and all these men were statesmen, and
as such ranked among the highest and foremost in

Venice. Poetry flourished late in Venice, but towards the end of the *quattrocento* it had numerous followers, and more still as time went on. Cardinal Bembo, a Venetian and a patrician, held a high position among the Italian men of letters in the famous *cinquecento*. The riches and freedom of Venice attracted thither artists and *litterati* from all parts of Italy, who mixed in social intercourse with the citizens, and found hospitality and welcome in a soil congenial to their labours. But the literature peculiar to Venice is that relating to her history. In no other city is there extant such a mine of interest and information as in the papers and records of the Venetian chroniclers. The originality, the *naïveté*, the minutiæ of their writings, though without any literary pretension to language or style have a force and value that is wanting in the elegant and finished diction of the Florentine chroniclers ; and give a picture of life and customs and events of surpassing value and interest.[1]

[1] Special mention must be made of the " Diari di Marino Sanudo " now in course of publication. The original of this important work is at the Marciana Library, and consists of 58 volumes in folio, ranging from the year 1496 to 1533.

MURAL DECORATION IN VENICE.

XII.

THE ACQUISITION OF CYPRUS.

(1471-1486.)

CRISTOFORO MORO was succeeded in 1471 by Nicolò
Tron, whose short reign of two years is connected
with the fact that the first silver *lira* was then
coined in Venice, and it is of note that he is the
only Doge whose effigy is stamped on the money
coined during his dukedom,[1] an act of assumption
not allowed again, for in the *Promissione* of his
successor, the Doge is forbidden to engrave his figure
on any coin, except kneeling before St. Mark.

During the dukedom of Nicolò Marcello, Tron's
successor, the war with Turkey continued with
vigour, when Venice met with no succour from
her former friends. She entered into an alliance
with Ussunhassan, King of Persia, against Mahomet,
whereat the Florentines, jealous of the Persian
monarch, refused any longer to aid their old allies.
The Emperor Frederick III. too had been gained over
by Galeazzo Visconti, Duke of Milan, to thwart and
obstruct the Republic, which was only driven by these
hostile manœuvres to enter into still closer relation-

[1] There are a few but very rare exceptions of some coins stamped so
in Doge Moro's reign.

ship with Ussunhassan. Her first efforts supported by him were crowned with success, and flushed both parties with hopes of victory and triumph. These hopes however were soon to be crushed: the Persian arms met with a severe defeat on the plains of Tergian, and the Turks proceeded to invest Scutari in Albania, which was gallantly defended by the Venetians under Antonio Loredan. It is said that when the besieged were murmuring at the scarcity of food and a still greater trial in the scarcity of water, Loredan, hearing of the growing discontent, presented himself before the malcontents, and baring his breast, exclaimed, "If you are hungry feed yourselves with my flesh; if you are thirsty drink of my blood." The words acted like magic on the crowd, they returned with shouts of admiration and devotion to the defence of the city, and shortly after their arms were crowned with victory.

In this year Bartolommeo Colleoni, the famous condottiere of the Republic, died, and bequeathed to Venice his fortune, consisting of five hundred thousand ducats, besides jewels, plate, and lands. The legacy was of inestimable worth to the Signory, whose exchequer, emptied by the Turkish wars, was unexpectedly replenished in this way, and one hundred thousand ducats were promptly devoted for the continuance of the campaign. Colleoni had exacted that his statue should be erected in the Square of St. Mark, but this was not judged expedient, and it was placed instead in the Campo of SS. Giovanni e Paolo, where it stands, the finest equestrian statue which the world has yet seen, and proclaims to all ages the fame of its reputed designer, Verrocchio, and the glory of the great general.

Pietro Mocenigo had hardly succeeded in 1474 to the ducal throne before overtures of peace were made to the Republic from Constantinople, and chiefly owing to the persuasions of the Doge, who, as admiral of the fleet at the siege of Negropont and elsewhere in the East, had had ample opportunities for judging how affairs were tending in those regions, peace was signed with Mahomet, to the indignation of the rest of Italy and of the other states of Europe.

This peace was not of long duration, and the two years and a half of the dukedom of Andrea Vendramin, Mocenigo's successor, were taken up with wars against the Turks, in which the Venetians suffered frightful losses and defeats. The armies of the infidels invaded even the province of Friuli, when the fires of the hamlets and villages which they burned to the ground, were to be seen from the belfries of Venice; and they only retired after having had their fill of plunder and booty, leaving pestilence and ruin behind them.

Under the reign of Giovanni Mocenigo (Doge Pietro's brother) Venice experienced fresh disasters, and the siege of Scutari, renewed by the Sultan and following close on the loss of the town of Croja, proved convincingly to the Republic how powerful a foe now reigned at Constantinople, and how all hope of coping with him or of holding again her position of olden days was for ever at an end. Mahomet, enraged at the defeat he had suffered four years previously at Scutari, and determined to add it to his dominions, assisted in person at the siege, and only withdrew when all hopes that the town would surrender seemed impossible. But the besieged were driven to such straits, and Venice was so little able to afford them help or support, that they were obliged to capitulate, and on January 25, 1479, another treaty was signed between the Sultan and Venice. The Republic had to surrender Scutari, Stalimene, together with other possessions in the Morea, and pay an annual fine of ten thousand ducats for trading rights ; while all that was accorded her was the power to retain her Bailo at Constantinople, and to receive again the places formerly marking the confines of her territory.

So ended a war that had lasted sixteen years, that had proved unfortunate to Venice, and that she had had to maintain alone and unaided by any outside help. On the contrary the rest of Europe, far from assisting her with men and money, cavilled only at the peace she now signed with Mahomet ; and exclaimed against her with fresh wrath and bitterness when in 1482 she renewed it again with Mahomet's son and successor, Bajazet. This behaviour of Venice in regard to the treaties and leagues she made with the new powers at Constantinople has been severely criticised ; often with justice, oftener still with harshness. Some historians, among them Sismondi, have urged that no people were so interested as the Venetians in withstanding the Turks, and acting as a barrier between them and the rest of Europe. He goes on to point out how her colonies had to be protected, her frontier guarded, her commerce defended, and that in all these respects Venice was not wanting. Again and again she sent forth fleets and war vessels worthy of her great name, and that too at moments when the rest of Europe stood with folded arms and absolute indifference to the cause wherein all were interested, and around which the fate of the Western world was so closely woven. But the error committed by Venice lay specially in her manner of setting to work, and less perhaps in her mode of warfare than in her inability to secure to herself the sympathy and co-operation of her colonies and subjects in outlying districts. She did not extend to her fiefs and possessions in the East that patronage and protection due from a parent state to its dependencies ; the conquered peoples and provinces were not enfolded in the parental arms of the home government ; and this policy of estrangement bore sad fruit at the moment of Venice's need, when she stood unsupported by vassals and subjects, who neither possessed nor professed devotion and loyalty to a state which they regarded as a taskmaster and despot, never as a guardian or parent.

Events in Italy now occupied the Republic, and called her attention from affairs in the Levant to scenes nearer home. Galeazzo, Duke of Milan, owing to his tyranny and excesses, had fallen beneath the knife of the assassin ; and in Florence the conspiracy of the Pazzi had brought about the murder of Giuliano de' Medici, and only just failed to accomplish that of his brother, Lorenzo the Magnificent. The Republic, horrified at this scandalous act, an act countenanced by Pope Sixtus IV.

himself, sent an embassy to Florence to condole over
the event ; and endeavoured, but in vain, to arbitrate
between the Pope and the Florentines. Venice then
gave more material tokens of her friendship by
forming an alliance with Florence against the Pope,
the Emperor, the Kings of France and of Naples, and
the Duke of Milan. The command of the forces,
contrary to the advice and wishes of Venice, was
entrusted to Ercole d'Este, Duke of Ferrara. The
war was an unlucky one for the allies, and the
Florentines, disheartened at their ill-success, made
peace with Ferdinand of Naples. This step was
taken without the counsel or knowledge of the
Venetians, who, indignant at such treatment and
ingratitude, avenged themselves by offering no opposition to the taking of Otranto in 1480 by the
Turks. This action or rather inaction aroused a
great outcry against Venice ; rumour even hinted
that the Venetians had gone so far as to suggest this
step to Mahomet from motives of personal vengeance ;
and the fact that their ships, cruising in the neighbourhood, and seeing the approach of the Turkish
fleet, gave no intimation of the impending danger,
does not exonerate them altogether from such an
accusation. Their refusal also to assist in driving
the infidel out of the town gives colour to the charge ;
but, on the other hand, there are proofs that would
seem to exculpate them, and several facts point to
the improbability of their sharing in such a deed.
Otranto underwent a fortnight's siege, and then it
fell before the numbers and fury of the Turks. The
excesses and butchery that followed were wholesale,

and all Italy trembled before a danger that appeared universal. Pope Sixtus, filled with dread, and fearing another invasion of barbarians into the Eternal City, thought of flying for refuge to France, but the terror that reigned in every mind was suddenly allayed by the death of Mahomet, and the withdrawal of the Turkish troops from Otranto. Bajazet succeeded to his father's throne, and the first power to acknow-ledge him as Sultan, and to renew with him treaties of peace, was Venice, who despatched Antonio Vetturi as her ambassador to Constantinople.

The Turks had hardly retired from Otranto than Venice was again at war : this time with Ercole d'Este, lord of Ferrara. It is supposed that Fer-dinand of Naples incited Duke Ercole against the Venetians, and aroused his jealousies and fears in regard to a neighbour of such increasing territory and domain as Venice was now proving herself. Her rights and privileges too in the town of Ferrara fomented the bad feeling entertained for her by the house of Este ; and Ercole further determined to annoy the Republic by setting up salt distilleries in opposition to those of Venice, and in direct rivalry to those owned and monopolised by her. The works were erected at Capodargine, near the mouth of the Po, and the fury created in Venice by this act was only to be appeased by war. A slight pretext served to bring this about, when the Venetian consul settled at Ferrara, caused a priest in that town to be arrested for debt. The Bishop of Ferrara declared that the consul Gian Vettor Con-tarini, had infringed on ecclesiastical rights, and

thereupon excommunicated him. Contarini appealed
to the duke, saying that, if he were not granted full
redress, he would leave Ferrara. Ercole's only reply
was that the gates were open, whereupon Contarini
instantly left for Venice, and related all the story
to the Senate. Ercole meanwhile repented of his im-
prudence, and sent ambassadors to Venice to explain
and apologise; but Venice was bent on war, and in
spite of numerous embassies to and fro, and many
efforts to wipe away the offence, war was declared, "and
never," says the chronicler Malipiero, "was it resolved
on with such unanimous acclamation." It was, indeed,
a most popular movement; the greed of increased
possessions on the mainland was waxing ever more
prominent in Venetian minds; they were keen too to
wipe out the defeats that of late had invariably
attended their arms; and they accepted fresh taxes
for the levies of men and munition, and subscribed
money and stores as well with a willingness and
alacrity that showed the popularity of the campaign.
Two hundred and forty thousand ducats of Colleoni's
legacy were contributed besides towards the war
expenses, and Venice saw herself supported by the
Pope, by Girolamo Riario, lord of Forlì and Imola, by
the Marquis of Montferrat, by Count Pietro de' Rossi,
lord of Parma, and by the Republic of Genoa; while
opposed to her were the Duke of Ferrara and his
kinsman, Ferdinand of Naples; the Florentines;
Lodovico Sforza; Frederick Gonzaga, Marquis of
Mantua; Giovanni Bentivoglio, head of the Republic
of Bologna; and the house of Colonna. On May 2,
1482, Robert of Sanseverino was named as the

Venetian commander-in-chief, and with him were associated Antonio Loredan, the defender of Scutari, and Damiano Moro, admiral of the fleet. Though no great prowess was performed on either side, the Venetians were generally successful ; and the Duke of Ferrara, beginning to fear for the safety of his. state, and supported by King Ferdinand and Lodovico Sforza il Moro, regent of Milan, employed secret and crafty negotiations to induce the Pope to withdraw from the Venetian alliance. Sixtus yielded to their persuasions, and announced to his former allies his decision to remain at peace, advising them at the same time to abstain from further warfare against Ercole d'Este. But the Venetians were too intent on war to heed a counsel that would arrest their victorious arms, and they pressed on to the siege of Ferrara, with every possibility and chance of success in their favour. The Pope, unable to persuade the Venetians to accept his advice, determined to exercise his authority, and force from them an obedience which they refused to his counsels. He accordingly pronounced an interdict on June 22, 1483, against them, with a threat of excommunication if within fifteen days they had not raised the siege of Ferrara. The strictest measures were adopted by the Council of Ten to prevent the Papal Bull from being proclaimed or even known of in Venice. It was sent to the Patriarch from Rome, threatening him with every possible evil, if he did not instantly communicate it to the Doge and the Signory. But the Patriarch was a loyal servant of the Republic, and placed his duty to St. Mark before that to St. Peter. He feigned illness, and sent secretly to acquaint the Doge and the Council of Ten with the communication he had had from the Pope. They enjoined on him the greatest secrecy in regard of the brief, bidding him continue all his sacred functions and offices as heretofore ; and when in Rome the Bull was affixed to the church door of St. Pietro in Vinculis, and its publicity could no longer be withheld, the Signory sent notices to all the principal courts of Europe to explain and justify their conduct under the circumstances. It is interesting to note the indifference so often shown by Venice in regard of Papal threats and excommunications ; she simply refused to be cowed by them, and pursued the even tenour of her way as though such things had nothing to do with her. She gave examples of this behaviour at the time of the Fourth Crusade ; at the siege of Ferrara in 1309 ; in the present instance ; and again in 1606, when Paolo Sarpi upheld the Republic against the anathemas launched against her by Pope Paul V.

In the meanwhile she had conquered Gallipoli, and continued to press the siege of Ferrara. But she was almost single-handed in the fight ; and by way of strengthening her cause she committed the fatal and short-sighted policy of inviting Charles VIII. of France to come and make good his pretensions in Italy to the throne of Naples. She also suggested to Louis, Duke of Orleans, to urge his claims to the dukedom of Milan and establish his rights against Lodovico Sforza. All these complications and strifes were however adjusted for the moment by the peace

signed at Bagnolo on August 7, 1484, when the confines already determined by the treaty of Lodi (1454),
were renewed with the exception of reserving to
Venice the Polesine and Rovigo together with her
trading rights at Ferrara ; while she was to restore
Gallipoli and the seaports she had conquered in
Apulia.

Pope Sixtus IV. died in this same month of
August, leaving Venice still under an interdict, but
his successor, Innocent VIII., speedily removed the
sentence that had in no sense weighed heavily on
the Republic.

Doge Giovanni Mocenigo died shortly after. His
reign, that had been agitated by wars and tumults,
had also witnessed a disastrous fire, when a large part
of the ducal palace was destroyed ; numerous valuable paintings and other treasures perished, and the
Sala dei Pregadi and St. Mark's were only saved
with the greatest difficulty. A discussion was raised
as to rebuilding the palace, and, regardless of the
want of funds, many opinions were expressed as to
the advisability of erecting a new abode for the
Doges, which was to exceed in size and magnificence
the ruined edifice, and involve an enormous cost.
This scheme was overruled by a wiser judgment, and
it was decided to repair the palace. Antonio Rizzo
or Ricci was appointed as architect ; he built the
Giant Stairs, and then absconded with a large sum of
the public money, whereupon Pietro Lombardo was
installed in his room.

A long period had elapsed in Venetian history
since two members of the same family had followed

each other on the ducal throne. This precedent was restored for the moment in the Barbarigo family when two brothers, Marco and Agostino, succeeded each other. Marco, the elder of the two, was the first

CHIMNEY-PIECE WITH THE BARBARIGO ARMS IN THE DUCAL PALACE. (*From Yriarte's " Venise," op. cit.*)

Doge crowned at the head of the Giant Stairs. He died a few months after his election, when his brother Agostino became Doge. This unusual event has been ascribed to the jealousy evinced by the " new houses," as opposed to the "old houses," and was a movement made to keep these latter out of the dukedom.[1]

The chief event in Agostino Barbarigo's reign was the acquisition of the island of Cyprus, and the way Venice made use of one of her fairest and most unhappy daughters, Caterina Cornaro, to possess herself of the isle is, though perhaps one of the best known, also one of the least creditable pages in her story. The island had been sold in 1192 by Richard Cœur de Lion to Guy de Lusignan. His family acquired by marriage the titles of King of Jerusalem and Armenia to add to that of Cyprus, and for two centuries the Lusignans reigned over the island. In 1432 King John II. of Cyprus died, leaving an only daughter Charlotte, married to Louis of Savoy, and an illegitimate son James. The youth who was very beautiful was also very popular in the island; and his sister and her husband to be rid of so dangerous a rival caused him to be expelled, and endeavoured to get themselves proclaimed sovereigns. James, supported by the Soldan of Alexandria, and by Venice, to whom he had applied for help, established himself on his father's throne, and offered to marry Caterina

---

[1] The old houses "case vecchie" numbered twenty four, and dated their nobility from the time of the Tribunes ; they were as follows : Badoer, Basegio, Barozzi, Bragadin, Bembo, Contarini, Corner, Dandolo, Dolfin, Falier, Gradenigo, Memmo, Michiel, Morisini, Polani, Querini, Salomon, Sanudo, Soranzo, Tiepolo, Zane, Zeno, Zorzi, Zustinian, in all of whose families (with five exceptions) there had been one or more Doges. In 1450 sixteen of the principal families of the new houses "case nuove" conspired to keep the old ones from the dukedom, and these were : Barbarigo, Donà, Foscari, Grimani, Gritti, Lando, Loredan, Malipiero, Marcello, Mocenigo, Moro, Priuli, Trevisan, Tron, Vendramin, Venier.

Cornaro, the niece of Andrea Cornaro, a Venetian nobleman, trading in Cyprus, and one of James's most trusted friends. The Signory willingly accepted the offer, and announced their intention to adopt Caterina in consequence as a daughter of the Republic, and give her a dowry of one hundred thousand ducats. King Ferdinand of Naples disapproved highly of this measure, and to counteract an alliance which he wished to secure to his own interests, he suggested to James a marriage with one of his natural daughters. For four years James wavered between the offered brides, though his marriage contract with Caterina had been signed in 1468, when Doge Cristoforo Moro had himself witnessed the deed, and the ceremony of betrothal had been carried out with regal pomp. At last, in in 1472, James elected in favour of his Venetian bride, who arrived in Cyprus with all the honour befitting her new dignity, and for one short year all went well and happily with the young and beautiful couple. But the following year King James died, and accusations have been made that he was poisoned by Venice to facilitate the acquisition she unlawfully intended to make of his kingdom. He left his wife with child, and in his will bequeathed the realm to this unborn child; with reversion to his natural children. In August, 1473, Caterina bore a son; and rebellions immediately arose on all sides to defraud the boy of his right. Charlotte of Lusignan claimed the throne as the only lawful heir of that house; while another rising, headed by the Bishop of Nicosia and Ferdinand of Naples,

threatened Caterina with still greater danger. They
seized on the town of Famagosta, forcibly entered
the Queen's apartment, when her physician, who
clung to her skirts for safety, was cut in pieces
under her very eyes, and murdered her uncle, Andrea
Cornaro, and his nephew, Marco Bembo. The infant
king was taken from his mother, who was herself
imprisoned ; and Alfonso, Ferdinand's natural son,
was proclaimed Prince of Galilee (a title only bestowed on the lawful heir), and his marriage with
the late king's natural daughter determined on.
Hearing of these seditions, the Venetian Republic
ordered the fleet, under Pietro Mocenigo, to sail
instantly to the Queen's rescue ; and Mocenigo
succeeded in obtaining her liberty, and in restoring
her son to her. Only for a short time though, for the
boy died the next year (1474), some say by fever,
others by Venetian poison. Mocenigo was also instructed to sow the seeds of Venetian power, and to
establish Venetian authority over the whole island ;
while under the pretext of guidance and help he
was to deprive the luckless Caterina of all that yet
remained to her of queenly privileges and position.
But Venice wanted more than this ; and fresh plots
on the part of Charlotte and of Alfonso of Naples to
secure the kingdom and dispossess Caterina, gave the
Republic the excuse for assuming more and more the
control and administration of Cyprus, and removing
altogether the shadowy figure of the queen who
stood between them and actual sovereignty. A
scheme in which Caterina was supposed to bear a
part served as an excuse for accomplishing their

purpose. Rizzo da Marino, a confidential servant of the King of Naples, and who had also shared in the former rebellion, was entrusted to repair to Cyprus, and concoct a marriage between Alfonso and Queen Caterina. This intrigue was soon discovered by the Republic, who caused Rizzo to be arrested and sent to Venice, where he confessed his machinations, and was then strangled by orders of the Council of Ten. After this Giorgio Cornaro, Caterina's brother, was despatched to Cyprus, with orders to induce his sister to renounce her crown and retire to Venice. But his task was no easy one ; Caterina had endeared herself to her subjects, and in spite of the trials and vicissitudes thronging around her ill-secured throne, the land of her adoption was dear to her ; and the empty honours held out by the Senate were poor compensations for the loving hearts, by whom she was surrounded in her island home. Opposition and resistance were however useless, and the queen had no choice but to surrender and to abdicate all her rights in favour of Venice. On February 2, 1489, after a touching sad farewell to her devoted subjects, Caterina Cornaro set sail for Venice, and St. Mark's standard was hoisted with much ceremony in the towns of Nicosia and Famagosta, in token of the possession taken by the Republic of the island of Cyprus. Caterina herself was received with all the pomp and state promised her by the Signory ; the Doge went out to meet her in the *Bucentaur*, and every demonstration of honour and respect was paid to her to compensate for a loved and lost crown. Arrived in Venice, she was called on to perform again in St. Mark's the act of abdication already performed by her at Famagosta, after which she was invested for life with the owner-ship of the castle of Asolo, though, till it was ready for her reception, she was assigned a palace on the Grand Canal, now used as the Monte di Pietà, and called after her Palazzo Corner della Regina. She passed most of the rest of her life at Asolo, where her goodness, gentleness, and charities en-deared her to the people, and when, in 1509, she was forced by the League of Cambray to leave her mountain home, she retired to Venice, where she died July 10, 1510. Her funeral was celebrated with all the pomp and ceremonial due to a queen, who had endowed Venice with one of her fairest possessions, and her remains, first laid in the Church of the Santi Apostoli (where the family vault of the Cornari was situated), were afterwards transferred to that of S. Salvatore, where a tomb over the door leading into the sacristy marks the resting-place of " Caterina, Queen of Cyprus, Jerusalem, and Armenia, and lady of Asolo," as she was wont to sign herself.

The laws passed by Venice in regard of her new possession, refute the accusations so often brought against the Republic of oppression and harshness towards her conquered subjects ; and the relation of the provisions made for the exercise of justice, for the defence of the weak, for the relief of the poor and needy in Cyprus would seem to assert that, if Venice were not better, she certainly was no worse than other victorious states placed in similar circum-stances.

XIII.

PRINTING, PAINTING AND ARCHITECTURE.

(1486–1521.)

Two events fraught with all-important results to Venice were to effect at this epoch a change in her relations to the whole world ; full of harm and injury to her trade and prosperity, though of advantage and profit to the rest of mankind. These were the discovery of America, and of the passage to India by the Cape of Good Hope. The consternation caused in Venice by the news of this latter discovery is recorded by Priuli in his chronicle where he says, "when this news reached Venice the whole city felt it greatly, and remained stupified, and the wisest held it as the worst news which could ever arrive." And so indeed they might well consider it, for till this moment all Eastern goods coming into Europe had passed through the monopoly of the Venetian market. Now these necessities and luxuries from the East, instead of paying for caravans, and being subjected to the taxations exacted by the cities of Syria, Egypt, and other countries through which they travelled, had found a cheaper way ; and the uninterrupted sea journey open to all was patronised by all, while Venice was left stranded and deprived of her most fruitful source of income.

At a moment when the commerce which had formed the chief strength and glory of Venice is about to slip out of her grasp for ever, it may be well to glance at her position in the world of politics externally, and in that of arts and letters within the city. The close of the fifteenth century is of special interest in the story of Venice as marking the apogee of her glory, and the commencement too of a decay, hardly visible at first, but which moved on by well-nigh imperceptible stages, till it crept into the heart of the great Republic, and closed over it like a pall. Her possessions in Italy over and above the actual "Dogado" and the sea-line of the lagunes consisted of the provinces of Bergamo, Brescia, Crema, Verona, Vicenza, Padua ; the " Marca Trevisana," comprising Belluno, Feltre, and Cadore ; the Polesine and Rovigo, and the principality of Ravenna ; while further to the north east she owned Friuli and Istria, with the exception of the towns of Aquileja and Triest ; on the east coast of the Adriatic, Zara, Spalato and all the Dalmatian isles, the coast of Albania ; the islands of Zante and Corfu in the Ionian Sea ; in Greece, Lepanto and Patras ; in the Morea, Moron, Coron, Nauplia of Romania, and Argos ; several small isles and settlements in the Archipelago ; and lastly, Candia and the kingdom of Cyprus. Thus from the mouth of the Po to the eastern extremity of the Mediterranean Sea she was mistress of the sea coast. But her old neighbours had also become more powerful, while the proximity, power, and enmity of the Turk was a new danger of more weight and alarm than most of the others.

And while this enlarging and spreading of her territories on the mainland was extending the possessions of Venice, a development was taking place within her walls of a wider, more elevating nature than that of conquered cities and enslaved subjects. The impulse given by the Humanists and Greek scholars to study and literature in Venice, paved the way to an incalculable degree for the reception of printing. The craving on all sides to possess copies of manuscripts and codices was a fit preparation for an art that would propagate among the many the treasures till now only obtainable for the few ; and the reproach occasionally laid against Venice of coldness and indifference to poets and writers, may be more than wiped out by the patronage and encouragement the infant art of printing received from her hands.

Printing from wood-blocks or engraved plates had doubtless been practised in Venice at an early date in the fifteenth century, and the production of playing-cards was so important an industry that in 1441 the card-makers petitioned the state for protection against foreign competition. After the invention of movable types by Gutemberg in Mayence about 1456, the new art quickly followed the road of commerce across the Alps. The first book, printed with movable types in Italy, was printed at Subiaco in 1465 ; soon afterwards the new art was practised in Rome, but it was in Venice that it was most warmly wel-

[1] See Daru, tom. iii., livre xix.

comed, nurtured, and developed. The first to introduce the art of printing with movable types into Venice was John of Spires, and his first book, an edition of Cicero's " Letters," was printed in 1469. He was followed by his brother Wendelin, and he again in 1470 by the Frenchman, Nicolas Jenson, who had learnt the art at Mayence, settled in Venice, and brought about many improvements in the art, including the perfecting of the round or Roman type, and the first casting of Greek characters. Subsequently the art spread rapidly and was carried to great perfection in Venice under John of Cologne, Erhard Ratdolt, and other printers ; the words " Impressum caracteribus Venetis " being sufficient guarantee for the excellency of an edition. During the first twenty-five years since the introduction of the art, 164 printing-presses were set up in Venice, and fifty were at work in 1500. It has been estimated that during the first thirty years about two millions of books were issued from the printing-presses in Venice.

It is, however, to Aldo Manuzio, born in 1450 at Bassiano in the States of the Church, that Venice owed the highest reputation to which it attained in the art of printing. When tutor to the young princes of Carpi, Teobaldo or Aldo Manuzio had conceived the idea of setting up a press with the chief object of issuing fine and correct editions of classical works. He naturally, in spite of offers of assistance at Carpi, turned to Venice as the place for such an enterprise, and settled there in 1489. From that date he began to issue the numerous editions which have made the

ALDVS·PIVS MANVTIVS · R·

PORTRAIT OF ALDO MANUZIO.
(*From an engraving of the fifteenth century.*)

Aldine press famous throughout the world. He also improved the types, especially the Greek, and was the first to introduce the cursive, or *italic* characters. Manuzio died in 1515, and his work was carried on by his descendants for many years. Throughout all the early history of the printing press in Venice numerous *privilegi* granted to printers are proofs of the careful and lavish patronage given by the state of Venice to the art which had settled in its midst. Another notable improvement in the art made at Venice was the invention of musical types by Ottaviano de Petrucci of Fossombrone in 1498.

The same age that witnessed the development and perfecting of printing witnessed too the development and perfecting of that wonderful school of painting which has left so celebrated a name in the world of art. The family of the Vivarini of Murano were the first to raise the study of painting from the crudity and stiffness of former periods ; and their efforts, specially in regard to colour, paved to a large extent the path for the great masters who followed in their wake, and whose names are linked with the glory and richness of the Venetian school. The secret of painting in oils was introduced into Venice by Antonello da Messina about 1473 ; and shortly after the true history of Venetian painting began with the brothers Gentile and Giovanni Bellini, and with Vittore Carpaccio. Their works, which combine the deep rich colouring that distinguishes their separate schools, blend the elements of devotion, grace, quaintness, and simplicity in unending beauty and originality. The art brought by them to such a height was faithfully maintained by Cima da Conegliano, Jacopo Palma the elder, Bonifazio, Paris Bordone, Sebastiano del Piombo, and reached its culminating point in Giorgio Barbarelli (Giorgione), and Titian.

During the latter half of the sixteenth century, when Venice was rapidly declining from her high position as a power in Europe, she was lavishing vast sums of money in the decoration of her palaces, churches, and public buildings. It was then that the festive gorgeousness of Paolo Veronese and the un-rivalled dramatic genius of Tintoretto were called into play, which has preserved so much of the glory of Venice for the instruction and admiration of posterity. With the ruin of Venice the art of painting ran riot in decay, and quickly came to extinction. It flashed out again once more beautifully in Tiepolo, topo-graphically in Canaletto, picturesquely in Guardi, and as a chronicle of life and manners in Pietro Longhi. With the fall of the Republic it died for ever.

Another great feature characterising in a very special way the town of Venice is the architecture of the city. The history of architecture in Venice follows closely the course of her rise and development as a state. The earliest decorated buildings existing to this day show traces of the influence exercised by the East; especially in the pierced marbles and fretted slabs ornamenting the façades. The transla-tion of the body of St. Mark brought about the erec-tion of a church, imitative of that dedicated to the saint at Alexandria in Egypt, but which soon yielded to the Byzantine style then paramount, and in this form became one of the wonders of the Western world. The constant intercourse maintained by Venice with Byzantium (Constantinople) had caused the Byzantine style of architecture to be largely employed both for public and domestic use in the days when Venice was only rising into power. In the thirteenth century Nicolò Pisano introduced the

TOMB IN SS. GIOVANNI E PAOLO OF THE DOGE MARCO CORNARO; DIED IN 1368.

pointed arch into Venice, and originated that special kind of Gothic which henceforth assumed so beautiful and peculiar a character throughout the city, and to which she owes some of her stateliest and most renowned churches. Moreover as her inhabitants amassed wealth and distinction there rose along the Grand Canal and in favoured spots of the city those matchless palace fronts, over whose details the eye wanders from Byzantine to Gothic in bewildered ecstasy. With the completion of the Doge's palace, after repeated fires in the fourteenth and fifteenth centuries, architecture in Venice reached its highest point. In this same ducal palace another style of architecture is visible, that of the "Lombardesque," which followed at a short distance of time on the Gothic, and which taking its name from the famous family of Lombardo gave many a grand specimen of church and palace to "the city in the sea." With the classical Renaissance it declined in beauty if it gained in solidity, in spite of the genius of such architects as Sansovino and Palladio. In the seventeenth century with Longhena, a clever but eccentric architect, the "barocco" style became prominent in Venice as elsewhere, and with painful frequency left tokens of its influence throughout the city. During the eighteenth century efforts were made to rise above the influence of the "barocco," but the attempt failed for want of power and originality.

The increase of territorial possessions on the mainland had an immediate effect for Venice in bringing her into contact with the wars and politics of her neighbours ; and they on their side turned to court the alliance of a power whose affairs and interests were now bound up with their own. As has been said, Venice had foolishly and short-sightedly called on Charles VIII. of France to claim the kingdom of Naples in right of his succession from the house of Anjou, and in this call the peninsula now joined, inviting the French monarch to bring war, ruin, and misery into their country. Charles was only too ready to answer such a summons, though anxious first to ascertain what states would really stand by him when he entered Italy. He had formed a strict alliance with Lodovico Sforza, regent of Milan, who it was well known aimed at installing himself as duke in the room of his fatherless nephew Gian Galeazzo, as soon as the occasion warranted his so doing. On April 25, 1493, Lodovico also entered into an alliance with the Pope and the Venetian Republic, and strove to persuade the King of France to become a party to this alliance, which had for its object the formation of a counterbalancing power against the increasing preponderance of the kingdom of Naples. To induce the Venetians to help him in his negotiations with Charles, Lodovico despatched his wife, Beatrice d'Este, to Venice with full powers to act for him, and to relax no efforts to induce the Senate to add their entreaties to his, and gain Charles of France over to their cause. Beatrice was received with all the honours paid to a reigning sovereign ; the Doge went out in the *Bucentaur* to meet her, and the jewels, dresses, and brocades displayed on the occasion are rapturously dwelt on by the old chroniclers. The Duchess was lodged in the palace of the Duke of Ferrara, it having been presented to him by the Republic in return for the help which he had accorded Venice in supplying grain to her troops during the Chioggian war ; a palace afterwards ceded to the Turks for the warehousing of their stores ; and now restored as the Museo Correr, or Civico. The Senate were much staggered at the literal way in which

Duchess Beatrice executed her office of envoy. She insisted on addressing them in person ; she explained to them in her husband's name the King of France's intention of invading Naples, and offered them certain privileges if they would assist Lodovico in the undertaking. But Venice had already repented of her rashness in inviting Charles, and both to the Duchess and to Perron de Baschi, Charles's ambassador, who arrived in Venice to gain allies for his monarch, the senators replied with evasive words, not meaning to commit themselves to either side till events should somewhat determine the wisdom of selection.

Charles, unable to obtain a definitive answer from Venice, despatched another ambassador in the person of Philippe de Commines, who stayed eight months in Venice, and whose observations and admiration of the city are well known and often quoted. But even he was not able to obtain for his master any other assurance from the Venetians than that of a lukewarm friendship, for Venice had determined to be an onlooker, and in that capacity refused to be inveigled into action or partizanship. But Charles's unexpected success in Naples induced the Republic to assume a definite attitude, and served also to rouse the entire peninsula to unite and expel the man whom they had themselves invited into their midst. Lodovico Sforza (whose nephew had died under strong suspicions of having been poisoned) was now Duke of Milan, and he saw in the French invasion and in the person of the Duke of Orleans dangers that urged him to establish himself firmly on his usurped throne. Maximilian of Germany likewise dreaded lest Charles, triumphant in Naples, should claim the empire; and the Italian states trembled in their turn before the might of a conqueror, who so far appeared invincible. Consequently all determined (in 1495) to form a league to drive their invited ally out of Italy and provide against a danger that they had themselves so eagerly courted. Francesco Gonzaga, Marquis of Mantua, was appointed commander-in-chief of the forces, to which Venice, who had joined the alliance, contributed, besides men and money, a body of Stradiots, or Albanian light cavalry. Charles, realising at last his danger and the gravity of the situation, began his march out of Italy; and how it came about that the allies did not again and again impede his progress and intercept, as they might easily have done, his passage across the Apennines, is a matter beyond all comprehension. When however the town of Novara opened its gates to the Duke of Orleans, who claimed through his ancestress, Valentina Visconti, superior rights than those brought forward by Lodovico Sforza to the duchy of Milan, the allies felt that the supremacy of the French must be checked, and a battle was resolved on. The engagement took place at Fornovo in the Apennines, and it is curious to read the different accounts of this battle and then decide who remained victorious. The French maintain that their foes met with a crushing defeat, while the allies claim a splendid victory, and the only point whereon all seem to agree is the number of victims who fell in the fight, the capture made by the Venetians of the French king's jewels, and the escape and safety of Charles himself, who throughout the battle had shown a courage and valour little expected in so weak-minded and irresolute a monarch. The victory however brought little advantage or result to either of its claimants ; neither party followed up their triumph ; Charles continued his retreat to his own country, and the Venetians despatched their mercenaries to assist in the siege of Novara. At the same time they also "responded generously to the appeal of Pisa" (for help against Florence) "by sending both ambassadors and troops, but as the Republic of the Lagunes was never quixotic, we must look for the explanation of her policy in the determination to prevent an alliance between the Duke of Milan and Pisa." [1]

The relief brought to Italy by the withdrawal of the French king and his troops was not so universal as might have been imagined, for hardly was the country freed from this invasion than Milan and Venice suggested to Maximilian of Germany that he should enter the peninsula and restore peace and order. He accepted the proposal, but as the task required of him proved one beyond his powers, and as his summoners found in him a charge and annoyance not to be endured, they strenuously advised his retiring to his own dominions, an advice he was only too glad to follow. A fresh alarm arose soon after of another descent of Charles VIII. into Italy, but from so dreaded an evil the peninsula was delivered by the death of that monarch at the early age of twenty-eight. Charles was succeeded by Louis, Duke of Orleans, who lost no time in making good his

[1] Story of the Nations, "Tuscan Republics," chap. xxvii. p. 367, by Bella Duffy.

claims to the duchy of Milan; and the rage of Lodovico Sforza can be well conceived when he learnt that the Venetians had signed a treaty with France, and bound themselves to support Louis's rights against their old ally. In exchange for their services they were to receive part of the conquered lands of Lombardy. This conduct of the Venetians can neither be admired nor defended: they withdrew their support from the Pisans, who were left to maintain singlehanded their gallant struggle for liberty; and without a moment's warning they deserted Sforza, when they perceived that his cause was a losing one.

For this perfidy Venice was to pay dearly. Lodovico, overcome by the league formed against him by Louis XII. and the Venetians, in which Pope Alexander VI. had also joined, determined to be avenged, and for this intent called on the powers at Constantinople to wage war on the Republic. The Turk, never backward to force his way into Europe, made secret preparations for war, and then awaited an opportune moment wherein to respond to Sforza's instigations. That moment soon presented itself, and hostilities commenced between Venice and the Turks. The Venetian forces were commanded by Antonio Grimani, under whom they received a severe defeat close to Sapienza, where Venice once before had met with terrible defeat from Genoa, and severe accusations were brought forward against Grimani, whose want of order and method in organising the attack, according to some, and whose cowardice, according to others, lost the day to Venice.

The warrior chronicler Malipiero, at the end of one of his despatches dated Zante, September 2, 1499, declares that eight hundred gallant men had died, that both money and reputation were gone, and that three hundred thousand *stara* of wheat annually drawn from this gulf were lost as well. The news of this disaster caused intense consternation and grief in Venice ; the Council of Ten ordered the return of Grimani in irons, an order his son Vincenzo entreated him to obey, and on his declining to do so, the son himself placed the fetters on his father to mitigate by this outward sign of obedience the wrath that he knew was hot against him.[1] A few days later another disgrace occurred in the surrender of the town of Lepanto to the Turks, and then the indignation in Venice burst forth, denouncing Grimani as the author of the mishap. "Antonio Grimani, ruina de' Cristiani" was shouted in every mouth, and these cries of condemnation only waxed louder when it was rumoured that he had lost the battle through his jealousy of Andrea Loredan, a

---

[1] Grimani might pass in some respects as the original of Shakespeare's Merchant of Venice. His youth had been spent in extreme poverty, but as he advanced in years he acquired immense wealth, and his luck as a merchant was so great that his dealings as to investments, acquisitions or speculations were closely imitated by all his neighbours. His wealth procured a cardinal's hat for one of his sons, his daughters were brides of three of the oldest patrician families in Venice, and he himself was raised to the dignity of Procurator of St. Mark. He had commanded the fleet on previous occasions, and always with success and honour. But now fortune forsook him, and it is said he shrank from accepting the command against the Turks, though when forced to do so, he contributed a sum of twenty thousand ducats from his private means towards the equipment of the fleet.

man more popular than himself in the navy, and who, as his colleague, would have shared the glory with him had their arms been victorious.

Terms of peace were solicited by the Republic with Turkey, but the demands of this latter were so exorbitant no treaty was possible, and the concluding speech made by the Turkish Vizier to the Venetian envoy shows how " old times were changed, old manners gone," and how Venice had now to accept in silent submission words of insult and disdain where of old she had ruled and dictated. " Till now you have wedded the sea," said the Vizier ; "henceforth it appertains to us, who have more thereon than you." And to this painful truth Venice could offer no reply, but had only to witness fresh losses when, under Melchior Trevisan, she lost Modon, Pylos, and Coron. She was unsuccessful too under Contarini, Trevisan's successor, but when he was replaced by Benedetto Pesaro fortune smiled for awhile on the Republic, and the likelihood of some help from her Christian neighbours against the infidels somewhat raised her position in the eyes of these latter, and peace was concluded between them in 1503.

Doge Agostino Barbarigo had died two years previously, when his successor had been named in the person of Leonardo Loredan, a man anxious to secure peace on every side for his country. His talents had no small scope for such practise in reassuring the King of France on the one hand, and Cesare Borgia on the other, of the goodwill and amity borne to them by Venice. The sudden and unexpected death of Pope Alexander VI., and the gradual downfall of the house of Borgia, altered materially the aspect of affairs for Venice in Italy. The encroaching policy of the Republic, and her desire to possess herself of more towns and districts on the mainland, had been shown in the advantage she took to acquire for herself the lands and cities that had owned Borgia's sway. These possessions, also claimed by the Holy See, proved a source of growing irritation on the part of Rome towards Venice, and when Julius II. was firmly seated on the Papal throne, this enmity to Venice took effect in the shape of the League of Cambray. The causes that conduced to the formation of this famous league had been collecting for some time previous to its accomplishment, but in October, 1508, the powers unfriendly to Venice met at Cambray, and no longer made any secret or mystery of the plot organised against the Republic. The larger part of Europe joined in this league, which had for its object the overthrow of a power that had aroused alike the hatred of the King of France, the Emperor of Germany, and the Pope. Venice had exasperated Maximilian by refusing him a safe conduct through her territory, when he had applied for one to go to Rome to be crowned, unless he came peacefully and without an armed retinue ; and, though at one moment she declined to forsake an alliance formed with France for one with Germany, she had afterwards provoked Louis by signing a treaty with Maximilian without first consulting him. The sentence in which the confederates avowed the object of the league ran as follows: "In order to put an end to the losses, the injuries, the plunderings, the damages caused by the Venetians, not only to the Holy Apostolic Chair, but also to the Holy Roman Empire, to the House of Austria, to the Dukes of Milan, to the Kings of Naples, and to many other princes, by occupying and tyrannically usurping their goods, their possessions, their cities and castles, conspiring, as it were, for every one's ruin, . . . we have found it not only useful and honourable, but also needful, to summon all to execute a just vengeance, and extinguish, as one would extinguish an ordinary fire, the insatiable cupidity of the Venetians, and their thirst for dominion."[1] Then followed the division to be made of the Republic and her territories. The Pope was to recover the lands in Romagna, of which the Venetians on the downfall of Cesare Borgia had possessed themselves, including Ravenna, Cervia, Faenza, and Rimini, together with Imola and Cesena, though these latter were not then under Venetian rule ; to the Emperor of Germany, Padua, Vicenza, Verona, Roveredo, Treviso, Friuli, and Istria were apportioned ; to the King of France, Brescia, Bergamo, Crema, Cremona, the Ghiaradadda, and all the dependencies of the Duchy of Milan ; the King of Spain and Naples was to have Trani, Brindisi, Otranto, Gallipoli, and the lands which the Venetians had received in pledge from Ferdinand II. ; the Kings of England and of Hungary were invited to join and to share in the

[1] Declaration of Maximilian, January 6, 1509. Ann. Ecc. Raynaldi anno 1509, tom. xx. p. 64.

partition of the Republic, Dalmatia being allotted to the latter if he entered the league ; the Duke of Savoy was to have Cyprus ; and, to strengthen the undertaking, the Pope promised to add his spiritual as well as his temporal arms to the success of the enterprise. It was stipulated that each state was to conquer for itself the portion assigned to it, and hostilities were to be commenced by France on April 1, 1509.

The blow about to crush Venice, and to weaken her beyond all possibility of ever rising again to her old position, had fallen. The seed sown by that fatal policy, against which Tomaso Moccnigo's dying warning had been uttered in vain, and which Foscari's ambition had fanned and propagated, was now to be reaped in terrible earnest. Venice had been warned again and again to withdraw from becoming a land power, and from measuring her forces in ways neither adapted nor intended for them ; but she would not heed, and rushed blindfold and headlong to a ruin which she herself had courted, and from whose effects she never entirely recovered. Weighed in the balance of forethought and sagacity, she was found wanting, and the price she had to pay for this culpability was the very life-blood of her prosperity and existence.

To make head against so formidable a danger Venice tried to provide by negotiations and diplomacy. She endeavoured in turn to soften the Pope, the Emperor and the King of Spain, and induce them to withdraw from the league. She sent to the King of England, and suggested his invading the French territory while King Louis and his troops were engaged in Italy; she applied to the Sultan Bajazet to join his cause to hers, pointing out that as the league was also inimical to him, it would be wise to unite against the common foe; but finding these arts and stratagems unavailing, she boldly prepared to meet single-handed a peril threatening her with total annihilation, and of a nature to daunt even the boldest spirit. This was the first instance, says Sismondi, since the Crusades that the European powers had united for the purpose of dismembering an independent state. Of old a nobler, higher aim had engrossed them in the wars they waged against the infidel; now their real object was the spoliation of a power weaker than themselves, and their own consequent profit and aggrandisement.

Against this "most crying injustice" Doge Loredan made a gallant resistance. He convened the Great Council, and in a noble speech called on his people to prepare for the emergency, and make ready for war. He applied all his fortune to his country's needs; he sent all his plate to the mint to be melted into coin for the war expenses; and set on foot communications to try secretly to gain over the Milanese general, Gian Giacomo Trivulzio, to command the Venetian forces. The immense wealth possessed by Venice helped in no small degree to strengthen the confidence of her citizens. She knew that by means of money she could secure the best "condottieri" of the day to lead her troops, and by the same means raise an army strong enough to oppose even that of the allies. But this confidence must have been sorely tried by signs and tokens which in that age would seem to denote that the wrath of heaven was working in co-operation with that of man against the Republic. An explosion at the Arsenal caused a fearful loss of store and ammunition, and the ashes and burning brands thrown into the town by the explosion filled the inhabitants with alarm and dread. The fortress of Brescia was blown up ; a vessel conveying a large sum of money from Ravenna for the payment of the troops went down ; and the building containing the public archives was destroyed by fire, when numerous precious papers and documents belonging and relating to the Republic perished irretrievably.

In order to support his party, as he had promised, with spiritual as well as temporal arms, the Pope issued an excommunication against Venice. The Signory, being unable to mitigate the Pontiff's anger and activity against them, resolved to prevent as far as possible any general knowledge of Julius's Bull ; they forbade its circulation, with orders to secrete the fact of its publication, so as to hide almost from themselves the existence of so injurious a decree. Hostilities began in April, 1509, when the Venetian troops, under Orsini, Count of Pitigliano, and Bartolommeo d'Alviano, marched to oppose the French on the banks of the Adda. The two Venetian commanders were men of totally different temperaments: Pitigliano was cautious and prudent to a degree approaching timidity ; Alviano bold and prompt almost to rashness. But little sympathy or concord could exist between them, and while Pitigliano was always for avoiding any engagement

with the French, Alviano would plead the advisability of attacking the foe without loss of time. On
May 14, 1509, the two armies met in the district
of Ghiaradadda, and at the battle of Vailate, or
Agnadello, the Venetians were terribly defeated.
The defeat blasted the bright hopes with which the
campaign had begun, and was a sad and true fore-
runner of the disasters in store for the Republic's
arms. Her position externally became daily more
serious; one after another of the cities subject to
her fell away from their allegiance, and soon the
important question arose as to providing for the
safety and maintenance of the town itself. The
surrounding fortifications were put into repair and
order, large provisions of wheat were conveyed into
the city; and while nobles and commoners alike
prepared for the defence of their homes and hearths,
negotiations were opened on every side to break up
the league, and prevail on each of its members in
turn to withdraw from it.

Venice adopted also another line of policy at that
moment, which has in turn obtained for her the
reputation of excelling in the art of diplomacy and
statecraft, and the accusation of having allowed terror
and fright to overcome every other impulse. This
was the resolution she now took of relinquishing all
her possessions on the mainland, and freeing all her
subjects from their oath of fidelity. By this act she
enabled the towns to bow to the storm, and left them
at liberty to avoid the horrors of a siege without
dreading the after consequences of accusations of
treachery; she allowed her vassals to yield to the

pressure—and it was a severe one—of circumstance and might, and even if the step were dictated by fear, the result justified it in the end as a masterstroke of generosity and wisdom.

A faint ray of hope about now began, however, to be discernible : the Pope, who in his heart was loath to see Italy overrun with foreign armies, was not disinclined to hearken to proposals from Venice ; two or three towns once more acknowledged the authority of St. Mark ; Padua, after a severe siege, when Maximilian himself was present, was regained to Venice, while ambassadors were despatched to every European court to implore the good offices of their rulers, or urge their withdrawal from the league. An envoy was sent to Constantinople to plead for help from the Turk against Venice's Christian neighbours, and she appealed likewise to Henry VII. of England, beseeching him not to allow the overthrow of a state to whom Christendom owed so much.

The defeat of their navy at Polesella, when their admiral, Angelo Trevisan, was routed by the Cardinal d'Este, made the Signory doubly anxious to conciliate at least one of the confederates, and their hopes centred round the Pope who now recommenced negotiations to forsake the league, and even hinted at removing the sentence of excommunication. But the actual safety of the Venetians lay in the position of their town, and as has been well said: " The situation of their capital, surrounded by the waves of the Adriatic, secured them from the apprehensions of total destruction."[1] The strange spot, which centuries ago had

[1] Roscoe, " Life of Leo X.," vol. i. ch. viii. p. 238.

offered escape and safety from the invasion of the barbarians, was now from its very remoteness and difficulty of access to prove the safeguard and salvation of its people and of its own existence. Venice, in the midst of her lagunes and encircled by her watery defences, could bid defiance to all assault and remain impregnable in her canal-girt fortress. She had however to strive in every way to crush the formidable league, which threatened her with so alarming a fate, and the possibility of gaining Julius over to her cause was one to be encouraged and fostered to the utmost extent. After much entreaty and negotiation the Pontiff at last consented to detach himself from his former allies and also to remove the interdict. To obtain these concessions however Venice had to renounce several privileges and rights which she had enjoyed till now, and only by humbling herself both in word and deed to Julius did she obtain formal revocation of the sentence on February 10, 1510. The Pope's secession from the league then became a recognised fact. But the Republic had still much to fear from the King of France, and from the Emperor of Germany, and she could in nowise relax from her warlike attitude in regard of these monarchs. On Pitigliano's death in February, 1510, Gian Paolo Baglioni was appointed to the command of the forces, and under him the Venetian arms were generally successful.

While her attention was engrossed and her thoughts absorbed by these wars and political dilemmas it is strange to read of the life that went on in the heart of the city. Feasts and entertainments were held

VENETIAN LADY.
(*From Yriarte's " Venise," op. cit.*)

regardless of expense, the gorgeousness of the dresses, the display of riches, and the lavishness squandered on all occasions would form an ironical contrast to the actual state of things were it not taken into consideration that the sixteenth century was now drawing upon Italy ; that age when a pure art and morality were to give place to debasement of every kind, and when manners, dress, art, and morals were alike to sink to a lower platform, and the high standard hitherto required was to fall to one inferior in every way.

But outwardly the tone of courage and valour was maintained ; the warlike movements of the forces then gathered in Italy assumed only fresh impetus and activity from the defection of Pope Julius from the league. The anger aroused by his conduct in the minds of his former allies took different forms : Louis XII. assembled a council at Tours to consider how best to avenge such conduct, and whether under the circumstances it were not lawful to wage war upon the Holy Father ; and Maximilian sent messages to Constantinople to urge the Sultan to join him in annihilating the Venetians. These measures roused the wrath and fiery spirit of Julius II., and in spite of failing health and advanced years he entered into military operations against the French at the town of Bologna with a courage, ardour, and skill superior to that of any of the generals engaged in the siege. The Papal and Venetian forces gained possession of Bologna in January, 1511. They then turned their arms against Ferrara, where, however, they were unsuccessful, and Italy was again torn in two by the troops of her own sons and of strangers warring throughout the land, while fresh councils and leagues only raised fresh and false hopes of peace by treaties made only to be broken.

In October of this year (1511) the Pope renewed his alliance with Venice, in which the King of Aragon also joined as well as the English monarch Henry VIII. " for the defence and support," he declared, " of the Holy Mother Church." By virtue of this treaty, known as the " Holy League," Ferdinand agreed to send a large force of cavalry and infantry, for whose maintenance the Pope and Venice were responsible, into the kingdom of Naples. This force was commanded by Raimondo di Cardona, Viceroy of Naples, and was to operate with the Papal troops in Romagna, while a body of Swiss mercenaries was to descend into Lombardy, where Gaston de Foix, Duc de Nemours was governor.

Early in the following year the memorable siege of Brescia took place, when Gaston, indignant at its loss, determined to regain it for his master from the Venetians, by whom it had been reconquered owing to the skill and courage of Andrea Gritti. Gaston was at Bologna, which he had retaken from the allies of the Holy League, when he heard of the capture of Brescia, and hurried instantly to the scene of action. In a march celebrated for its rapidity (it occupied but nine days) and for the dangers therein overcome, Gaston repaired to Brescia, and, assisted by the Chevalier Bayard, attacked the town, which Gritti defended with ingenuity and vigour. After a desperate fight the French remained victors of the field and stained their victory by sacking the town, sparing neither age, sex, nor sanctuary. Gaston then returned to Romagna, and having failed to induce Cardona to engage with his troops, he resolved to besiege Ravenna, persuaded that the Viceroy would be drawn into action by such a step. The manœuvre succeeded perfectly. The allied troops of the Pope, Ferdinand and Venice met the allied French and German forces in the great battle of Ravenna, fought April 11, 1512, when the latter remained victors. But their victory cost them dear, for Gaston de Foix remained dead on the field of battle with many a gallant knight and soldier around him. The following day Ravenna surrendered to the French, the towns of Imola, Forlì, Cesena, and Rimini did the same, and the loss of the battle and of these towns so disheartened the Pope, that he was ready to make peace on any terms. But the Venetians urged him to resist, they reminded him of the succour promised from England and Switzerland, and represented how they could still make head against a foe, whose losses well-nigh outweighed the gains that should have accrued from the victory. And indeed the French were little able to profit by their triumph. Their loss of men had been heavy ; the troops who survived were weary of sojourning in a foreign land ; the booty gained by them at the sack of Brescia had greatly demoralised them ; the towns they had conquered were soon reconquered by the Spanish and Papal forces, and negotiations were opened by France with the Republic, while Maximilian in his turn made overtures of peace to Venice. But his terms were too hard to accept, and again the Emperor, more than any member of the league, showed himself both a difficult and dangerous man to deal with. His constant need of money, from whence came his surname, "The Penniless," led him into shifts and stratagems, when Imperial pledges and promises were given, but not kept. He was always in debt, and the expedients, to which he resorted to obtain funds for his court expenses and for the requirements of his armies, were not always calculated to raise him in the estimation of his neighbours. Most of his negotiations with other powers were conducted with the sole aim of raising money, and he now offered terms to the Venetians, based on the condition of receiving from them a large sum. To this Julius urged them to agree, volunteering to lend the required sum himself, if Venice would but be reconciled to Germany. This momentary pacific inclination of the Pope was turned to account in November of this same year by an agreement between him and the Emperor to restore Maximilian Sforza to the duchy of Milan, and in December, 1512, this descendant of the Sforza was recognised as duke. This act exasperated Louis XII., who was by no means disposed to renounce the rights he had put forward to the duchy, and was about to reassert them with the help of the sword, when the aspect of affairs was changed by the sudden death of Pope Julius II. in February, 1513, and the appointment of Giovanni de' Medici under the name of Leo X. as his successor.

The first step consequent on the death of Julius II. was a treaty of peace signed between Venice and France at Blois on March 23, 1513, and a notification of it was sent to the new Pope proposing to him to adhere likewise to it for the restoration of peace and tranquillity to Italy. But hostilities continued nevertheless, and though the French had retired from the peninsula they were soon recalled by the Venetians to assist them against Maximilian. After several engagements the French were severely defeated at Novara, and Cardona advanced upon Venice, which lay open to the conqueror as far as Mestre and Marghera. But the impregnability secured to Venice by her position saved her again from an invading foe, and Cardona, after opening his cannon upon the town and firing some shots which fell short of their mark, had no choice left but to retire by way of the Brenta, when Alviano tried, though in vain, to cut off and harass his retreat. The war dragged on with weary monotony for eight years, and on the death of Louis XII. (1515) and the accession of Francis I. hope again revived that peace would be concluded in earnest. But Francis's designs on Italy dispelled this hope, and fresh battles, fresh sieges, fresh treaties signed and then broken, occupied the Republic till 1517, when, after long negotiations, Francis succeeded in arranging a treaty between Venice and Germany for five years. By this treaty both countries retained possession of the towns and districts acquired by them during the war; commercial dealings were reorganised for the mutual convenience of both states; all prisoners were set free; and as long as the treaty lasted Venice was to pay an annual fine of twenty-one thousand ducats to the Emperor. The Republic had shortly before regained possession of Brescia and

Verona, but the question of her authority over the larger part of Friuli was still unsettled when in 1519 Maximilian's death gave a new turn to the aspect of affairs. His throne was claimed by Charles V. of Spain and Francis I. of France, and both aspirants sought the alliance of Venice to strengthen their pretensions. But Venice was now embarking on that policy of caution and evasiveness, which she soon developed to the full, and returned only vague answers, declining to commit herself to either cause. In 1519 Charles was universally acknowledged as Emperor, and successor to his grandfather, Maximilian; in 1521 Venice renewed with him the treaty signed with his predecessor; and though she ceded to him Aquileja and some other towns, she was confirmed in her possession of Friuli and Istria.

In this year (1521) Doge Loredan, whose reign of more than twenty years had extended over a most momentous period of Venetian history, died, and was followed by Antonio Grimani.

COIN OF THE EMPEROR LODOVICUS.
(*Coined in Venice.*)

XIV.

VENICE AFTER THE LEAGUE OF CAMBRAY.

(1521–1585.)

FROM this moment the position of Venice was changed. Although courted alternately by France, Spain, and Germany, at moments when her participation in their wars and politics was considered desirable, and when she still played a part in European history, the vigour and independence of old was gone. The brilliancy and boldness that formerly distinguished her actions gave place to a course of statecraft and strategy hampering every movement of her policy, betraying her weakness, and forming a striking contrast to the energy and resolution of bygone days. She now began, says Daru, a system of timid and unstable policy, mistaking irresolution for prudence, and inconstancy for dexterity ; a fatal system, which finally reduced her to being alternately a useless ally, an uncertain friend, and a despicable foe. The League of Cambray forced Venice to sink bit by bit from the foremost rank, where she had stood so proudly and so long, into a second-rate power, always adopting a course of irresolution and vacillation, and anxious to maintain an even balance in the political scale, no matter in how troubled and agitated a manner that scale might be working for other nations. The mystery and importance she now attached to all questions, great or small, with which she came in contact developed too a taste for intrigue and manœuvre that made her statesmen the most observant and discursive of their time, and their reports and despatches the most faithful and minute records that exist. Venice becomes now, as it were, the special reporter and correspondent of the age ; her archives are stored with accounts of the doings, sayings, even dresses of the chief actors on the European stage, and she chronicles with an unequalled minuteness and exactness the deeds of other countries, though her share and interest in those doings no longer exist.

A proof of how humbled the great Republic had become (and all who love her cannot read such facts without sadness and regret) is evident in her behaviour towards Suleiman the Magnificent after his conquest of Rhodes. He besieged the island in 1522, when the Knights made a gallant resistance ; but their efforts were useless, the island was conquered, and their order abolished. The loss to Venice was great ; the tenure of this isle by an enemy instead of an ally involved a fresh shock to her Levantine commerce, and, as though to acknowledge her weakness, she was forced to send her orator, Pietro Zeno, to Constantinople to congratulate the Sultan on his victory, and express her satisfaction at the way he would now be able to make head against the corsairs.

The efforts which Venice still made to take a

prominent part in European matters occupied her considerably concerning the league that Pope Adrian VI. endeavoured to form among the states of Italy to protect their country against Sultan Suleiman. But Venice hesitated to become a party to this scheme ; she had lately entered into an alliance with Suleiman, whom she considered a more sure and profitable ally than a number of small powers, who would but leave her in the lurch the moment it suited their convenience so to do. After nearly a year's hesitation, during which time Doge Antonio Grimani died and was succeeded by Andrea Gritti, a treaty was signed in July, 1523, between the Emperor, his brother, the Archduke Ferdinand, Francesco Sforza, Duke of Milan, and Venice, by which the confederates agreed to arm for each other's mutual defence, but only against Christian powers, a clause inserted by the Venetians to save themselves from joining in any attack on the Turks, with whom they were determined to keep on good and friendly terms.

A few months later Adrian VI. died, and Giuljo de' Medici, under the name of Clement VII., succeeded him as Pope. His first endeavour was to effect a reconciliation between Francis I. and Charles V. ; a hopeless endeavour though, for neither monarch desired peace. Francis sighed for an opportunity for giving proof of his personal prowess, an opportunity soon to be gratified at the battle of Pavia ; while Charles kept demanding and obtaining money from the Republic for the subsidies needed for wars and campaigns, wherein he meant to signalise his superiority over the French king. In these long and intricate wars Venice took no special part. Leagues and treaties, broken as soon as signed, filled up the intervals between the battles ; sieges and assaults returned with a frequency in turn bewildering and wearisome, and Venice only joined in occasionally. She was now chiefly of account for what she could pay or provide, not for what she could do or effect ; and while the Pope, the Emperor, and the King alternately regarded her as their enemy or ally, they mentioned or omitted her name in their treaties with a disregard as contemptuous as it was marked. This treatment of a power once so formidable and dreaded shows clearly how her day of importance was over, and her day of usefulness of such small moment as to inspire neither respect nor consideration for one so palpably an inferior. A signal proof of this was given in 1529 at the Peace of Cambray (known too as " La Paix des Dames," since the negotiations were conducted by Louise, Queen Dowager of France, and Margaret of Austria, the Emperor's aunt), when Charles and Francis finally settled their disputes, and divided their own and their neighbour's territories with no thought beyond their own advantage. The selfishness and heartlessness displayed by Francis throughout the transaction was scandalous ; no thought was shown, or provision made, for any one of those who had sacrificed everything in his interests. His ingratitude to Venice was the more marked as she had constantly proved herself a faithful and efficient ally towards him, and his forgetfulness of past services was the harder to bear now that the State was weakened and no longer able to avenge such

slights and insults. Not till the close of this year
(1529) were the Venetians included in a treaty of
peace by which in December the Pope and Emperor
ratified at Bologna the treaty signed a few months
previously at Cambray. In this they had to cede
to Clement the towns of Ravenna and Cervia ; and
to Charles the ports on the Adriatic conquered by
them in Apulia, together with a sum of three hundred thousand ducats. Only at such a price, and by
the surrender of money, possessions, and dignity,
could Venice obtain "the blessing of peace." But
although she was no longer a foremost actor on the
stage of the world's history, her position and conduct
were marked by peculiarities all her own, and when
from time to time Venice moves again to the front
her actions are tinged with a reflection and colouring
essentially characteristic to herself. The way her
alliance was courted by France and Germany can be
explained from her geographical situation ; the isola-
tion procured by her surroundings brought with it
a safety and security unknown to other localities.
Unlike any other town of importance, Venice never
suffered either siege or sack ; no invader ever desecrated her hearths or homes, and the advantages
resulting from such a position gave her still a weight
and consideration in the eyes of the nations that stood
her in good stead when her day of power had passed
away.

She had still too an interest to guard and a commerce to protect in the East, and when, to the indignation of all Christendom, Francis I. had leagued
with Suleiman and urged him to harass his old allies,

Venice decided to fit out a fleet, though alleging that she did so merely for prudence, not for war or aggression. But her fleet coming in contact with the great Turkish corsair, Chaireddin Barbarossa, an engagement took place, and though the Venetians remained victors they gained nothing by it, and Barbarossa passed on to assault every island that owned Venetian sway in the Archipelago ; and in August, 1537, proceeded to assail Corfu. The island was taken and devastated by the Turks, but after a severe fight the Venetians were able to expel the invaders, who retaliated by ravaging the adjacent isles ; and Venice was too feeble to do more than rejoice over her conquest not having power to follow it up, or avenge the insult and injury done to her dependencies. The year after she entered into a treaty with the Pope and the Emperor against Suleiman, and a fleet sailed to Turkish waters to establish the claims and demands of the allies ; but at Prevesa the Spanish forces under Doria so hampered and hindered the operations of the Venetians under their admiral, Capello, that the issue of the fight was doubtful, the Turks claiming the victory, while the allies were compelled to withdraw to Corfu. Negotiations for peace were set on foot, but not concluded till October 2, 1540, when terms most disastrous to Venice were agreed on.

A strange bit of diplomacy in connection with this treaty came to light shortly after, as well as a glaring act of treachery, which led eventually to the expansion of the Council of Ten. Alvise Badoer was despatched as Venetian envoy to Constantinople to conclude the affair, when he was to demand before all things the restoration of all Turkish conquests. If this proposal were rejected he was then to offer a tribute of six thousand ducats for the towns of Nauplia and Malvasia, with a further offer of three hundred thousand ducats as a war indemnity. But beyond this he was empowered, though in absolute secrecy on the part of the Council of Ten, with full powers to cede the two towns if necessary, and to make beside every concession required for the attainment of peace. The Turks however refused every offer; and the surprise and wonderment of the Venetian ambassador were great when these refusals were persisted in unflinchingly, and he had no choice but to make greater concessions and deliver up some Dalmatian fortresses into the bargain to attain the desired end. When the news of this transaction was known in Venice public indignation was aroused at the humiliating terms agreed upon, and this indignation, though quieted to some extent by the Council of Ten announcing that Badoer only acted by their instructions, blazed forth with unabated fury when it was known that the reason of these hard terms was the result of treachery, and that the impossibility of dealing with the Turks arose from the fact that they were all the time well aware of the two instructions entrusted to Badoer. It now transpired that Nicolò Cavazzo, secretary to the Ten, and Maffeo Leone, secretary to the Senate, had sold the secrets of their Government to the French court, who in its turn passed them on to the Sultan. This treason in high places could not be tolerated, and stringent measures were adopted to bring the miscreants to justice.

Cavazzo was seized and imprisoned ; but the incidents attendant on the capture of another of the accomplices, a certain Agostino Abondio, were more involved, and have a special interest as demonstrating the state which matters had reached in Venice, and illustrating in a deplorable manner the signs of the times. This Abondio fled to the palace of the French ambassador, then in the Calle di S. Moïsè, for safety, and thither the Council of Ten sent Bernardo Zorzi, one of the Avogadori del Comun, to seize him. Zorzi left his guard in the courtyard, and entering the house declared his office, and expressed a desire to speak to the master of the house. The porter rushed upstairs, shouting and giving the alarm, followed by Zorzi, who endeavoured in vain to silence this noisy herald. Hardly had he ascended a few steps before an armed servant of the ambassador appeared, to whom Zorzi repeated his wish to speak to his master on behalf of the Council of Ten. The man retired, whereupon, as at a given signal, armed men appeared from every corner and rushed at the Avogador. In vain he ordered them back, maintaining he came with no ill intent ; he had to retire and summon the rest of his band, when a free hand-to-hand fight began. The men of the embassy had decidedly the best of it, and Zorzi had no choice but to withdraw and relate to the Doge and the Signory this defiance of order, and appeal to them to uphold the honour and dignity of the State. A larger force was thereupon despatched to S. Moïsè, and the ambassador, after debating whether he should not strangle Abondio to prevent his making revelations compromising to his sovereign, decided to deliver him up to justice. The confessions made by Cavazzo and Abondio led to fresh arrests, and the town was in a state of agitation and anxiety for many months, which was only allayed by the execution of the chief traitors and the exile of the rest.

The treaty signed at Constantinople between Suleiman and the Republic contained many and minute details as to Venetian and Turkish subjects, their trades, the shipping interests of each country, the suppression of corsairs, and so on ; but though it brought in its train a peace of thirty years to Venice, it was severely censured by many as having robbed Venice of some of her fairest territories in the East, as well as of an enormous sum of money. Others again pleaded that it was better so : Venice could not stand the cost and strain involved in outlying possessions, nor could she support the burden of encountering alone a foe of such strength and resources as the Ottoman Turk.

The consternation produced in Venice by the discovery of traitors in the very midst of her administration did not die away with the punishment of the offenders, but led to the introduction of a measure calculated to make the recurrence of such treachery well-nigh impossible. This was the institution of the Inquisitors of State, known also as the Council of Three. The sound of their name suffices to raise visions of a dread, mysterious tribunal seated in chambers, where a feeble light sufficed to reveal secret staircases leading only to the sack and the canal ; or whose drawn curtains only opened to show vistas of a scaffold and an axe; all this and much more have imagination and unfriendly representation woven around the Venetian Inquisition of State. But in reality things were not so. All the authority possessed by the Three emanated solely from the Council of Ten, who ruled and directed them absolutely in everything. Their office was to judge all persons suspected of guilt or treason in matters of state, or who revealed state secrets. They were composed of three nobles, two chosen from the Council of Ten, and one from the Doge's Councillors. The two former, from their dress, were called the "Blacks"; the third was called "the Red," and always sat in council between the other two. All sentences passed by them were published in the Great Council, and together with the heads of the Ten they may be considered as the strongest supporters of public liberty, of the observance of laws, and also as a guarantee for the discipline of the nobles. They were elected for one year, and could be reelected ; and as the habits and morals of the town degenerated, and plots and conspiracies concerning foreign politics increased, their powers also expanded, till no subject was too minute or peculiar for the investigations of the Three, and comprised examinations into state crimes equally with prohibitions to Venetian ladies to go to the theatre unless dressed in a certain fashion and closely masked.

For some time after the institution of the Council of Three the history of Venice proceeded in an uneventful tranquil manner. One Doge succeeded another without furnishing much material for record either in his public or private capacity ; the religious

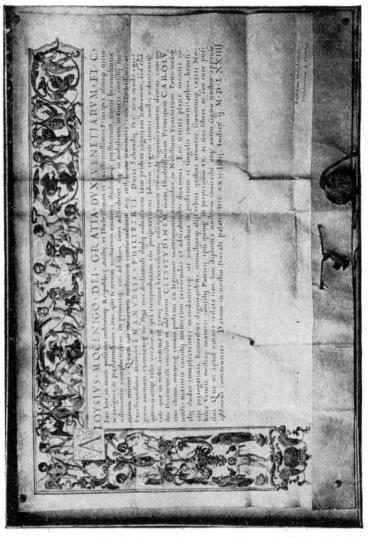

DECREE OF DOGE ALVISE MOCENIGO I., ADMITTING EMANUELE FILIBERTO, DUKE OF SAVOY TO THE
"LIBRO D'ORO" (1570). (*From the original in the possession of the Mocenigo family of S. Stae.*)

controversies agitating and distracting England and
Germany aroused but feeble interest in the heart of
the lagunes; by statecraft and diplomacy the Republic managed to evade becoming involved in the
wars and disputes occupying her neighbours, and not
till 1565 was she disturbed from the calm in which
she had contrived to enwrap herself, and compelled
to take an active share in disputing with the Turks
for the possession of Cyprus.

The ill-feeling that had been growing between
Venice and Constantinople since 1540, had been fed
by constant and petty warfares during which defeats
and successes had proved equally unavailing for the
conclusion of existing differences, or for inducing
either nation to sue for peace. A war waged upon
Venice by the Uscocchi, pirates of Istria, had increased the offences real or imaginary entertained
by the Porte towards the Republic. The Uscocchi
had pillaged with equal indifference the Venetian
and Turkish territories. The Turks ascribed these
depredations to the Venetians, who had thus the
mortification of being identified with the pirates,
and classified as their allies while in reality they
were their deadly foes. It was not till after long
and frequent protestations that Venice was able to
persuade the powers at Constantinople that she
had neither part nor parcel in the doings of these
corsairs; but in spite of all their strivings and
yearnings after peace the Venetians were involved
in war; and once embarked in action they displayed
a courage and heroism worthy of all praise and
admiration.

On the death of Suleiman the Magnificent in 1566, his son, Selim the Drunkard, succeeded to the throne, and though at first his actions seemed friendly, he soon showed himself in his true colours as a deadly foe to the Republic. Rumours of an alarming nature reached Venice: the Sultan was said to be preparing a large fleet; his longing to possess himself of the island of Cyprus, and of its fair vineyards and vintages, which appealed temptingly to his drunken tastes and habits, was no secret among his minions; and it was hinted that he had already apportioned the island, and named one Nassi, a Jew, his satellite and favourite, as the king who should reign there in his name. Notwithstanding the attempts to keep these plans and preparations secret, the Venetian Bailo, Marc' Antonio Barbaro, got knowledge of them, and communicated them to his government without delay. The alarm was given. An armament was got ready and placed under the command of Girolamo Zane, while Giulio Savorgnano was despatched to Cyprus to inspect and put in order the fortifications there. The Turks commenced operations by sending an emissary to Venice to demand nothing less than the surrender of the island. They chose their moment for this exorbitant demand at a time when Venice was in a sorry plight. The year had been a bad one for the harvest, and the town had suffered severely from scarcity of food, followed by much sickness and mortality among the people. A most disastrous fire too had broken out in the Arsenal and wrought wholesale damage and havoc. The flames are said to have been seen even at

Verona, and the smoke and noise and conflagration spread such ruin and dismay, many thought the end of the world was at hand. The cause of the fire was unknown, but it was ascribed to the Turks, who, though probably guiltless of the evil, did not hesitate to profit by it and turn it to their own account. While Venice was suffering under the weight of these misfortunes, and dejected both morally and materially, they prepared a large fleet under the command of Mustafa Pasha, and sent it to besiege Nicosia, the capital of Cyprus. The Republic, on realising the danger of her position, implored the help of her Christian neighbours against the infidel. Beyond some feeble reinforcements from the Pope, and the King of Spain no further assistance was forthcoming, and the rivalry and discord between Colonna, Doria, and Zane, the admirals of the Papal, Spanish, and Venetian forces were so great as to work more woe than weal to the cause which they had undertaken to aid. The Governor of Nicosia was Nicolò Dandolo, a man ill adapted for a position requiring courage, promptness, and skill ; he either ignored or feared to seize the opportunities that might have led his troops to victory, and in spite of some acts of might and valour the town fell after a fierce assault by the Turks, when a horrible carnage and butchery disgraced the arms of the victors. Dandolo was executed and his head cut off, and sent as a warning to Famagosta, whither the Turks now proceeded, and closely invested the town which was held for Venice by Marc' Antonio Bragadin. Bragadin was, however, a man of a widely different stamp to Dandolo, and the heroic way in which he conducted the siege and raised and supported the courage of its inhabitants, together with his cruel fate, has made his name famous. The besieged in Famagosta were but a handful, while the number of their opponents was countless, and after enduring every possible privation, and performing feats of heroism and devotion, helped too by the women and children, the garrison were compelled to capitulate on August 18, 1571. Honourable terms were secured to the gallant little band, but when Bragadin and his captains were led before Mustafa to deliver up the keys of the city, he caused them to be seized regardless of a promise assuring them of their safety, and Querini, Baglione, Martinengo, and Tiepolo, Venetian patricians, who had helped their leader in his brave defence, were hacked in pieces on the spot, while a worse destiny awaited Bragadin. His nose and ears were cut off, and after having been made for eleven days to labour like a beast of burden and carry loads of earth on his back to and from the fortifications that he had so nobly defended, amid the jeers and scoffings of a hooting crowd, he was finally flayed alive, his skin was then stuffed with straw and paraded on the back of a cow under an umbrella (in parody of his office) through the city. After that it was fastened by the Pasha to the prow of his galley, to serve as a trophy wherewith to swell his triumph on his return to Constantinople. Long afterwards it was bought (some say stolen) by his descendants from the Arsenal at Constantinople, where it had remained for many years, and finally deposited in an urn in the

Church of SS Giovanni e Paolo, where it rests to this day over the third altar on the right-hand side of the church.

With the tragic death of Bragadin and the loss of Famagosta, Venetian rule came to an end in Cyprus. The island was henceforward lost to Venice, not so much for want of courage and bravery on her part, as by the indifference of Spain and Rome, who displayed a selfishness and apathy widely inconsistent with the characters which they had assumed of allies and friends.

The Venetian fleet had been unable to come to the rescue of its countrymen at Famagosta, and while the horrors just related were being enacted there the naval force had been swelled by fresh supplies from Spain, and another league had been formed which bade fair to act in earnest, and contribute deeds instead of mere words. This league was composed of Pope Pius V., Philip II. of Spain, and the Republic of Venice ; Don John of Austria, Philip's natural brother, was named commander-in-chief of the expedition, and the announcement of this union of forces and interests was published in Venice on July 2, 1571. The dilatoriness displayed by the League however filled the Venetians with dismay ; they saw the fall of Nicosia and of Famagosta, and the sacrifice of time and lives never to be replaced, while the fleet still tarried for Don John, who arrived only after a delay which cost the Venetian contingent dear. The squadron then proceeded towards Cephalonia to meet the Turkish fleet anchored in the Bay of Lepanto. The Venetians were commanded

IL GENERAL VENETIANO I MARE NELa GRAaNAa VITORIA

NON
NOBIS
NON NO
BIS.

SEBASTIAN VE.
NIERO

INVEN.FIA.TRE.
TARIA PER CESA.
RO VECELIO
DISVERSIT.VELIBROS

PORTRAIT OF SEBASTIANO VENIER.

(*From a woodcut by Cesare Vecellio.*)

by Sebastiano Venier, who keenly urged Don John to attack without delay, and following his advice, on the morning of October 7, 1571, he engaged the enemy, and the famous battle of Lepanto was fought. The Turks were defeated with great loss, their commander-in-chief, Ali Pasha, was slain, and the triumph of the allies was complete. The battle raged for five hours, and most of its success was owing to the prowess and bravery of the Venetians, whose despair may well be imagined when Don John, instead of following up the splendid opportunity thus opened to him to crush and annihilate the Turkish force, made no effort whatever to profit by the occasion. Acting apparently on his own responsibility, but more probably on orders from Madrid, he pursued a cautious, inactive course, which convinced the Republic more than ever of the want of loyalty and affection on the part of Spain towards her. Venice tried to divert the flood of religious zeal bubbling over against Protestants and Huguenots into channels more worthy of such fervour, and pointed out that the wrath and indignation of both Philip and Charles would further more nobly the Christian cause if directed against hordes of Turkish heretics than against loyal Netherlanders and staunch Huguenots. But both monarchs were absorbed in the pursuit of holiness in their own fashion ; they had no desire to make their piety subservient to the ambitions of Venice. She had so far to smile approval on their doings, that when, on the night of August 23, 1572, Charles IX. gave orders for the massacre of St.

Bartholomew, she judged it expedient to simulate approbation, and sent a letter of congratulation to the King, ordering at the same time a solemn procession to parade the town in celebration of the event. But Venice's efforts to obtain aid against the Turk were in vain.

Christendom was too busy to be occupied with the clamours and suggestions of a state unable to keep at bay a foe of extraordinary vigilance and capacity, and the only course open to Venice was to act independently, and study her own interests regardless of allies who had proved themselves hindrances sooner than helps. She was also alive to the fact that the Turks emboldened and strengthened by their successes might easily deprive her of Candia and other possessions, and to avoid such a peril she resolved to conclude a peace with the Sultan. By this treaty, signed on March 7, 1573, the whole of Cyprus was ceded to the Turk ; the fortress of Sopoto, the only conquest which the Venetians had retained in Albania, was also given up ; and during the next three years Venice agreed to pay a tribute of one hundred thousand ducats. Well might Voltaire commenting almost two centuries after on this transaction remark : " It would seem as though the Turk had won at Lepanto." The only gain, if such it can be called, reaped by the Republic by this deed was a cessation from war which enabled her to turn with undivided attention to pleasures, pageants, and revelries in strange contrast to the miseries and horrors so lately experienced. A love of merry-making and display formed a marked characteristic of the Venetian temperament in bygone days ; and an opportunity was given them to exhibit this taste to the full, when in 1574 Henry III. of France escaped from his kingdom of Poland, and to avoid traversing through Protestant countries elected to pass by Venice on his way to claim the French crown vacant by the death of his brother Charles IX. The Republic resolved to greet him with a reception and welcome worthy of his rank and position. He was met at Marghera (the fortress half way between Mestre and Venice) by a concourse of people and senators, these latter in gondolas decked from prow to stern with satin, damask and cloth of gold, and escorted by them to the palace of Bartolommeo Capello at Murano. That island was far different then to what it is now, and those who know its squalid poverty stricken appearance of to-day may with difficulty realise that at the date we are speaking of it was the fashionable suburb of Venice, where the nobles had their villas surrounded by gardens, and where in the midst of beauty, luxury and pleasure, they believed that life was worth living.

In Capello's house, decked with hangings of gold and silver cloth, sixty guardians, dressed in the French colours and all in silk, were appointed to watch over the safety of the king's person, while forty noble youths also in sumptuous attire were told off to wait on him. The monarch seems to have been much struck with the ingenuity of the glass-makers of Murano, who made proof of their skill before him, and all of whom in his delight he ennobled for their prowess ; after that, it being Sunday, he attended mass, and then proceeded

A REGATTA AT VENICE.

(*From Giacomo Franco's " Habiti d'Huomeni et Donne Venetiane," &c*
Venice, 1609.

to Venice where he was lodged in Cà Foscari,[1] and entertained in princely style. The feasts and revelries that took place in honour of this visit have acquired a historical importance as showing the riches and luxury that reigned in Venice at that epoch; and, while poet and painter have depicted the scenes in connection with it in lines and colours familiar to most readers and travellers, the historians of Venice have devoted page upon page to celebrate the sojourn of the French monarch in their city and record the splendours and glories displayed in his honour. Henry III. remained ten days, when he must almost have been wearied by the endless processions of the different guilds and trades, who in turn filed before him illustrating their handicrafts and professions in devices and symbols that reflected credit on their invention and originality. Illuminations, serenades and regattas were in turn set forth before the king; and a platform of boats in front of the palace, draped and hung with beautiful tapestries, and with the arms of France and the Republic intertwined overhead, enabled Henry to witness all the aquatic sports provided for his delectation in ease and comfort. Inside the Foscari palace the hangings in the principal rooms were of leather, gilt, and adorned with decorations and heraldic patterns, and with cloth of gold and silver; the bedrooms were ornamented with a profusion of gold and silk that must have seemed almost oppressive from their gorgeousness; and the two

[1] "Cà" the Venetian for "Casa" (house) is prefixed to a house which takes its name from, and was the habitation of some patrician family, such as Cà Giustinian, Cà Capello, Cà Pisani, and so on.

adjoining Giustinian palaces were also placed at the disposal of the Royal guest and his suite.   King Henry also assisted at one of the national water jousts between the " Nicolotti " and the " Castellani," the two factions between whom the Venetian populace were divided according to whichever side of the Grand Canal they were born.   These fights took place on three or four different bridges, and resembled wrest· ling matches, with the difference that in Venice the pugilists hurled each other off the bridges into the canals below.   The " Ponte dei Pugni " at S. Barnaba was one of the chief centres for this sport, and it was here that Henry III. witnessed the sight, and acted as umpire between the combatants.   The footprints that mark the vantage ground beyond which the wrestlers might not pass, are still to be seen on this and two or three other bridges in Venice.   When these matches were abolished towards the middle of the eighteenth century balustrades were added to the bridges for the security of the passengers.

The King was also feasted in regal pomp at the ducal palace, when a peculiar and perhaps somewhat uncomfortable innovation was practised in that all the knives, forks, napkins and other accessories for the banquet were made of sugar.   Having revelled to the full in all that Venice could put forth to demonstrate how she was indeed " of joy the sojourn, and of wealth the mart," Henry III. proceeded to France to claim his throne ; and the Signory to record his visit erected a slab in the wall of the ducal palace facing the Giant Stairs, where an inscription chronicles the happy event to all posterity.

The following year (1575) an awful pestilence raged through the city. Forty thousand citizens died, among them being the painter Titian, who, at the advanced age of 99, fell a victim to the disease. The plague was appalling in its virulence and intensity, but the courage shown by high and low in the face of death and infection was admirable. The nobles remained at their posts of office, endeavouring to alleviate the evil, and to attend to the affairs of state regardless of the danger continually around them. Many a time those who were present at a morning's sitting at the Great Council were absent in the evening, death having summoned them to a higher tribunal : but though the members of the Council were reduced by hundreds, the rest stayed gallantly on, trying by their example and calmness to restore confidence and courage to the people. Every precaution was taken to prevent the spread of the disease, and when all seemed of no avail, prayers and votive offerings were made in abundance to propitiate Divine wrath and remove the scourge. Alvise Mocenigo, who was then Doge, decreed the erection of a church to the Redeemer of mankind, if only the plague might cease. As shortly after the malady began to abate, Palladio was ordered to build a church on the island of the Giudecca as a thank-offering from a grateful people and state for their deliverance from death and destruction. The Church of the Redentore was begun on May 3, 1577, when Doge Mocenigo laid the first stone, and when it was ordained that a visit should be paid to this church on the third Sunday in every July by the civil and ecclesiastical powers, that date being the one on which the town was pronounced free from the plague. This ceremony was continued for many years with strict ritual and pomp, but has degenerated in these days into a popular fair during which a bridge of boats connects the Giudecca to Venice, and the people hold holiday by night as well as by day.

Doge Mocenigo did not live to see the cessation of the pestilence in his native city; he died in May of that same year, and Sebastiano Venier, the hero of Lepanto was named Doge in his stead. Venier was an old man of eighty when he was raised to the dukedom, and his short reign of little more than a year was clouded by a disastrous fire which destroyed nearly all the ducal palace and so greatly saddened the Doge that it is said to have hastened his end. The fire began in a room adjoining the hall of the Great Council, and a wind blowing from the east unfortunately fanned the flames to such an extent most of the building was destroyed. The thickness and excellence of the walls preserved them however from the fury of the fire though little else remained beyond the shell of the palace when after only two hours' duration the flames were extinguished. The damage done in that short space of time was incredible; and the pictures and documents alone destroyed in the fire involved a loss to art and history quite irreparable. Measures were immediately taken to repair as far as possible a building whose erection had occupied such years, and whose destruction was all but effected in so brief a moment; and under the direction of the architect Antonio da Ponte the work proceeded well and rapidly.

Doge Venier saw but little of the restorations, as he died in 1578. He was followed by Nicolò da Ponte, a man aged eighty-seven, but who in spite of his years made a vigorous stand against Pope Gregory XIII., when that Pontiff wished to assume the right to send a Papal nuncio to inspect the convents and monasteries in Venice and the Veneto, instead of leaving that office as heretofore in the hands of the Venetian Patriarch. The difficulty was only smoothed away by concessions on both sides, the advantage however being more in favour of Rome than of Venice.

In the meantime disturbances were arising among the ruling powers within the town, and the rivalry and emnity that for some time had been smouldering between the Great Council and the Ten now broke out in earnest, and lasted till the fall of the Republic. The Council of Ten had gone on adding to its numbers and increasing its strength in a way far from reassuring to the Great Council. In September, 1529, the *Zonta* or *Giunta* (that body of twenty extra members till then only called in on great emergencies) had become permanent by the addition of fifteen members to the original member of the Council ; and backed by numbers, custom and quiet assertion the so-called " Ten " ruled as absolutely and arbitrarily as though no other Councils existed. But the Great Council had no intention of being shelved, and when in 1582 matters had come to a critical pass, they resolved to show themselves in their old light of

rulers and dictators, and resolved without exciting
tumults or seditions to suppress the *Zonta* and
reduce the Ten to their original numbers and powers.
Certain events happened in this year which gave them
the opportunities they needed, and they did not let
them slip. The first opportunity was this : the Great
Council refused to nominate Andrea da Lezze to
form part of the *Zonta*. Da Lezze however was
rich ; and the Ten, who stood in need of his money,
augmented, unlawfully, the number of the Procurators
who sat in the *Zonta ex officio*, and thus secured the
votes for their candidate. But the Great Council
refused to ratify his election, and the Ten had to
submit. Other annoyances and differences between
the two councils aggravated the condition of affairs,
but the following incident led to the final split. A
party of young nobles armed, and accompanied by
their retainers, went to the Lido, where they fell in
with a party of " Bravi." One of the young nobles
having insulted a woman in the company of the
" Bravi," these latter fell upon the nobles and gave
them a thrashing. Both parties referred the matter to
the Council of Ten, who sided with the " Bravi," and
told the nobles that they had got what they deserved.
And so perhaps they had, but the slight shown to
members of their own class and rank irritated the
Great Council, and they resolved to readjust the state
of things. Old laws and statutes were brought
forward and enforced, and matters were finally
arranged by the suppression of the *Zonta*, though
the ill-feeling between the councils became ever more
intense and emphatic.

It was during the dukedom of Nicolò da Ponte that the story of Bianca Cappello was enacted, a story that reflects but small credit either on the chief actors, or on the Republic of Venice herself. The outlines of the tale are as follows : Bianca Cappello, the daughter of a rich Venetian patrician, fell in love with Pietro Bonaventuri, a Florentine youth engaged in a bank in Venice, and of a rank and standing very inferior to that of Bianca. Her father vehemently opposed the marriage, but Bianca found means to escape from the paternal roof, and fled with her lover to Florence. Here they were married, and Cappello, enraged at his daughter's conduct, renounced her as his child, and by his entreaties induced the Council of Ten to place a reward on the heads of both Bianca and her husband. She on her side appealed for protection to Francesco de' Medici, Grand Duke of Tuscany, and he, fascinated by her beauty and charms, which even her enemies allow she possessed in no common degree, fell hopelessly in love with her, and neglected his wife, Joanna of Austria, in order to devote himself mind, body, and soul to the fair Venetian. He appointed Bonaventuri to some high office about his person, lodged Bianca in a magnificent palace close to his own, and openly paraded his devotion to her in a way that scandalised the whole town. After the lapse of a few months Pietro Bonaventuri was found murdered in the streets of Florence, and it is still matter for doubt whether he fell a victim to the pursuing vengeance of the Council of Ten, or whether the Grand Duke removed him from his path so as better to continue his amours with Bianca, or again whether she herself directed the murderer's blade.

The death of the Grand Duchess occurred soon after and removed all further obstacles for Francesco and Bianca, and but two months after the death of his wife the Grand Duke married Bianca. He then applied to Venice to adopt his bride as the child and daughter of the Republic, and accord to her the honours due to her exalted position, a request to which the Signory acceded with a promptness and eagerness in strange contrast to the treatment which they had accorded to Bianca when she had left her father's house in exile and poverty.

The Grand Duke had no children, and though Bianca, by a series of contrivances and deceits, wicked as well as horrid in their details, had endeavoured to pass off a spurious boy as their offspring, the deception was well known, and Francesco still sighed for an heir to his name and throne. Again Bianca strove to persuade him that his hopes were about to be fulfilled, but before he could be either deluded or enlightened he died at his villa at Poggio a Caiano, and Bianca only survived him a few days. Some accounts ascribe their deaths to natural causes, but others again accuse the Cardinal Ferdinando de' Medici, Francesco's brother, of having poisoned his brother and sister-in-law to possess himself of the succession, and to put an end to the excesses and crimes of Bianca, for whom he had always entertained a violent hatred.

Bianca was denied the right of sepulture among the Medici family; she was buried in the common burial-ground outside S. Lorenzo at Florence ; and at Venice the Signory, thinking it wise to maintain friendly relations with the Cardinal Grand Duke and with Florence, forbade the wearing of mourning on her account. In Florence her name and arms were erased and obliterated from every place where they had been set up, and the silence and oblivion thus invoked over her memory form the most appropriate shroud wherein to envelop one whose beauty was only equalled by her crimes.

A MODERN GONDOLA.

XV.

THE INTERDICT.

(1585–1623.)

DURING the reign of Doge Pasquale Cicogna, who succeeded Nicolò da Ponte in 1585, the town of Venice underwent a series of embellishments and alterations. The damage caused by the fire in Doge Venier's dukedom was repaired, and the ducal palace, restored within and without, was beautified by Tintoretto, Paolo Veronese, the two Palmas, and others, with masterpieces which remain to this day. Another notable feature in Venice, namely, the Rialto bridge, was added at this date, but opinions are divided as to whether this work, consisting of a single span and uniting the two halves of the city, is due to Antonio da Ponte or Giovanni Alvise Boldù. The biography, as it were, of the bridge can be briefly summed up as follows: The first bridge existing at Rialto was built in 1180 of boats; it was removed in 1264, and one on piles was erected; this was renewed in the same way in 1450; and, finally, in 1588, the first stone was laid of the marble construction now familiar to us.

But while these alterations were being effected within the city, Venice was being tormented without by foes of two different kinds, the first of whom, the Uscocchi, gave her no little trouble. The Uscocchi were Slavonian pirates, who had their hiding-places and smugglers' caves on the mountainous coast of Croatia, from whence they infested the Adriatic sea, pillaging every ship which fell into their clutches, and working untold evil to Venetian traffic. Bold, warlike, and barbarous, they proved a cruel and dangerous foe, and Venice was engaged in no less than three severe wars with them—in 1545, in 1593, and again in 1606, before she was rid of them.

A still more troublesome and persistent opponent, however, now came to the fore in the person of Pope Clement VIII., who considered himself injured and slighted in several ways by Venice, and who was only restrained by the caution and prudence of his nature from openly avenging his so-called wrongs. The close proximity of the Pontifical and Venetian territories was one cause of great irritation between the two powers. This neighbourhood had been brought about in 1597, when Alfonso II., Duke of Ferrara, died, leaving his possessions to his nephew, Cesare d'Este. Clement opposed Don Cesare's succession, and he, to make head against the Holy See, applied to Venice for reinforcements and aid. The Republic, foreseeing the danger of admitting so powerful a next-door neighbour as the Pope of Rome in the stead of a more or less feeble duke, was disposed to support this latter; but before matters came to a crisis the Pope had induced Don Cesare to cede all his rights to Ferrara, and content himself with the duchies of Modena and Reggio. He accordingly agreed to do so, and all warlike preparations were suspended.   In 1598 Clement took possession of his new domain, and soon after quarrels and disputes began between him and the Venetians as to their respective rights of fishing and dredging in the Po, the Venetians urging the need of making a canal to remove the accumulation of soil and gravel deposited in the river-bed, the Pope objecting to the work on the ground of injuries to his lands.   Other difficulties were also forthcoming as to the taxation of the clergy for the national defences of their country, the Pope maintaining that they should be exempt from such taxes.   The Venetians argued that since these defences guaranteed to them the safety and protection shared equally by them with the rest of the community, it was but fair that they should contribute towards the expenses ; and the Venetians gained their point.   But Clement was too wary to come to open rupture with the Republic ; and notwithstanding the opposition he encountered and the rebuffs he endured, he managed to keep the peace, and to smother the resentment which he must often have felt towards a state that openly defied him, but with whom he strove to remain on friendly terms.   The cloak of his dislike to the Republic fell on his successor, Paul V. (for Leo XI., who succeeded at Clement's death in 1605, only reigned twenty-six days, and can hardly be counted among the Pontiffs).   During his reign the dissensions and disputes between Rome and Venice reached their height, and culminated in the famous Interdict and in the resistance made to the Curia by the Republic of Venice under the rule and direction of Fra Paolo Sarpi.

As has already been seen, the attitude taken by Venice all through the course of her history with regard to Rome is one peculiar to herself, and of extreme interest from its independence and originality. Venice was religious and Catholic in the wide sense of the words, but the exigencies and welfare of the state, or of interests dependent on it, generally proved paramount when they collided with questions of religion or Catholicism; and the celebrated answer made by the Venetians when, in 1454, they signed a treaty of peace with the Turk and announced : " Siamo Veneziani poi Cristiani," is the keynote to their conduct in ecclesiastical matters throughout most of their history. The indifference shown by Venice to Papal wishes and wrath was first manifested at the moment of the Fourth Crusade ; in 1308, under Doge Gradenigo, she pursued the same policy, and in 1351 she was again wrangling with the successor of St. Peter as to how far the clergy were to profit by " death money " or succession duties, and to these subjects of discord and ill-will others were soon to be added.

Though the Venetian clergy were trained and drilled to grasp that the commands and wishes of the home government were paramount to those of the Holy See, Venice was, broadly speaking, a dutiful daughter of the Church, and it was only when their mutual interests were in direct opposition that she swerved from blind submission and asserted her duty to the state before that to the Pope. At the Council of Trent however her conduct had pleased and conciliated the Pontiff; she had sent thither Nicolò da

Ponte and Matteo Dandolo as her representatives, and when in 1563 the Council closed its long sitting of eighteen years, Venice issued throughout her dominions the Bull drawn up by the Council, and enjoined its observance on her subjects. But matters had not run so smoothly in 1595, when divisions arose over the town of Ceneda, a town in vassalage to the Republic, though governed by a bishop. In 1546 the people and their bishop had rebelled against Venice, who, to punish this insubordination, deprived the bishop of all temp ral power, and sent a Podestà to rule in his place. For several years the bishops endeavoured to regain their forfeited position, and applied to Rome, who espoused their cause against the Republic. The people of Ceneda in the meanwhile appealed to Venice to save them from exactions and taxes levied by the bishop with the approbation and support of the Pope. Excommunications and interdicts were threatened by Rome, which the citizens of Venice and Ceneda resolved to treat with absolute disdain. Things began to wear an ominous aspect when Clement, to avoid as far as possible all cause for offence, consented to waive his claims, and for a while the controversy ceased.

But another difference brought the Curia and the Republic again into collision this same year, when the Pope issued a Bull forbidding all Italians, under pain of excommunication, from travelling in countries inhabited by " heretics," unless they had first obtained a license from the local inquisitors. This edict was one particularly noxious to Venetians, whose trade with England, Germany, Switzerland, and Holland took them perforce into lands which had shaken off the Papal yoke. The difficulty was one that had to be met and grappled with, and the Signory decided that the best way to do so was to issue an order to the Holy Inquisition in Venice to reject and ignore all denouncements made on this head, whether coming from Rome or from foreign countries.

Another bull published soon after was destined to meet with equal failure and disregard. Clement decreed that all books with a heretical tendency, and whose publication was prohibited in other places, should equally be prohibited in Venice. But the advantages of printing and selling were of prior consideration to the mandates promulgated by the Head of the Church, and Clement had to content himself with seeing the matter settled in the following year according to the terms and agreements dictated by Venice. He had also to accept, though he did so under protest, the forbearance shown by the Republic to the English Ambassador, Sir Henry Wotton, who not only was allowed to reside in Venice, but also to celebrate the rites and services of his own church within the walls of his embassy.

A fresh source of annoyance was also forthcoming in regard of the Uscocchi, who were now working great damage to both Turks and Venetians, and who were protected by Austria. The Pope who was desirous to form a league against the Porte, which was to consist of Austria, Poland, and Venice, sent subsidies of arms and money to the Uscocchi to enable them to continue their molestations upon the Turks. This succour sent by Clement to their foes caused much vexation to the Venetians. They expressed to the Holy Father how the support he granted to their enemies was prejudicial to their cause; and when the Pope announced his scheme for the league against Constantinople, they promptly and decisively rejected the idea, and utterly declined to interrupt the friendly relationship existing between them and the Porte. They were moreover unwilling to embark in a war, wherein—as former experience had taught them—they were but too likely to be left to engage alone against a foe mightier and stronger than themselves.

It can hardly be matter for surprise that, when the cautious conciliating policy of Clement VIII. had given way to the overbearing, ambitious rule of Paul V., the enmity and distrust between the two states broke into open strife and contention, and that the reprisals between them waxed ever keener and sharper. Camillo Borghese, who became Pope in 1605 under the name of Paul V., was of a character different in every way to that of his predecessor, Clement VIII. While the one was wary and cautious the other was fiery and irascible; and whereas Clement would cede in order afterwards to recover what his leniency had accorded, Paul would snatch at any rights which he considered owing to the Papacy, and eagerly avenge slights which he conceived had been offered to his office. The behaviour of Venice had displeased him for some time past, and while still a cardinal he smarted under the disregard and disrespect shown by the water-city to the Mistress of the World. A story goes that he one day remarked

A DOGE OF VENICE.

(*From Giacomo Franco's " Habiti d'Huomeni e Donne Venetiane," &c.
Venice,* 1609.)

to Leonardo Donato, then ambassador at Rome from Venice, that were he Pope he would place the city under an interdict. "And were I Doge," was Donato's quick retort, "I would treat your interdict with scorn and contempt." Both eventualities came about, and both men kept their word.

Paul V. was determined when he became Pope to bring Venice into a state of respect and humiliation to Papal orders and decrees ; but there was opposed to him a man who for keenness of intellect, and for wisdom, knowledge, and goodness, withstood him with so steadfast a will, and so marked an individuality, that he carried the whole of Venice with him, and set her for awhile again to the front, with power to hold her own against Roman statecraft and wiliness. This man was Fra Paolo Sarpi, a Servite monk, and withal one of the first scholars of the day, a mathematician, linguist, astronomer, and anatomist, as well as a theologian and a statesman in the highest, best sense of both words. His knowledge of anatomy and medical science was so great that many ascribe to him the discovery of the circulation of the blood and the valvular action of the veins ; his understanding on all astronomical matters was such that Galileo looked upon him as his master, and called him "Padre and Maestro"; while he was besides "the great political leader, whose unflagging energy and unbending courage piloted his native country through one of the stormiest and most dangerous epochs of its existence."[1]

[1] Adolphus Trollope, "Paul the Pope and Paul the Friar," London, 1870, ch. iv. p. 95.

An occasion was not wanting to bring the two men into contact, and enable the Pope to put forth his weapons of wrath and vengeance against Venice. Sarpi all the while defended her with an energy and intellect so courageous and so keen as to gain from his adversaries the surname of " the terrible friar." The first outburst of Papal indignation was occasioned by the appointment of a new Patriarch in Venice. On the death of Matteo Zane, who held that office, the Senate had named Francesco Vendramin as his successor, and applied to Paul V. to confirm his nomination. The Pope insisted that in compliance with a Bull drawn up by Clement VIII. the new Patriarch should proceed to Rome to be examined by him as to his fitness for the post. The Venetians considered such a statute as directly opposing the laws of the Republic, and the Senate refused to allow their Patriarch to present himself in Rome for any purpose than that of tending to the Pope the homage and reverence due to him as head of the Church. These differences, following on the discussions and wranglings which had occupied so much of Clement's reign, in no way smoothed the mind of Paul towards Venice ; but the crowning point of offence was reached when the Republic refused to deliver up two Venetian priests guilty of most foul and heinous crimes to the Roman tribunal, and elected instead to judge them before the Council of Ten. Before this offence had reached a climax some courtesies however passed between the disputants, and to the Pope's satisfaction (at least so say the Venetian chroniclers) the Borghese family were inscribed among the patricians of Venice.

This favour had also been demanded by Henry IV.
of Navarre, and the entire body of the Great Council
to the number of sixteen hundred declared unanimously that his name and family should be entered
in the *Libro d'Oro.* Other courtesies had also
passed between the French monarch and the
Venetians. They had been among the first to
recognise his claim to the crown of France, and
had stood by him with gifts of money and recognition of his royal rights when the other sovereigns
of Europe refused to acknowledge him as king.
For such help and loyalty Henry was not un-
grateful, and he was not slow to manifest this
gratitude when in later times the Republic stood
in need of his good offices to arbitrate between
herself and Rome.

In the meantime Paul V. endeavoured to force
from Venice the debt of respect and allegiance considered by him as owing to the Holy See ; a debt
Venice was in nowise minded to acknowledge or to
pay. The question of the two ecclesiastics, Scipione
Saraceni, Canon of Vicenza, and the Abate Marcantonio Brandolin of Narvesa, alluded to above, was
the point whereon the Pope resolved to take his
stand, and as in the same matter Venice was equally
determined not to yield, the resolution displayed on
both sides could not fail to bring about a collision.
The Pope had other causes beside for complaint. In
1603 a law had been passed in Venice forbidding the
erection of either new churches or monasteries without the permission of the Government. And two
years after this another edict had forbidden alike

donations and legacies of money or property to any religious institutions. These combined grievances were more than Paul could endure ; he complained to Agostino Nani, the Venetian ambassador at Rome, and demanded that the prisoners should be handed over to him, and that the decrees should be revoked. Nani replied that the Republic could not relinquish the right of judging the delinquents, a right possessed by all princes, and one that Venice, with the sanction of former Pontiffs, had exercised from time immemorial ; that the offences committed by the priests being of a temporal not spiritual nature, the sending them for judgment to Rome would be a renunciation of their sovereign rights, to which the Senate would never agree. As to the law relating to churches and monasteries there were already more than two hundred of such edifices in Venice ; they occupied half the town, and were in excess of the number required for either worship or worshippers. And lastly as to the legacies and bequests to the Church, this statute was neither new nor unusual ; a similar decree had been passed in 1357, and renewed since then in 1459, and again in 1515, in 1536, and in 1561. The law was founded on the right possessed by every state to provide for the well-being of its subjects ; it existed among other nations, and Clement VIII. had himself made use of such a law, when he had forbidden the Church of Loreto to receive fresh donations and gifts.

But none of these arguments satisfied the Pope, whose indignation against Venice was fanned in the Consistory by the enemies of the Republic, especially the Spanish faction who considered the liberality shown by Venice to people of other creeds and opinions an offence against religion, and a painful contrast to the bigotry and fanaticism advocated and practised in Spain. Paul accordingly issued two briefs, one demanding the handing over to him of the culprits, the other the revocation of the two laws. These briefs reached Venice on the night of December 25th, 1605, but as the Doge, Marin Grimani, was then on his death-bed, they could not be opened in the Great Council, where the presence of the Head of the Republic was necessary for such an act. Doge Grimani died on December 26th, and no time was lost in appointing as his successor Leonardo Donato, the man who had threatened Camillo Borghese with firm resistance should the occasion require it, and who, having served on no less than seven embassies at the court of Rome, was well qualified to direct the affairs of state in so complicated and difficult a moment. No time was now lost in opening the two briefs, and great was the general surprise when they were found to be identical; a mistake having occurred in despatching the original and its duplicate instead of a single copy of each. Before proceeding further however the Senate resolved to appoint Paolo Sarpi, theologian of the Republic, to assist them by his advice and knowledge in a matter which they clearly foresaw was one of extreme gravity and import. And so indeed it proved; for the Signory refused to heed a threat made by the Pope sentencing them to be placed under an interdict if within fifteen days they had not subscribed to his wishes ; and he had no option but to put his threat into execution. Accordingly on April 17, 1606, the sentence was promulgated. Venice and all her territories were declared excommunicate ; the Venetian ambassadors were dismissed from Rome, and notices of the sentence were sent abroad the same day throughout all Italy. When the fact was known in Venice the behaviour of the Senate was dignified and spirited to a degree: an order was published forbidding the opening of any bull, brief, or other document from Rome, and directing all such to be instantly handed to the Senate ; a vigilant watch was to be kept to prevent any such document being appended in any place, and should it be found it was straightway to be torn down under pain of the Signory's extreme displeasure. The Doge in a bold speech told the Papal Nuncio that not only he, but all the nobility and people of the land were unanimous in their action ; that the excommunication counted for nothing, and would meet with no consideration from them. The Nuncio was given to understand that his presence in Venice was no longer needed, after which a decree was issued to all the clergy in the Venetian domain, informing them of the publication of this sentence against the Doge and the Republic, and "that as the welfare of the state must be considered, and the Doge recognised no superior in things temporal after God, the sentence was declared invalid, and every ecclesiastic was enjoined to continue as heretofore his cure of souls. The state declared its firm determination to remain

in the Holy Catholic and Apostolic Faith, and in the
observance of the Holy Roman Church, praying God
Almighty to inspire His Holiness to recognise the
uselessness of his brief, his ill-doing against the
Republic, and the justice of that Republic's cause."
And this decree the Nuncio had the mortification to
see affixed to his door ere he departed. The next
step was the expulsion of the Jesuits, who refused to
obey the mandate just published and for the same
reason the Theatines and Capuchins were also
expelled shortly after, while decrees were issued
announcing the same fate to all who ran counter
to the orders of the Government. These orders were
strictly enforced as the following examples will
show. The Podestà of Padua informed the Vicar-
General there of the mandate passed by the Senate,
and the need of obedience. " I shall proceed," said
the Vicar, "as the Holy Spirit inspires me." "The
Holy Spirit," replied the Podestà, "has already
inspired the Council of Ten to hang all refractory
subjects." Another case was that of a priest in
Venice, who dared conform to the interdict, and
closed his church. The following morning he found
a gallows erected in front of his church. He took
the hint and resumed his services.

The conduct of Venice had attracted the interest
and attention of all Europe. Opinions and ideas had
changed since the days when the thunders of Rome
had thrilled all Christendom with their weight, and
when kings and emperors had trembled before the
anathemas from the papal chair. The strife was one
of keen and universal interest, for on its issue would

depend the release from the superstitions paid to a power, whose abuse of its authority had led things to the present climax, or the relapse into fetters and shackles unworthy of the civilisation now scattering the light of liberty and knowledge in its ever-advancing march. The greater part of Europe was in sympathy with the Republic : the Netherlands offered their help ; a league was proposed by the English ambassador, in which England, France, the Grisons, and some German princes would support Venice ; and France and Spain offered their services as mediators. From Spain little could be expected beyond words ; and France was looked upon as the peace-maker most acceptable to the Republic, and whose good offices could most be trusted by both parties. Rome eagerly desired a peace-maker. A year had now elapsed since the interdict had been pronounced, and in Venice no change was felt or perceived : the services of the Church were regularly and punctiliously performed ; no rites or ceremonies that religion required or enjoined were omitted ; and no sign was made by the people or their rulers to sue for the withdrawal of a sentence effete and disregarded. But in Rome things wore a different aspect. The Pope was sorely distressed at the failure of his anathema. The effort made by him to raise the dignity and position of the Holy See had met with signal defeat. One of the most powerful weapons wielded by his predecessors had shivered in his hand, and must henceforth be laid aside for ever as useless. To a man of Paul's temperament the revelation must have been a cruel one. His zeal for his office, however bigoted and narrow, was sincere and ardent, and it is no matter for surprise that the unconcern shown by Venice to his sentence weighed like a load on his spirit and crushed him to the ground with anguish and distress. He felt some steps must be taken to recover his lost dignity, and accepted the offices of Henry IV. of France to negotiate between him and the Venetians, empowering the French ambassador to submit to them the following proposals : An application was to be made to his Holiness through the French ambassador to remove the sentence of excommunication; the two ecclesiastics arrested by the Government were to be delivered up, not to the Pope, but to the king, and solely out of consideration for his Majesty ; the interdict should be continued for four or five days, when on a given day the Pope should remove it, while the Venetians should likewise revoke their edict against it ; the religious orders expelled from Venice for conforming to the interdict should be recalled ; and the laws against further church building and against endowments should be suspended till the previous stipulations should be carried out. But the Venetians only agreed to one of these conditions; they consented to hand over the offending priests to the King of France, but on no account would they listen to the other suggestions. The Pope was bitterly mortified at the rejection of his offers, and the negotiations became only more involved and intricate, till war seemed the only solution of the difficulty. Venice thereupon clung but more closely to France, whom she rightly considered her best ally ; and affairs only took a more pacific turn when Henry IV. despatched

Cardinal de Joyeuse, armed with full powers from himself to Rome to treat between the Pope and the Republic. The negotiation was one requiring great tact and diplomacy, and Du Fresne Canaye, the French ambassador, and Cardinal de Joyeuse had no light task to bring it to a peaceful conclusion, and preserve at the same time the appearances so eagerly adhered to by both sides and the dignity whi<h neither would abrogate. The Pope insisted that Venice should demand the removal of the sentence ; Venice flatly refused, and the only concession to be obtained from her was the addition of her name to those of his most Christian Majesty and of the most Catholic King, when these royal petitioners entreated for the cessation of the censures. Neither was their acquiescence as to the delinquents tendered in a way likely to propitiate Papal susceptibilities ; they agreed to deliver them up to the French ambassador on the clear understanding that they did so solely out of regard for King Henry IV. ; and as this question of the prisoners had been the chief cause of offence they were extremely punctilious to establish that the concession made out of respect and courtesy to the King of France was not to be confounded with a submission to the Curia, to whom they in nowise intended to yield. The culprits were accordingly handed over to the French representatives " out of respect to his most Christian Majesty," says the secretary of the Council of Ten, who gives a minute account of this transfer of the prisoners, " and without prejudice to the authority held by the state to judge ecclesiastics. Whereupon the ambassador replied, ' And as such I

receive them.'" After this the cardinal repaired to the Senate, where the assembled members received him sitting and with their hats on. He proclaimed the removal of the interdict, offering at the same time his congratulations on so auspicious an event. The Doge handed him the revocation of the edict, and accepted courteously the announcement which he had made, but all rejoicings were forbidden as uncalled for and inappropriate, and both the Doge and the Signory were conspicuous by their absence at the High Mass held by the cardinal to testify to the cessation of pontifical indignation. And thus the great controversy was over ; the interdict was withdrawn, and Venice might well be proud of the victory she had gained. For a great moral victory it undoubtedly was ; Venice had held her ground firmly and triumphantly, and made a gallant stand for what she considered her rights and *privileges* against Rome. She had gained her point in regard of maintaining the laws which she had passed as to Church property ; she had declined to plead for the removal of an interdict which she had never acknowledged ; she refused to readmit the Jesuits who had been disobedient to her and faithful to Rome,[1] and though she had given up the two criminals it was to her friend and ally the King of France not to the Head of the Church, thus upholding her dignity as well as her right to try her own delinquents, whether clerics or laymen.

The hand that had guided the helm through these troubled waters, and directed the Venetian Govern-

---

[1] The Theatines and Capuchins were allowed to return, but the Jesuits did not come back to Venice till 1657.

ment so wisely and safely at this critical juncture,
was that of Fra Paolo Sarpi, and consequently the
feeling aroused against him in Rome can be well
imagined. His learning in all matters, whether lay
or ecclesiastical, was so profound and so reliable ; his
mode of life and thought and conduct so upright,
pure, and irreproachable, that he could not fail to
raise a host both of friends and foes, while the respect
and love he created in Venice was only equalled
by the hate and distrust, not to say fear, that he
inspired in Rome. It was well known there how he
was at the root of the opposition so successfully
waged by Venice, and for such opposition and success
Rome was determined to be avenged. Affairs had
by no means settled down peaceably on the removal
of the interdict ; Venice was too lenient, too large-
minded in regard of other worships and dogmas to
suit the narrow behests of Rome. A rebuke was
administered as to the liberty of action allowed to
the English ambassador, Sir Henry Wotton, who
received packages containing heretical books, and
the Republic paid no heed ! To this accusation the
Doge plainly told the Nuncio that it was not their
affair to pry into the boxes and secret things of the
English ambassador, that they were aware of these
cases of books, but they knew too that the ambassador lived a retired quiet life, giving no occasion
for scandal or annoyance, and assured his reverend
listener that " in matters of religion we do not live
with our eyes shut." Other grievances were brought
forward, and again the Pope insisted on the Patriarch
going to Rome for examination before being appointed

CHURCH OF STA. FOSCA.
(From " Calli e Canali," op. cit.)

to his office. To conclude the affair the Signory finally consented to this, though stipulating that it should take place this once but never again, and Paul V. agreed, though he had his small revenge in nominating a Jesuit as the Patriarch's examiner.

But a more serious form of vengeance was brewing against Fra Paolo, whom his enemies in Rome had tried in vain to lure to the Eternal City, and whom they tried to seize either living or dead. On the evening of October 25, 1607, when returning to his convent, accompanied only by one of the brothers, Fra Marino, and an old patrician, Alessandro Malipiero, while crossing the bridge of Sta. Fosca, he was set upon by three assassins, and stabbed in three places. Two wounds were in the neck, but the third, which proved the most dangerous, passed by the right ear, through the cheekbone, and out by the nose. The dagger was left in the wound, for the murderers fled on the alarm being given by some women who saw the attack from their windows. Fra Paolo fell as though dead on the bridge, but Malipiero, who extracted the dagger, saw that life was not extinct, and had him conveyed to the convent. The indignation and excitement caused throughout the town when the news was known was intense; crowds thronged the convent to hear how the beloved Frate fared; the Council of Ten immediately took upon themselves the expenses of his cure, and no pains were spared to discover the assassins. These however found safety in the house of the Papal Nuncio at S. Francesco della Vigna, from whence they afterwards escaped by sea to the papal territory, where the protection extended to them against Venetian law and revenge left no doubt as to the authors and originators of the plot. Fra Paolo himself, on seeing the "stiletto" which had so nearly proved fatal to him, said jokingly that he recognised the "Roman style," but all idea of vengeance was far from his thoughts, and he opposed most strenuously the wishes of the state to inquire more fully into the matter. On his recovery the Senate insisted on his being accompanied by an escort to guard so valued a life from further attacks, and much as this precaution distressed Fra Paolo the need of it was but too evident, as a fresh attempt upon his life in 1609, and again the year after, showed how desperate his foes were, and how eagerly they sought to compass the death of a man whose loss to his native town they knew would be irreparable. Extra vigilance however was instituted to watch over the safety of their beloved theologian, though the life now led by Fra Paolo was much secluded, and was spent absorbed in his studies and devotions, employed up to the last in the guidance and enlightenment of the Republic which he loved so truly and devotedly. He died on January 14, 1623, his last words expressing thoughtfulness for those around him, bidding them go to rest, since he was "returning to God, whence we all proceed," and then with all the brothers of his convent kneeling, weeping, and praying around him, he joined in a low voice in their prayers, and on the brink of eternity his thoughts again dwelt on his beloved Venice, and with the words, "May she endure" (*esto perpetua*), he passed away. In him Venice lost one of the best and greatest of her sons ; great in the possession of an intellect and mind exceptionally clear and gifted ; great in the use he made of his varied talents ; and great in the unselfish, absorbing, truly patriotic love which he bore to his native city, for whose welfare and advancement no sacrifice was too costly, no effort too arduous. Venice might well be proud of " Il terribile Frate," though all her desires to do him honour after death and erect a monument to his memory were again and again frustrated by opposition from Rome, and his tomb at S. Michele records only that his bones rest there after they were removed from the demolished Church of the Servites. This opposition has however been overcome at last, and but a short while ago (November, 1892) a statue in front of the Church of Sta. Fosca has been erected to Fra Paolo Sarpi ; a record of one of the most enlightened men of any age, and one who freed the civilised world from the superstitions and trammels of a tyrannical and prejudiced power.

A VENETIAN GALLEY.
(*From Medina's " Arte del Naveger."*)

XVI.

WAR AGAINST THE USCOCCHI.

(1610–1631.)

THE external relations in Europe immediately
affecting Venice underwent a great change in 1610
by the murder of Henry IV. of France, whose friendship for the Republic had acted to such purpose as
a bulwark against the enmity of Pope Paul V., as
well as against the jealousy of Spain. Henry's death
also involved more than his own personal loss, for
the entire policy of his kingdom was now altered,
and during the regency of Marie de Medicis, as well
as during the reign of her son Louis XIII., France,
Austria, and Spain were in close alliance ; and the
marriage of the young king with an Austrian
princess, and of his sister with the Infant Philip,
cemented this alliance only more firmly. This
change of policy and feeling on the part of France
was of important advantage to Spain and Austria,
and strengthened by it this latter became more
unfriendly and inimical to Venice in regard of the
Uscocchi, and supported these pirates more deter-
minately than heretofore in their depredations against
Venice and against Turkey. The horrors and bar-
barities practised by these corsairs, and the damage

wrought to Venetian trade, raised against them the anger and indignation of all the inhabitants of the lagunes. This fury reached its height when, in 1613, a Venetian force sent against them under the command of Cristoforo Venier, was surprised by the pirates, the men all put to death in cold blood, and the commander beheaded, his heart torn fron his body and devoured by his victors, who finished the fell repast by dipping their food in his blood. But Venice at that moment could make no active reprisals; she was alarmed at the prospect of a war with Spain, and Austria protected the Uscocchi, against whom Venice dragged on a weary war, during which she assaulted Gradisca in Friuli then held by the Austrians. The treaty, known as that of Madrid, though actually signed in Paris in 1617, overthrew the power and piracy of the Uscocchi, and concluded a war which had occupied the Venetians for almost a century, and had cost them twenty millions of gold. The gallant stand which they had made against these barbarians and buccaneers showed however that the old spirit of independence and valour still ran in their veins, and proved them worthy of their ancestors.

Their hostilities with the house of Austria had suggested to the Venetians the advisability of allying themselves with a power who could furnish them with men and money in the case of need, and on whom they could rely should their Austrian foe prove too strong for their somewhat limited resources. In 1617 they consequently entered into a league with Holland, and four thousand Dutchmen landed on the Piazzetta under the command of

Count John of Nassau. The sight of these new allies
in their very midst seems however to have inspired
the Venetians with more dread than confidence.
The fear arose lest these new friends might wish to
possess themselves of the city, and without loss of
time the Senate hurried them on to Friuli to aid in
the siege of Gradisca ; an undertaking however terminated this year by the treaty of Madrid, when the
differences between Venice and Austria were smoothed
over for the moment.

The following year (1618) the Spanish conspiracy
occupied the attention of Venice, and increased the
dislike and distrust that for so many years had been
growing between the two peninsulas. The accusations and exculpations that abound with regard to this
conspiracy cannot fail to arouse suspicions as to
what can be called truth in relation of it, and creates
a longing to pierce the mystery enveloping a plot
which affords more play for historical controversy
than for elucidation of facts. The hatred on the side
of Spain, had of late been increased by the part
taken by the Republic in assisting the Duke of
Mantua to maintain his rights to Montferrat, and in
preventing its possession by the Spaniards ; and
though the Court of Madrid took no active measures
for vengeance, three of the most powerful Spaniards
in Italy were bent on doing so. These men were
the Duke of Ossuna, Viceroy of Naples ; the Duke
of Toledo, Governor of Milan ; and the Marquis of
Bedmar, Spanish ambassador in Venice. The chief
agent employed by them was one Jacques Pierre of
Normandy, a famous corsair, of a bold, daring spirit,

MILKSELLERS.

(*From " Le Arti che vanno per via nella Città di Venezia."*

always absorbed in plotting and scheming. This
man's life had been spent in one adventure after
another; he had taken part in designs against the
Porte, Spain, Austria, and Venice alternately, and
had seen much service under the Duke of Ossuna,
from whom however he had parted in disgust. He
then sought employ under the Republic, together
with another Frenchman of the name of Régnault,
and though at first they were looked on with diffi-
dence, **they** succeeded in being appointed to subordinate positions in the navy (the only ones accorded to
foreigners) with a stipend of forty ducats a month.
To ingratiate himself with the Government, Pierre
pretended that he was possessed of some secret
designs planned by the Duke of Ossuna against the
city, which he would communicate to the Senate ; but
when his offers met with no attention, he addressed
himself again to the Duke, and laid before him a plan
for possessing himself of Venice. He assured him
that the city, having no means of defence, would fall
an easy prey, and only claimed for himself the booty
when the town was taken. The Viceroy entered
fully into the plan ; ambition, fanned by the idea or
the reality of unrequited services in his own land, is
supposed to have been at the root of his actions, and
he sent Pierre supplies of money wherewith to gain
over the Dutch troops still quartered near the city,
and to seduce other mercenaries. The Marquis of
Bedmar was also privy to the plot, though veiling
his share in it with an astuteness and craftiness that
did him credit, and even the French ambassador, Léon
de Bruslast, connived at the affair. Pierre encouraged

and supported in so material a way matured still further his designs, and suggested to Ossuna to sail from Naples with the fleet, which for some time had been preparing there, land unexpectedly in Venice, set fire to the Arsenal, the Mint, and the ducal palace, massacre the nobles, take possession of all the exits and entrances of the city in the name of Spain, and sweep Venice away as a power for ever.

But Ossuna did not act with the promptness and rapidity urged on him by Pierre ; whether he doubted the possibility of the Frenchman's scheme, or suspected him of exaggerating the facility of his design, is not known. The matter dragged on and on, and suspicions began to awaken in Venice. Pierre and his two principal associates and accomplices, Régnault and Langdale, were absent on their naval duties, when two other Frenchmen, Balthassar Juven, a near relation of the Maréchal de Lesdiguières, and one Montcassin, revealed the conspiracy to the Doge and to the Council of Ten. The announcement of such active hate and treachery on the part of Ossuna and Bedmar caused dismay and consternation to the Government, but they lost no time in dealing swiftly with the danger ; and without perhaps investigating as closely as they might have done into the matter, took prompt measures for vengeance. Jacques Pierre and Langdale were ordered to be executed instantly on the vessels whereon they were embarked, time not being even granted them first for confession ; Régnault and several others, who were known to be in the confidence of the Viceroy, were strangled in their prisons, and their bodies, suspended by one leg

on a gallows between the two columns, marked that
they died the death of traitors ; while others again
who were judged innocent were set free. When the
news became know that Spaniards were at the root
of the evil, popular indignation and fury knew no
bounds ; Bedmar's life was in peril from the rage
of the crowd, and he had to be protected by the
Government till he could withdraw in safety from
Venice, whither he never returned, deeming it more
prudent to accept another embassy in Flanders.
The French ambassador too found it well to consider the moment a fitting one wherein to pay his
devotions at the shrine of Loreto, and leave Venice
till things had returned to their normal state of quiet.

And so ended the Spanish conspiracy of 1618,
over which the Council of Ten saw fit to utter no
revelations, and this silence on their part has been
ascribed either to a sense of having acted in too
hasty and ill-judged a manner, or from a desire to
cover a scandal whose publication could but embitter
still further the animosity between their state and
Spain. The conspiracy, though at an end, left one
fatal consequence behind it in the shape of suspicion, distrust, and doubt as to who was in league
with Spain, and how far the taint of her gold had
corrupted the hearts of Venetian citizens. And these
fears were not altogether unfounded. Spanish gold
had found its way into the hands of many a noble
of Venice, and a lower tone of morals and principles
had laid a foundation for bribery and corruption, that
reflected but little credit on those who gave or those
who took. Public offices were made accessible to

those unfitted to hold them through gifts of Spanish money, gifts to be repaid by the disclosure of secrets never intended for Spanish ears. That that was the case was proved by a conspiracy which came to light in 1620. A certain Giambattista Bragadin had procured through Spanish means the number of votes required to admit him as member of the Great Council. Bragadin had been recommended alternately to the Marquis of Bedmar, and to Luis Bravo, Bedmar's successor, as a man entirely devoted to the cause of Spain, thoroughly trustworthy, and well up in all the sayings and doings of the Venetian councils. The manner he selected for transmitting his information was this : he was observed to attend frequently the Church of the Frari, where it was noticed he was particular in always paying his devotions at one special faldstool. It was also noticed that when he withdrew, the secretary of the Spanish ambassador would enter the church and always kneel in seeming reverence at the faldstool just vacated by Bragadin. The curiosity of one of the monks in the church was aroused ; he went to investigate the cause of this fervour, and found a document placed in a corner of the stool. He carried it to the Doge, who laid it before the Council of the Pregadi, and Bragadin was arrested. He made no attempt to excuse or exonerate himself, but pleaded guilty, and was hung between the two columns. On the affair being made public, the Spanish ambassador retired from Venice, and some time elapsed before his vacant post was refilled.

Venetian justice was not, however, always infallible,

and a terrible example of erring judgment on the part of the Council of Ten is recorded in the story of Antonio Foscarini, unjustly accused and executed in 1622. Foscarini had been ambassador from the Republic both in France and in England, and in both countries had fulfilled his duties with honour and credit. In England he had gained the esteem of James I. and of his queen ; but while at this court a suspicion had arisen as to the fidelity of his secretary, one Scaramelli, who was dismissed, and a certain Giulio Muscornò sent in his place. At first Foscarini was well pleased with him ; he was clever, attractive, good-looking ; but besides that he was treacherous, crafty, and revengeful. He ingratiated himself with the queen and the ladies of her court, being a " cunning musician," and evidently an amusing mimic and story-teller. His head became turned with his successes, he grew careless as to the duties of his post, and on one occasion, Foscarini having refused to grant him a favour, Muscorno swore that he would be revenged, and would never rest till he had worked him abiding woe. For this intent he left England and repaired to Venice, where he laid the foulest accusations against Foscarini before the Council of Ten, declaring that his behaviour in England was a disgrace to their state, that his life was licentious and irregular, his way of speaking to the queen insulting and ungentlemanlike, and though these libels were not borne out by the investigations made by the Ten, they ordered Foscarini to be recalled to Venice, and placed on trial. For three years this trial lasted, when a series of the most contradictory reports were issued and received, but finally sufficient evidence was forthcoming to prove Foscarini's innocence, he was set at liberty, and his calumniator Muscorno was sentenced to two years' imprisonment in the fortress of Palma.

The former ambassador was for a while treated with honour ; he was named " Savio di Terraferma,"[1] after that senator, and was also employed to treat with foreign ministers, and granted full confidence by his own Government. But some unseen agency was at work to compass his destruction, and though Muscorno's name never transpires, there is little doubt that his evil influence helped toward his late master's downfall. While in England Foscarini had made the acquaintance of Alethea Talbot, wife of Thomas Howard, Earl of Arundel and Surrey. This lady was now living in Venice for the education of her sons, and Foscarini went to visit at her house, where he met, among other guests, the secretary of the Spanish Embassy. This fact was enough to create an accusation. Girolamo Vano, a paid spy in the employment of the Government, was set to watch Foscarini's doings, and reported that he frequented the Countess of Arundel's house for the purpose of conferring with the Spanish secretary, that he was often masked when going to the house, and that his whole demeanour suggested deceit and secrecy. Foscarini was accordingly seized one evening when leaving the Senate, imprisoned by order of the Council of Ten, accused by them of holding intercourse with foreign ministers, of resorting to the

[1] An officer who attended to the affairs of peace and of war on the mainland territory of the Republic.

houses of foreigners in disguise, and of betraying the secrets of the Republic in return for money. In vain Foscarini pleaded his innocence ; he was condemned to be strangled in his prison, a fate that he endured with calmness and courage, having first demanded leave to draw up his will. The sentence was then executed ; and his mangled body was hung up next morning by one leg between the columns, to the rage and horror of the Venetian nobles.

The part taken by the Countess of Arundel when she heard of Foscarini's untimely end, and the accusations thrown upon the visits paid to her house, show her to have been an active stirring lady. Fearing evidently that malicious tongues might put a more spiteful interpretation on the poor ex-ambassador's visits than the one it already wore, she lost no time in hastening to Sir Henry Wotton, and insisting (a good deal against that worthy's inclinations) on his accompanying her without delay to the ducal palace. Here he was to act as her interpreter and justifier, and extract instantly from the Doge and his Council a written declaration for her to transmit straight to England to exonerate her fair name from the gossip and rumours too likely, she feared, to be circulated by ill-natured tongues concerning her and the strangled Foscarini. By dint of forcing Sir Henry to interpret her reasons and explain her scruples the Countess of Arundel gained her object, and obtained an ample form of exoneration over conduct which perhaps would never have been called in question. Both her husband and King James seem thoroughly to have appreciated the courtesy shown to their wife and cousin on the occasion. A letter

signed by the King and dated from Greenwich, June
10, 1622, thanks the "Serenissimo Principe, amico
carissimo" for the "equity and favour shown to our
dearest kinswoman, the Countess of Arundel and
Surrey."

The malignity that had brought Foscarini to a fate
against which no appeal could profit, and where no
redress could avail, was about to be confronted with
the light of truth and justice. How the light first
broke in seems uncertain and vague, but four
months after Foscarini's murder suspicions began
to be aroused as to the honesty of the spy and
informer Vano, and it was discovered that his
evidence had been a mass of lies and calumnies from
beginning to end. He and one of his accomplices
were immediately strangled ; and the Council of Ten,
to atone for the fatal blunder they had committed,
made an open confession of their crime, proclaimed
the innocence of their victim, for whom they decreed
a public funeral, and restored to his family all the
marks of honour forfeited by their kinsman's death.

But in spite of the apologies and confessions of
error made by the Council of Ten their credit was
immensely shaken : revelations were made that
reflected shame and dishonour on their practices ;
and, when a reformer arose in the person of Reniero
Zeno, public sympathy was large enough to give hopes
that his mission would prove successful. Zeno had
filled some of the highest posts in his country's
service ; he had been twice ambassador to Rome,
where he had not hesitated to rebuke ambassadors
and cardinals, whom he suspected of accepting

bribes and of simony. Of a straightforward frank
nature, withal proud and haughty, he was the man
required for the occasion, and his fearless attempts to
restrain the unlawful deeds of the Ten, and restore
the rights possessed of old by the Great Council, show
him to have been of the stuff of which reformers are
made. The reigning Doge at that period (1624) was
Giovanni Cornaro, several of whose sons were filling
posts and offices prohibited to them by reason of
their father's dignity as head of the Republic. Zeno
eagerly spoke against the infringement of a law
asserted and reiterated by one ducal *Promissione* after
another, thus drawing upon himself the odium and
animosity of the Doge and his party. When at
that moment one of the ducal councillors died, and
Zeno applied to be nominated in his stead, he met
with great opposition ; but his friends outnumbering his foes he was elected to the office. Shortly
after however new differences arose between him
and the Doge, and on his refusing to appear and
answer a summons brought against him he was.
banished for a year to Palma. This sentence did but
enlist further sympathies on behalf of Zeno, with
fresh displeasure against the Council of Ten, whose
assumption of powers beyond their province and
arrogance of conduct became ever more and more
unbearable. At this moment Pope Urban VIII.
offered a cardinal's hat to Federigo Cornaro, one of the
Doge's sons, an honour that should have been refused,
but which the Doge and his Council found means to
justify and accept ; while other honours were added
to those already too numerous in the Cornaro family.

The public clamoured for the recall of Zeno; and on August 1, 1627, he returned to find himself elected to the Council of Ten, and lost no time in availing himself of his new position to denounce the irregularities committed by the Doge and his sons. To some of Zeno's remonstrances heed was paid; and the Doge gave orders to elect two new senators in the room of two of his sons who sat unlawfully in the Great Council. When Zeno endeavoured to obtain further concessions and sweep away further abuses his efforts gave rise to most stormy harangues and scenes in the Council. After turbulent discussions, during which party spirit and words ran high, Zeno secured a victory, and the Doge's party had to give in and own their discomfiture. But he had to pay for his victory. One evening while standing under the Porta della Carta he was assaulted by five assassins, who dealt him such severe blows with their hatchets that he fell fainting to the ground, and was left for dead. The impossibility to discover the murderers, and the flight of the Doge's son, Giorgio, left little doubt in any mind as to the authors of the crime. On recovery from his wounds Zeno set to work with redoubled zeal to accomplish his reforms; an order enjoined on him by the Ten to keep silence with regard to all their doings and judgments he refused to heed, and a tumultuous meeting took place in the Great Council, when each faction endeavoured to drown its adversary's voice, the Doge's party by belabouring the benches with hammers, and Zeno's party by declining to be silenced. All was riot and confusion. The sitting had to be dissolved, and, to punish Zeno for the uproar, and for the part he had always taken against the abuses of their office, the Council of Ten ordered him to be banished for ten years to the fortress of Cattaro. This sentence provoked just indignation, whilst the enmity that it produced against the Ten well-nigh caused the overthrow of that Council ; and had it not been that they foresaw their peril, recognised the advisability of concession, and agreed to modify some of their statutes and actions, it is probable they would have been abolished, and their power brought then and there to an end. A committee was appointed to reduce the extent of their control, but beyond doing away with the *Zonta* little change really was effected in the authoritative administration of the Council, and the effort made to free the people and the *Maggior Consiglio* of a taskmaster to whom they had grown accustomed was unavailing ; the bondage had become part of the system, the chain was preferable to the free motion of the limbs, and Venice clung to the fetters from which Zeno had tried in vain to liberate her.

The ill feeling that already existed in Venice towards Spain at the time of the conspiracy of 1618 had received an impetus from that act of treachery not modified by after events. The antipathy and distrust felt by Venice had but grown and increased with every movement and action of her governing body. Yet Spain, linked as she was to Austria by bonds of relationship as well as of policy, was a power with whom the Republic could not safely come into violent collision, and with whom her instincts of self-preservation bade her deal warily and with caution. This wariness was now called into play in regard of a war threatened by Spain for the possession of the Valtelline.

The province of Valtelline is that strip of land watered by the Adda, and extending from the Tyrol to the head of the Lake of Como. Connecting as it does the Duchy of Milan with Austria, its possession was eagerly desired by Spain as a stepping-stone by which she or Austria could communicate or manœuvre on to Italian and Venetian soil whenever inclination or ambition tempted them so to do. It was equally in the interest of Venice to prevent such a measure, for the Valtelline once possessed by Spain all exits and egresses into Venetian territory would be in Spanish hands, who would also have the support of Austria ; and thus all communication with France, Germany, and Switzerland would be hopelessly cut off. The province, though strictly Catholic, had placed itself under the League of the Grisons. From this yoke it now desired to free itself, and was backed in the wish by Spanish and Austrian troops ; while Fuentes, the Spanish Governor of Milan, commenced building a fortress on the confines of the province. War and bloodshed devastated the country ; a terrible massacre of the Protestants took place, and the Grisons, who were in league with Venice, applied to her for aid and support in a cause affecting them so vitally. Venice was by no means willing to put herself in opposition to Spain and Austria without first ascertaining the intentions of France. But while negotiations were delaying all action the Spaniards, and

Austrians took possession of the Valtelline, out of
zeal, they said, for the Catholic faith and for the protection of the Valtelline Catholics against the Grison
Protestants ; and Venice was too weak to attempt
either resistance or rescue.   Through the intervention
however of Richelieu the province was restored to
the Grisons, and a treaty for the fulfilment of this

TOMB OF THE CARDINAL ZENO (DIED IN 1501) IN THE CAPPELLA
ZENO IN ST. MARK'S.
(*From Yriarte's "Venise," op. cit.*)

arrangement was signed at Monson in 1626, though
it was not carried out in its entirety till eleven years
later.   Venice was not consulted as to this treaty, nor
informed of its accomplishment till some time after ;
her sanction or disapproval were no longer of weight

among the great powers, and they disregarded alike her satisfaction or mortification.

Shortly after the conclusion of the Valtelline war Venice had to battle with a still deadlier foe in her very midst, for in 1629 the plague broke out in the land with a virulence and fury not to be withstood. No less than a quarter of the inhabitants were swept way, and skill and science were alike unavailing to grapple with an evil which has obtained notoriety from the accounts left us of its might and horror by contemporary and modern writers. Another and more evident memorial of it exists in the Church of the Madonna della Salute, which was erected now, and which, in spite of all its architectural blemishes, gives a finish and completeness that otherwise were lacking to the town, and adds its weight to the testimonial of gratitude and thankfulness paid by Venice for the removal of so dire a calamity from among her people.

A VENETIAN GALLEY.
(*From an old Chronicle at the Marciana Library.*)

XVII.

THE WAR OF CANDIA.

(1631–1718.)

THE scenes of the great drama enacted between Venice and the East were now drawing to their close, and the noble way in which the Republic played her part and maintained the struggle against the Turk in Candia and in the Morea, shed a ray of glory over actions and conduct worthy of the brightest days of the Republic. Her relations with the Porte, though friendly on the whole, had been frequently interrupted by skirmishes and disputes on the high seas that often left much irritation and ill-feeling between the two powers, who, not always strong enough to avenge the insult at the critical moment, brooded over wrongs neither forgiven nor forgotten. In 1644 the Venetians were accused of an offence for which they had to pay the penalty, though perfectly guiltless of the deed. Some ships, belonging to the Knights of Malta, were cruising in the Archipelago, when they fell in with some Turkish vessels laden with pilgrims bound for Mecca. A fight ensued, and the Maltese remained victors. Several Turks, among them some favourites of the Sultan, were slain, and the rest made prisoners. When the news of the event reached Constantinople the rage of the Sultan Ibrahim was unbounded. He summoned all the ambassadors and representatives of the different courts into his presence, and held them responsible for the offence. In vain they pointed out the innocence of their respective governments. Ibrahim persisted that among the Knights of Malta were men of all nationalities and belonging to divers countries, but his anger was especially directed against the Venetians, as after the engagement the Maltese conquerors had attempted to put into one of the ports on their island of Candia. The Venetians argued that this was no fault of theirs. The Sultan wanted an excuse for possessing himself of that island, and the injustice and triviality of the excuse mattered nothing to him. He did not however declare war against the Republic, but asserted that the warlike preparations now commenced by him on a large scale were directed against Malta. The Venetian Bailo, suspicious of his good faith, inquired as to his intentions, but he maintained that his cordiality, nay friendship, for Venice was unimpaired, and that his hostilities were preparing against Malta. But the Venetians were not so easily duped. They suspected the Sultan of plotting against Candia, and the Senate gave orders to repair the fortresses there, to build new ones where they were required, and to equip and man the fleet. Supplies of men, money, ships, and victualling were despatched at the same time, and Andrea Cornaro, the governor of the isle, was ordered to spare no efforts to provide for its safety, and to render the defences as impregnable as possible.

On April 30, 1645, without any declaration of war, the Turkish fleet, consisting of over four hundred galleys, and carrying fifty thousand soldiers, sailed out from the Dardanelles, and in June anchored off Canea, the north-western point of the island. No further doubts were now entertained as to the intentions of the Porte, and the dismissal of the Venetian Bailo from Constantinople at the same moment confirmed every fear. Canea was ill prepared to resist such an invasion, and, though all that could be spared of men and ships were sent to its rescue, it was all in vain. The winds and waves fought against Venice, for the supplies could not reach the desired haven; and Biagio Zuliani, captain of the fort, seeing the hopelessness of the situation, blew up the citadel, preferring to die with his men and under his country's colours than fall into the hands of the enemy. But no courage or heroism could avail to save the town, and the commander Navagero, after straining every nerve for its defence, was obliged to capitulate. He was however accorded honourable terms, and allowed to leave the town with all the honours of war. For the Turks the capture of Canea was all-important. They had now a footing in the island, and were possessed of a harbour where their ships could lie in safety, and from where they could obtain stores of food and arms, thus securing themselves against all danger of blockade or famine. The Signory were fully alive to these advantages gained by their foes. They mourned over the loss of Canea, and no price seemed too high to pay for its recovery, and for providing against further perils. In order to raise money to levy fresh troops and equip fresh ships every expedient was resorted to in Venice : each citizen was called on to contribute three-fourths of his plate to the mint ; the highest dignities of the state were offered for sale ; and admission into the ranks of the nobility was obtainable for money. The office of Procurator of St. Mark's could be bought for twenty-five thousand ducats, while the privilege of being enrolled among the Venetian patricians, though at first only offered to five families, was eventually extended to eighty, on condition of their maintaining a thousand soldiers for a year, and for that purpose depositing in the treasury the sum of sixty thousand ducats. The only stipulation required from the purchasers of this honour was that they should have been born in lawful wedlock, and be able to prove that neither they, their fathers, nor their grandfathers had been engaged in any mechanical profession. The same privilege was extended, though at a somewhat higher price, to a few foreigners, but no Jews, Turks, or Saracens might be admitted as nobles, no matter what sum they might be ready to pay.

The new armies now levied for the war stood in need of a commander, and as in cases of unusual need unusual measures have to be adopted, it was decided to appoint the Doge commander-in-chief of the expedition. The Doge, Francesco Erizzo, was an old man of eighty, but he gladly acceded to his country's wishes, and commenced preparations to

sail for Candia. Erizzo however had over-estimated
his powers, the flesh was weaker than the willing
spirit, and he died while making ready for the undertaking. Francesco Molin was named Doge in his
stead, and Girolamo Morosini generalissimo of the
forces, Giovanni Cappello being made captain-general.
The object of the Venetian fleet was to blockade
Canea, and close the passage to the Dardanelles, and
for this latter intent Tomaso Morosini was sent with
a squadron of twenty-four galleys. But he was
unable to hold the position, for the Turks, foreseeing
the damage threatening them by such a course,
forced a passage through the Venetian vessels, and
kept that passage clear. The town of Canea was
defended by Giovanni Cappello, a man ill suited for
so important a post, and whose irresolution and
slothfulness proved most injurious to his cause.
Through his mismanagement the town of Rettimo
was lost to Venice, notwithstanding the assistance
sent by Cardinal Mazarin of nine warships. Cappello
was recalled to Venice, sentenced to a year's imprisonment, and Battista Grimani was appointed to
command in his stead, while Andrea Cornaro, who
had fallen fighting valiantly at Rettimo, was replaced
by Nicolò Dolfin. The Dalmatian coast was also
fortified against the Ottomans by Venice, who applied
ceaselessly to the other European powers for help,
pleading how she had to guard the frontiers of
Dalmatia and Friuli, and preserve Candia and a
host of other islands, all in their turn forming a
barrier against the Turk, alone and unaided. But
her entreaty for succour in this unequal struggle met

THE DOGE RETURNING IN THE *BUCENTAUR* FROM ESPOUSING
THE SEA.
(*From Giacomo Franco's "Habiti d'Huomeni et Donne Venetiane," &c.
Venice, 1609.)*

with little response. Most of the powers were
absorbed with their own affairs, and Venice had to
prepare almost singlehanded to defend Candia which
was now besieged by the Turks. For over twenty
years she gallantly maintained the strife. Many and
frequent acts of valour and heroism were displayed
by the Venetians notwithstanding the terrible odds
against which they had to contend ; for not only did
the Turks outnumber them in men and ships, but the
very elements fought against them. More than once
they were prevented by stress of weather from engaging the foe, and in 1648 a fearful hurricane
deprived them of one of their best admirals as in a
gale close to the Dardanelles, Grimani with twenty-
eight ships and all on board were lost. In the
previous year another gallant life, that of Tomaso
Morosini, had also been lost to Venice. He had
attacked the enemy regardless of fearful odds and
overwhelming numbers, and his dismantled ship,
with broken masts and torn sails and rigging, was
only saved from falling into the enemies' hands by
the skill and bravery of her crew, who avenged their
captain's death by rescuing his vessel. Another
brilliant action was the victory obtained off Paros
by the two Mocenigo brothers, Alvise Leonardo and
Lazzaro, but for that too the Venetians had to pay
dearly, Alvise Mocenigo having died in the engagement.

Victories and defeats followed each other in quick
succession, varied occasionally with overtures for
peace. But both sides declared that the demands
were too exorbitant and the conditions too hard, so

war was always resumed, and continued by Venice
with an energy and vigour, that reflect the more
credit on her when the strain under which she
laboured is taken into consideration. Except for
some small and inefficient help from the Pope, the
Grand Duke of Tuscany, the Knights of Malta, and
from Spain, she had met with no encouragement but
fair words from those to whom she might well have
looked for aid and support. In 1657 she had been
victorious at the battle of the Dardanelles, but at a
heavy cost, for the Admiral, Lazzaro Mocenigo, was
killed in the action. He had been one of the boldest
and bravest of the Venetian leaders ; a few years
previously in joint command with his brother Alvise
he had gained the battle off Paros, after that his plan
of campaign had been to advance with his fleet to the
very walls of Constantinople, and insist on an advantageous peace for his country. But death cut short
all his designs, and no one was found to carry out a
scheme too daring for any hand but his own to
attempt, and which, had it proved successful, would
have changed the whole aspect of affairs. After the
battle of the Dardanelles offers of peace were made by
Constantinople, and a long discussion took place in
Venice as to continuing or concluding the war. It had
lasted for nearly fourteen years, and several pleaded
that the Republic had done more than enough for her
honour and renown ; the lives of many of her bravest
and best had sealed their country's cause with their
blood ; no help from without was forthcoming, and
it was better to conclude hostilities while some
advantages could be gained rather than await total

annihilation. But the war party, headed by Giovanni Pesaro, swept away these arguments; the terms offered by the Porte were, they urged, too hard to accept, and it was decided to reject them. So the war was continued, and in 1660 Francesco Morosini was named general of the Venetian forces in Candia, and two years after the first help deserving of the name was proffered to Venice by France. This help consisted of a force of four thousand men, under the command of Prince Almerigo of Este; but the troops failed in displaying the quiet endurance requisite for a long drawn-out war, they clamoured for prompt and rapid action, and when their wish was granted and they assailed the Turkish lines, they were repulsed notwithstanding the force and impetuosity of their attack, and large numbers of them were slain. Their commander, who was killed in the flower of his manhood, was buried with pomp and honour in the Church of the Frari, where a monument was erected to his memory. A contingent sent soon after by Leopold I., Emperor of Germany, proved equally unavailing, though the want of success this time was due to the season being too advanced, when all attack was impossible. The Venetian Government, disheartened by these failures, recalled Morosini, and subjected him to a court martial, but after awhile he was honourably acquitted, and in 1666 returned again to his post in Candia. In his absence the command devolved on his brother Giorgio, and afterwards on Angelo Correr, and fresh negotiations were started with the object of effecting peace, but always in vain. This same year some practical help was given to Venice;

France sent four thousand *scudi*, the Viceroy of
Naples eight thousand, Cardinal Barberini despatched
a large supply of grain, the Emperor of Germany
contributed a force of three hundred men, and the
Duke of Savoy sent two regiments to their aid.
While these recruits were strengthening the Venetian
arms, the Turks had been busy repairing their
defences, increasing their ammunition, and enlisting
fresh men and ships for the war. On May 28th,
with renewed forces, they attacked Candia, and
opened a furious cannonade of three hundred guns
upon Canea. The town had been assaulted and
defended times without number, and the special
means of both attack and defence consisted chiefly
of mines and countermines. A perfect labyrinth of
underground interstices had been formed in this
way, each side striving to forestall the mischief
threatened by its adversary by digging a deeper,
lower mine than that already made. The assailants
met constantly in these subterranean passages and
fought in the dark, till "the caverns ran down with
blood," says the chronicler Nani ; and when the mines
were sprung Venetian and Turk alike were buried in
masses in these ready-made sepulchres. From May
to November in 1667 the town of Candia, the capital
of the island, underwent thirty-two assaults, and seventeen sorties, no less than six hundred and eighteen
mines were sprung, and three thousand two hundred
Venetians perished, besides four hundred officers ;
while the Turks lost twenty thousand men. The eyes
of all Europe were now turned towards Candia. The
gallant defence of the city, the courage and constancy

of the Venetians, the heroism and endurance displayed by their rulers aroused the chivalry and admiration of Christendom. The Pope exhorted and encouraged the sovereigns of Europe to arm for the rescue of Candia ; and a gallant band of Frenchmen, led by the Duc de la Feuillade, set sail for the island. Again the French were determined to try and effect by brilliancy what could only be achieved by patience and endurance. Eager to give signal proof of their zeal, they clamoured to be allowed to make a sortie, certain that the mere dash of their arms would win the day and compel the Turks to raise the siege. Morosini strongly opposed the measure ; his experience had shown him the uselessness of these sallies, the loss of life they entailed, and the disheartening effect involved by their failure. But the French would not be gainsaid ; winter, they pointed out, was approaching, and they had not taken that long journey to consume their time in digging mines. They resolved to carry out the sortie, and having failed in inducing Morosini to join them, they attacked alone the enemies' trenches. The impetus of their onslaught gave them at first a slight advantage, but the contest was too unequal, the odds too uneven ; the larger number of them were mown down in handfuls, and only a few wounded officers and men crept back, disheartened and discomfited, and desirous only to depart. All that remained of that impetuous band, anxious to escape from the scene of their defeat, left Candia only to die of plague and sickness on their homeward route. To compensate as best he could for this

second failure of French forces, Louis XIV. determined to send fresh supplies to aid the Venetians.
The Pope, Clement IX., keener than most of his
predecessors for the success of the Republic, sent
also large subsidies of money, and urged the French
monarch in emphatic terms to execute his intentions.
His representations were warmly seconded by those
of the Venetian ambassador in Paris ; and Louis
ordered a contingent of twelve regiments of infantry,
three hundred cavalry, and even a detachment of his
personal guard to sail for Candia. They started
under the command of the Duc de Noailles and the
admiral, Duc de Beaufort ; other help being contributed at the same time from different parts of
Europe. These auxiliaries arrived to find the town
of Candia reduced to almost its last straits, and
further resistance well-nigh impossible. No building
of any sort remained intact ; the springing of the
mines continued with unabated vigour ; the streets
were strewn with the dying and the dead ; and the
odour arising from the unburied and wounded bodies
filled the air with pestilence. But Morosini still
held out. With a courage and devotion worthy of
his name and race, he still made head against the
foe ; and his hopes revived with the additional forces
at last come to his aid. His purpose was to divert the
enemy on the side of Canea, but the French insisted, as
their former comrades had done, on making a sally,
and in spite of all Morosini's entreaties and prayers
to desist from so unavailing a movement, they
refused to abandon their intention, and Morosini
had to yield. The same fate befell them as had

befallen their countrymen on two previous occasions ; and two hundred French heads, among them those of the Duc de Beaufort and some of his foremost officers, were paraded in ghastly triumph before the Grand Vizier. Even this defeat did not crush Morosini's spirit, and the prospect of a second contingent due from France continued to raise his hopes. His despair therefore can be imagined when the French announced their resolution to forsake the cause they had come to protect, and neither the supplications of Morosini, nor the prayers and entreaties of the garrison and of the people and clergy could prevail on them to stay. Only two months after they had raised the hopes of the besieged by appearing among them they sailed away, leaving desperation and desolation behind them, and setting beside an example soon after followed by the German, Maltese, and Papal troops, who all sailed off from Candia, leaving Venice again alone.

But the end had now come. All hope was over ; and it only remained to save the little garrison still left in the city and procure the best terms possible from the victors. Morosini resolved to do this. He was not possessed of actual powers to treat with the foe, but the moment was not one to be wasted in applying for an authority which might arrive too late, and he determined to act on his own responsibility. On August 28, 1669, he opened negotiations for peace with Achmet Kiupergli, the Grand Vizier, and, owing in a great measure to the respect which Morosini inspired and to the admiration felt for him by his foes, honourable terms were conceded to Venice. The

Venetians were to leave Candia, carrying with them their guns, their goods, and all the sacred vessels of their church. Venice was to retain possession of the three ports of Carabusa, Suda, and Spinalunga, together with the frontier towns conquered by her in Dalmatia and Bosnia, especially the fortress of Clissa, and friendly relations were to be resumed between the two powers. This treaty was ratified alike by the Venetian Senate and by the Sultan, but voices were not wanting in Venice to abuse Morosini's action, and to accuse him even of treachery, cowardice, and venality. The foremost among his detractors was Antonio Correr, but a powerful speech from Giovanni Sagredo silenced the injustice and vileness of such accusation, and Morosini was hailed in Venice with the honour and praise due to his patriotism and valour. On September 27, 1669, the keys of Candia were consigned to the Vizier, and the war which had lasted twenty-five years was finished. In it Venice had sustained almost single-handed a struggle utterly disproportionate to her forces, sustained it too with dignity and courage, and though in the end she had to succumb to overwhelming numbers, a " dying glory smiles " indeed over this last achievement of " Europe's bulwark 'gainst the Ottomite."

The end of the war with Candia found Venice on the verge of bankruptcy, but a period of fourteen years of peace somewhat restored her exchequer, and she strove in every way to revive and reanimate her commerce. But anxiety as to the purposes and intentions of her late foe could not be laid aside ; and though the friendly relations between them were

nominally restored, they were not so in reality.
Since their conquest of Candia the Turks had been
carrying on an almost constant war with Austria, and
had profited by the quarrels between Hungary and
Austria to harass this latter.   In 1684 the Pope, the
Emperors of Germany and Russia, and the King of
Poland formed a league against the Porte, and urged
on Venice the advisability of joining them against the
common foe.   The alliance was in every way acceptable to the Republic ; she agreed to join it, formally
declared war against Turkey, and appointed Francesco
Morosini generalissimo of her forces.   He sailed
straightway for Greece, besieged and took the island
of Sta. Maura, made himself master of Coron, and of
the fortresses of Zemata, Calamata, Chialafa and
others, and subjected all the province of Maïna.   In
Venice the efforts resorted to during the last war for
raising funds were again put into practice in order
to further the conquest of the Morea now contemplated by Morosini.   The office of Procurator of St.
Mark once more was obtainable by money, and by
the same means twenty-five new families were enrolled
in the *Libro d'Oro*.   Besides the levies raised by
these means Morosini was also supported by an able
commander, the Count of Königsmark, whose services
had been enlisted by the Republic to aid their general
in this campaign.   In 1685 the conquest of the Morea
was effected under the direction of these captains, and
the following year a brilliant series of victories at
Navarino, Modon, Argos, and Nauplia in the Morea
confirmed the possession of the peninsula to Venice.
Athens also was besieged and bombarded, and in less

than six days the whole town was in flames. The statue of the goddess Minerva by Phidias was destroyed, and the Parthenon, which had been used by the Turks as a powder magazine, was fired. Morosini was only able to save a few trophies from the general havoc, among them being the marble lions brought from the Piræus. These he sent to Venice, where they are to be seen to this day standing as sentinels to guard the entrance to the Arsenal. Further victories at Patrasso, Corinth, and Lepanto heightened the glory of Morosini's arms ; and when the news of these triumphs reached Venice the joy and exultation that spread through the town knew no bounds. Morosini was hailed as the greatest general Venice had ever had, and an honour, never before granted to any Venetian, was accorded him in the erection, during his lifetime, of his bust in the Hall of the Council of Ten. Over this was hung the banner taken from the Turks, and below it ran the inscription : " Francisco Mauroceno Peleponnesiaco adhuc viventi Senatus ;" while the praise and thanks of the nation were conveyed to him in a letter from the Doge.

The next year, 1688, the Doge, Marcantonio Giustinian, having died, public opinion with one accord named Francesco Morosini as his successor, though the Senate begged him, for the welfare of the state, to remain yet awhile in command of the forces. But with his appointment as Doge, his success as general began to wane. It was judged needful in a council of war that to insure the safeguard of the Morea, Negropont must be won to Venice. This was accordingly resolved on, but hardly was the campaign undertaken ere the plague broke out in the camp, and a third of the army was swept away, among the victims being Morosini's able coadjutor, the Count of Königsmark. The weakened and reduced forces attempted to defend themselves against the attacks of the Turks, and though they were able to repulse them on two occasions their losses were great, and in spite of a reinforcement of four thousand men from Venice, Morosini was obliged to raise the siege and retire to Malvasia. Here he was overcome with illness, and obliged to leave the army and return to Venice, where he was received with great rejoicings, and crowned Doge with all the pomp and state belonging to that ceremonial. Girolamo Cornaro succeeded him as commander, but to the regret of the army and of his country, he died of fever at Vallona, which the Venetians had besieged after possessing themselves of Malvasia. The command devolved upon Domenico Mocenigo, a man altogether unworthy of so important a position. He neglected in the most culpable manner to avail himself of an opportunity to reconquer Canea, and his irresolution and pusillanimity were so evident he was recalled to Venice, and the Doge was entreated to assume the command once more. Morosini gladly responded to the call, and on May 24, 1693, Venice witnessed for the last time all the pageant and magnificence attendant on the departure of one of her greatest Doges for war in a foreign land. The fleet sailed to the Archipelago, but before any occasion arose of encountering the foe, Morosini's health, which had long been ailing, gave way, and he died at Nauplia on January 9, 1694, aged 76. The mourning over his death was sincere and universal in Venice ; his funeral, attended by great and small, took place in the Church of S. Stefano, and an inscription was set up in the ducal palace in the Sala del Scrutinio to record his virtues and greatness.

Constant battles occupied the next five years against the Ottomans in the Archipelago ; and on most occasions the Venetians still proved by their successes the superiority of their naval skill and prowess. In 1699 the peace of Carlowitz was signed by most of the European powers, and Venice, anxious to lay down her arms, and dreading lest she should again be left to wrestle singlehanded against the Turks, gave in her adhesion to the treaty, though she had to relinquish several of her conquests and retain only the Morea, some towns on the frontier, and a few ports in Greece and Dalmatia. The peace of Carlowitz insured to Venice a period of tranquillity for nine years. From the war of the Spanish succession then engrossing the rest of Europe she kept aloof, and asserted a neutrality, which was remembered against her when some years later she required help against the Turks in the Morea. This neutrality was also totally disregarded by the contending armies, for the Marshals Catinat and Villeroi, the Dukes of Savoy and of Vendome, and Prince Eugene of Savoy in turn overran the Venetian territory, and the subjects of St. Mark endured all the trials of fighting and invading hosts without any redress or compensation, and without the consideration which they might have claimed had they been in the position of either enemies or allies. Venice had besides the mortification of being forced to submit to a violation of her rights in the Adriatic. Some Venetian vessels had been captured by the French under the plea that they were carrying supplies to Austria, and not till the Peace of Utrecht in 1713 (when Venice, though she had not participated in the war, was asked to send a representative) were these difficulties removed.

The Turks had by no means accepted with resignation the condition of things imposed on them by the peace of Carlowitz. Though the commencement of their decline may be dated from that moment, they were meditating and preparing to recover the Morea. In 1714 they pleaded the capture of one of their merchant vessels by some Venetians as an excuse to declare war against the Republic. Venice applied to the European states for assistance, but the fact of her neutrality during the war of the Spanish succession was brought up against her, and but for some feeble help from the Pope, the Grand Duke of Tuscany, and the Knights of Malta, she remained without allies.

The rule of the Republic had not been of a nature to gain the love and attachment of her new subjects. They were anxious to return to the Turkish yoke sooner than endure that of Venice ; and they profited by the opportunity now offered them to help the Turkish cause and expel the Venetians from Greece. One by one the provinces and towns gained by Francesco Morosini were wrested from Venice ; and the links

that had bound Venice to the East with a chain of
such splendid friendship and intercourse were severed
without one deed of heroism or of valour to colour the
recital or brighten the last scenes to be enacted on
that special stage. The island of Corfu proved however the one exception to the rule, and made a gallant
resistance against the Turks. The Venetian troops
were commanded by the Saxon Count Schulemburg,
and repulsed under his leadership a sharp assault of
the foe. Corfu was saved to Venice, and to mark the
Republic's appreciation of his services an equestrian
statue was erected to Schulemburg on the spot which
he had so gallantly defended. The victory gained by
Prince Eugene at the same time over the Turks at
Peterwaradin, confirmed the possession of Corfu to
Venice ; for the Turks, cowed by the constant defeats
dealt them by the Imperialists, withdrew their forces
from the Archipelago, and left Venice unmolested. But
she was unable to profit by the situation, for the rest
of Europe was bent on making peace, and she had
to accept the conditions imposed upon her without
power to expostulate or remonstrate. The peace of
Passarowitz, signed July 21, 1718, was concluded
regardless of the Republic's wishes, and she had to
submit to the limitation of her dominions to proportions which henceforth remained untouched till the
close of her political existence. By this treaty the
actual Dogado was assured to Venice, together
with Bergamo, Brescia, Crema, Verona, Vicenza, the
Polesine and Rovigo, the Marca Trevigiana, besides
Istria and Friuli. She was to surrender entirely the
Morea, but on the other hand, she preserved parts of

Dalmatia and Albania, with their island dependencies, and in the Ionian Sea, Corfu, Paxos, Zante, Ithaca, Sta. Maura, Asso, the rock of Cerigo, and the Strophades ; while her trading duties with Turkey were reduced from 5 to 3 per cent. Thus ended a war which had caused an enormous sacrifice of men and money ; a war reflecting but small glory to Venice, and which was but another step in the downward path she had now to tread towards decay and extinction.

THE OLDEST REPRESENTATION OF ST. MARK'S LION.
(*From the Belfry of Sant' Aponai, cir.* 1100 *A.D.*)

XVIII.

FALL OF THE REPUBLIC.

(1718–1798.)

THE public career, so to speak, of Venice was now all but closed; and the tone of her story assumes henceforward a hue of sombre, grey colouring, very dissimilar to the gorgeous, brilliant setting which had characterised it of old. Her object now was to avoid attention; and by a steady refusal to embroil herself in her neighbours' wars and struggles to retire into an existence of neutrality and exclusion. The spirit too of the Venetians of bygone times had died away; and the turn of men's minds and temperaments was of another mould; neither capable to adapt itself to the present necessity, nor to revive the energy and industry which had distinguished the early days of the Republic. The new nobility were of a totally dissimilar stamp to those among whom they had purchased the right to evolve themselves. The contempt they proclaimed for trade turned the tide of fashion and custom against one of Venice's chief means of income and wealth; and while they despised and spurned the ladder by which they had reached their present heights, they embarked in ostentation and display, undermining their for-

tunes, and, at the same time, courting the vices
and corruptions engendered by luxury and ex-
travagance. The old nobles, not willing to be
outdone by their monied compeers, entered into a
competition utterly beyond their powers to sustain,
and squandered in mistaken rivalry fortunes never
again to be accumulated or repaired.

The altered condition of men and manners in Venice
required also an alteration as to the laws. The rules
and regulations, adapted to the early centuries of
Venetian story, were no longer suitable to the tempers
and habits of later times. In 1761 the Inquisitors of
State had attempted acts of despotism and autocracy
which could no longer be tolerated by the advanced
thinkers of the day; and the Great Council now
determined to exercise that power of restraint and
restriction which they had essayed but failed to put
into practice in 1627. As then the indignation of
the governing body had prevented the nomination
of the members of the Council of Ten, and threatened
the existence of that Council with annihilation, so
now the same fate was imminent. But by concessions and adaptations the candidates managed to
secure election ; and the populace who considered
the Ten as the sole power able to hold in check
their oppressors, the nobles hailed the return of this
Council to office, and rejoiced over the confirmation
of rights granted to their coadjutors, the Three.

The Signory also endeavoured to keep pace with
the times in regard of trade. In 1689 the right, passed
thirty-one years previously, to allow free exit for all
goods leaving Venice was revoked, and a duty of

4 per cent. levied on all goods coming into the town. The folly of such an edict bore fruit in the following century when the stores of accumulated wares found neither purchasers within the town, nor any one sufficiently adventurous to risk the payment of export dues and carry the hoarded goods to foreign markets. The subject was discussed in 1733, but in spite of a hot debate setting forth the wisdom of removing the duty, at least on exports, the Bill was rejected in 1735. In the following year however more liberal measures were enforced, and Venice became almost a free port.

Other efforts at reform and amelioration were made concerning Church laws. The number of monasteries was curtailed ; and donations and legacies to pious institutions were forbidden to exceed certain limits. An outcry was raised in Venice and in Rome against the restriction of people's wills and intentions, but the wisdom of the measure commended itself so universally it ended by being adopted. At Rome the Pope Clement XIII., a Venetian of the house of Rezzonico, appealed to his countrymen against the passing of this law, but the Senate replied with dignity and firmness, regretting their inability to conform to his Holiness's wishes. Clement's successor, Ganganelli, who took the name of Clement XIV., a far more enlightened man than Rezzonico, raised no opposition to the decree ; and also supported the Signory in suppressing the exaggerated number of festivals and holidays then in vogue in Venice, as injurious to the cause of religion, and giving rise instead to idleness, debauchery, and crime. This

MASQUERADERS RETURNING FROM THE RIDOTTO.
(*From " Le Arti che vanno per via nella Città di Venezia.*"

moment saw the expulsion of the Jesuits from all the European states, and Venice joined eagerly in a movement entirely to her taste; and of which some years back she had given so forcible an example.

Another attempt to reform the manners of the age was made in the suppression of the Ridotto, or gaming house at S. Moïsè in 1780. The retirement into which Venice had withdrawn with regard to political affairs and interests with the outer world had not been maintained in the private life of her citizens. A passion for amusement, gambling, masquerades, and every kind of revel had absorbed the Venetian mind; the characteristic of the age was frivolity, licentiousness, and wantonness, and an indelible stamp has been left on the Venetian life of that century by this marked and universal characteristic. Never before were morals at so low an ebb: conjugal fidelity was an unknown quality; and the example set by the rich spread like a disease through all ranks of the town. An explanation for all this may be found in the fact that no other outlet for thought or ambition was then possible for a Venetian. Politics may be said to have expired; French opinions and ideas drove religion out of every mind; literature followed where fashion led; and high and low alike declared themselves devotees of the ruling god. An effort to check this in some way was resolved on by the Government, and the first step in that direction was taken in closing the gaming house at S. Moïsè. The taste for gambling was encouraged by the facility offered at this Ridotto. The house had been set up in 1676; and generally from sixty to eighty tables were set out, each one presided over

CANAL AND CHURCH OF S. BARNABA.

(*From " Calli e Canali," op. cit.*)

by a noble (for this was a privilege accorded only
to them) in the capacity of banker, dressed in his
patrician's robes and unmasked. These nobles were
not allowed to hold the bank on their own account,
but were in the pay of companies engaged in specu-
lation, or of Jews, and they were paid by the hour,
the month and the year. The other gamblers were
all masked ; and perfect silence reigned over scenes
where ruin, beggary and starvation went hand in
hand with the delirium created by the acquirement
of riches without honour, and wealth without dignity.
The decree that put a stop to this pursuit was hailed
by the common people with joy, and they paraded
the streets, rejoicing publicly over the suppression of
the Ridotto.

Another movement demonstrating the restlessness
and dissatisfaction of the times took place in this
same year, 1780, when a party of the older nobles
strove to assert their rights and suppress the power
of rivals who by wealth and influence bade fair to
eclipse them altogether. These poorer nobles, who
were known as the " *Barnabotti* " (from the parish of
S. Barnaba, where most of them lived), had neither
the talents nor energy to raise themselves from
the straits to which they were reduced. They were
jealous of the position whereunto the *nouveaux
riches* had attained, and their discontent was fanned
into flame under the leadership of Giorgio Pisani,
Carlo Contarini, and others. Availing themselves
of the state of public affairs, which certainly was far
from satisfactory, and on the plea of reducing the
taxes and alleviating the expenses of the poor, Pisani

and his followers conspired to overthrow the Doge, together with all the recognised forms of government, and exalt himself and his partisans to office. But the plot failed. Pisani, though he had attained to the rank of Procurator, was exiled to Verona ; the other ringleaders were also banished, and the conspiracy was silenced by the annihilating force of the Inquisitors of State.

The condition of political, financial, and moral weakness to which Venice had fallen in the eighteenth century has left a mark on the epoch which stamps it with a character at once peculiar and individual ; and gives it too an attraction that perhaps Venice alone can claim at that moment. The habits and customs of public and private life, the theatres, the "conservatoires" of music, the life both in the town and in the splendid "villas" which now arose in the plains of Padua and Treviso, the arts alike decorative and representative, the literary productions of the day, all offer a field of interest and study to the historian, the artist, and the philosopher that attracts and repels at the same time. Though neither greatness nor dignity leave their mark on the age, there is a gracefulness, a joyousness, a spirit essentially Venetian which gives—though not in a high sense— a charm to that period, notwithstanding the stamp of decay belonging to it.

A brilliant form of entertainment was indulged in on the occasion of the visit of Pope Paul VI., when Venice blazed forth once again with much of the brilliancy and pageantry that had distinguished so many bygone days of the Republic. The Pope

had been to visit the Emperor Joseph II. at Vienna,
and on his homeward journey stopped at Venice, the
Doge and Signory meeting him at the island of S.
Giorgio in Alga. The pomp and ceremonial, together with the feasts and revelries that took place
in his honour, are a proof that the water-city had lost
none of the love of show and display that ran in the
very veins of her citizens. No pope had been in
Venice since the time of Alexander III., whose
sojourn there in the twelfth century ranked among
the famous events in the Republic's history ; and the
city was bent on cordially welcoming the Pontiff,
and acknowledging a courtesy that had not been
exercised towards it for so many years.

In 1784 a vigorous sign of life was made by the
Republic in her raid upon the corsairs and barbarians
of Tunis and Algiers. The demands made by the
Bey of Tunis for sums claimed by him from Venice
goaded the Signory into action, and a fleet was
despatched under the command of Angelo Emo.
He was the last admiral of Venice who gained
honour for his country, and under his direction the
Lion of St. Mark was once more victorious and
triumphant on the high seas. The war lasted three
years, and to Emo and to Venice belong the credit
of having purged the coasts of Algiers, Tunis, and
Tripoli from the hordes of pirates and corsairs who
made these coasts dangerous and formidable.

This was the last act of Venice's greatness. The
mists were gathering fast round the fair city in the
sea, though a strange contradiction mingled with
those mists, and cast lurid lights athwart the dark-

ness of her decline. Never before had such floods
of revelry, gaiety, and light-heartedness swept over
Venice ; never before had the whole population,
high and low equally, sought so wildly after pleasures
of every kind ; while opposed to this craze stand out
the victories and triumphs of Emo, the efforts made
by the Senate by renewed laws and regulations to
adjust affairs in the Church, in the Arsenal, in the
council chambers, and in agriculture ; together with
the endeavours, always futile and in vain, to check
the looseness of manners and morals among the
patricians and their wives. But the age was that
of the French Revolution ; French ideas, French
customs, French habits were permeating every corner
of Europe, and Venice was not exempt from the
effects of so tremendous a movement. Her attitude
in regard of the French Revolution lacked the dignity
and straightforwardness she might have assumed, and
the vacillation and cringing she displayed alternately
were little in keeping with the traditions and memories of her past. In spite of the warnings and advices
of Antonio Cappello and Alvise Pisani, in turn her
ambassadors in Paris, to unite herself to some of the
other powers, or take up a position either of approval
or condemnation in regard of France, she clung to
her old policy of neutrality. When however the
ascendency of the French Republic was acknowledged Venice abandoned her policy of irresolution,
and assumed an attitute of respect towards France
widely different to the contempt she had shown when
that power seemed undeveloped and insecure. Some
excuse though exists for Venice when the peculiari-

ties of her situation are considered. For seventy
years she had maintained almost absolute peace
throughout her realm. Her soldiers and sailors were
unfitted by repose and inaction for the service of war ;
the laxity that had crept into all grades of society by
the avoidance of warlike thoughts and deeds was too
deep-seated an evil to be eradicated in a moment ;
her exchequer was exhausted ; and, to complete all,
Venice was afraid. She feared the French—and to
that fear was joined a strong element of hate—and
still more did she fear Austria, whose near proximity
to her frontier rendered her a formidable foe, and
kept alive in Venice the nightmare of being eventually
swallowed up by this more powerful neighbour. The
endeavours of the different states of Europe to persuade Venice to join with them against France, and
the same cautious refusals coupled with reasons for
preserving a strict neutrality, occupy pages of her
story, and form a wearisome episode at so stirring an
epoch of the world's history ; but the dying hours
of the great Republic must be respected, and the
end was not far off.

The question as to whether Venice would have
retained her independence had she adopted another
line of action is one not easy to answer, though there
is much whereupon to argue that such might have
been the case ; and there can be no doubt that, had
she avoided the timid, wavering policy of neutrality
and of submission to whatever power happened to be
in the ascendant, she would have fallen with dignity
and honour. A proof of her weakness and of her
cringing to France is shown in her behaviour to

the brother of the murdered King Louis XVI., when as Count de Lille he sought refuge in Verona. This town was subject to Venice, and the Count, welcomed by the Republic, lived here for two years in retirement. The authorities at Paris however demanded that he should quit Venetian territory, and Venice, willing to content a government whose preponderance among the nations gained weight from day to day, sent to request the Count to leave Verona. The answer sent by the exile to this request must have been galling in the extreme, and must have demonstrated most unpleasantly to the Senate the baseness of their conduct. The Count de Lille expressed his readiness to leave, but insisted that, before doing so, the *Libro d'Oro* should be sent to him that he might erase from its pages the name of his family ; and, secondly, that the armour presented by his ancestor, Henry IV., to the Republic should be restored to him. But Venice managed to evade both these demands, and the exiled prince quitted her inhospitable soil without obtaining the desired satisfaction.

The object of this act had been to propitiate the French rulers, whose irritation against Venice was twofold. They were irritated at the shelter given to the Count de Lille, and still more were they displeased by the passage granted through Venetian dominions to Austrian troops—a violation, they considered, of the neutrality professed by Venice, and fraught with injury and annoyance to France. The French troops were now commanded by Napoleon Bonaparte, and his haughty domineering spirit was by no means inclined to overlook conduct, which he considered damaging to his country and contrary to the rules and conditions of war. The victories of Montenotte, Millesimo, and Lodi were far from disposing him to leniency and forbearance, and the language which he used to the Venetian envoy, showed how little favour or consideration the Republic might expect from his hands. He railed against the vacillation and procrastination of Venetian policy, of the breach of neutrality in allowing Austrian troops to pass through the land ; he announced his intention to set fire to Verona and Venice, declaring at the same time the ease with which he could accomplish his threats. Fresh victories in the north of Italy gave force to these threats, and the Senate, alarmed at the aspect of affairs, thought it wise to comply with a demand made by Napoleon for a monthly supply of a million francs. In 1796 Verona was obliged to open her gates to him ; and his subsequent conquests in Lombardy placed the Venetian *terra ferma* at the mercy of his victorious armies. Bergamo, Brescia, Salò, and Crema renounced their allegiance to Venice, and the success, that on all sides attended Napoleon's arms and stratagems, increased the anger and irritation entertained by him for the town of Venice. In vain he had proposed terms of peace, and made offers of alliance to the Signory. They recoiled from all such proposals, fearing by these measures to become entangled in war ; and Napoleon, vexed at their refusals and annoyed at certain signs in the behaviour of the Senate, which he construed as inimical to himself and his country, determined more than ever to overthrow the Republic. Some of Venice's subjects, and specially those belonging to her mountainous districts, clung loyally to her, and appealed to her for help and stores to oppose the French. No aid was however sent from the lagunes ; and Napoleon, who resented the resistance made by the mountaineers, sent Junot to Venice to remonstrate in strong terms against the injuries done to his soldiers, and to threaten instant war unless his demands were granted. He also insisted that the supplies of men and arms, quietly collecting in Venice and in the neighbouring forts, should be disbanded ; but the Government disclaimed any warlike intentions as to these levies with regard to France, and gave evasive replies as to the general's other claims. These covert and constant grievances soon broke out into open and bitter reprisals ; and two events which followed in quick succession exasperated Napoleon and the French to acts of violence and vengeance against the Republic. The first of these was the rising in Verona of the inhabitants against the French quartered in their city. The cause of the insurrection is uncertain ; but the animosity reigning between the two nations ran high, and any trifle was sufficient to bring matters to a crisis. On the evening of April 17th the Veronese attacked the French, and massacred them indiscriminately, not even sparing the sick and wounded in their fury. The authorities in the town endeavoured vainly to check the cruelties and excesses of their fellow citizens and to silence the guns which poured a hot and relentless fire on the foreign invaders from the forts. The populace, goaded to madness and thirsting to deliver their town, were beyond control, and not till a fresh force of French troops had come to the rescue of their countrymen was the tumult appeased. "Les Pâques Véronaises," as the French stigmatised this outburst, comparing it for horror and villany to the Sicilian Vespers, had no effect but to increase the bad feeling existing between the two states, and heighten the desire for vengeance vowed by Napoleon against Venice.

The second cause of offence was the treatment experienced by a French vessel in Venetian waters. This vessel, the *Libérateur d'Italie*, commanded by a Captain Laugier, was cruising in the Adriatic in April (1797), on the look-out for Austrian men-of-war. A strict watch was always kept by Venice on all foreign ships sailing in the waters of the lagunes ; and on Laugier manœuvring his vessel close up to the Lido, Pizzamano, the governor of the fort, ordered him to withdraw. The French officer made as though he would obey ; but whether his intention was to assert his supremacy and enter the harbour in spite of opposition, or whether the ship was borne onward by the tide is uncertain. The *Libérateur* pursued her course into the harbour, and was immediately fired upon from the fort and from Venetian galleys. In the havoc and confusion that ensued Laugier and several of his men were killed ; the rest were made prisoners. Napoleon's anger knew no bounds. He had just signed with Austria the peace of Leoben ; when, unknown to Venice, all the *terra ferma* domains were transferred to Austria. Venice herself was to possess only her capital and the Ionian isles, and the mainland territory between the Oglio and the Po. Before the news of this partition was known in Venice, a message from Napoleon conveyed to the Senate his wrath and indignation over the death of Laugier, and his resolve to be avenged. The message, prompted by anger and revenge, was backed by forces and subsidies, against which the worn-out faculties of Venice could make but feeble opposition. Napoleon proclaimed that Venice should pay for the blood of the French slaughtered, through her treachery and with her connivance, on Venetian soil ; that all persons imprisoned for adherence to French views and opinions should be set at liberty ; that the English ambassador should be expelled ; and that the old institutions and forms of government should be abolished. He inveighed at the way his alliance had so often been rejected ; and declared his intentions against Venice in a manner which left no doubt of his animosity and hatred. " I will have none of your alliance now," he declared ; " I will have none of your projects ; I will have none of your state inquisitors ; none of your Senate. I will be a second Attila to Venice, whose old worn-out government must collapse." And these words were enforced by a declaration of war issued against the Republic on May 1, 1797.

When this declaration reached Venice, orders were given to provide as far as possible for the safety and defence of the city. Supplies of food, water, fuel, and ammunition, were provided in case of a blockade ;

the ships in the Arsenal were fairly numerous, though not all in repair and working gear ; and a gallant resistance might yet have been made had there not reigned throughout the entire city a spirit of weakness and decay eating into the very heart of the nation, and undermining any effort to strike for freedom and honour.

The order given to arm and victual the town was the last act of the Senate. The power, which for so many centuries had governed with a wisdom and authority rarely equalled, was now to be superseded by an illegal and irregular gathering of the Doge, his councillors, and most of the other chief magistrates ; who assembled in the Doge's private rooms, and dignified their meeting by the name of " The Conference." The pusillanimity of the Doge Ludovico Manin, and of most of the members assembled, revealed how vainly the people of Venice might hope for an example of courage or endurance from their so-called leaders. They debated as to whether they should resist, or yield to the threats and claims of the French general ; and the majority of voices advised submission. The sitting lasted into the night, and yet no decision was resolved on when a message came from the commandant of the fleet, announcing that the French had begun erecting forts and batteries on the marsh-land adjoining the lagunes ; and he only awaited orders from the Government to open a brisk fire upon them. The agitation caused by this communication was extreme. The Doge paced the room in terror, exclaiming that there was little hope that night of sleeping quietly in their beds ; more uneasy

for his night's rest than for the safety of the city committed to his rule.   Before an answer was returned to
the commandant, some shots of cannon showed that
he had found it necessary to act on his own responsibility.   After fresh debate a message was sent,
authorising him to employ force to stop the French
works, but empowering him at the same time to con-
tradict his actions by offering terms for an armistice.
The steady oncoming of the foe made it necessary,
however, to resort to extreme measures.   The time
for summoning the Great Council and applying for
advice was too limited; so it was decided to conform to Napoleon's wishes, to agree to most of the
claims dictated by him, and above all to yield to a
change of government.   The Doge and many of the
nobles urged the advisability of such a step, and for
the last time in Venetian history the Great Council
was convened, when only 537 members assembled.

Though no sitting was legal unless six hundred
members were present, the question as to continuing
the form of government was put all the same.   A
majority of 512 voices, as opposed to twenty negative
and five neutral, decided to do away with the constitution that had existed in Venice for so many centuries.   This took place May 12, 1797, and four days
after a proclamation announced that henceforward
the government would be administered by a temporary municipality.   All public decrees would begin:
" In the name of the sovereign people, the Venetian
temporary government," &c., instead of, " Il Serenissimo
Principe fa sapere &c. ; " as heretofore ; and the motto
would be, " Liberty, virtue, and equality."   These

municipal edicts would still have the Winged Lion for their badge ; but the words, " Pax tibi Marce," &c., inscribed on the book resting between the paws of the Winged Lion, were to be altered to " Rights of man and of citizenship." This change provoked from a gondolier the witticism that " St. Mark had at last turned over a new leaf ! " Under the new arrangement the nobles and members of the Great Council renounced their sovereign powers and hereditary rights of nobility, and acknowledged that they were one of an assembly of citizens. All they pleaded in return for these concessions was that the new Government should declare itself responsible for the public debt, and should continue the pensions allowed to the poor nobles. French aid was invoked to insure the security of the town ; and troops of French soldiers were to provide for the safety of the religion, the citizens, and all property, till such time as the new government had established its sway, and could maintain order on its own account.

The institution of this new magistracy was celebrated in Venice with the delirium of disorder and irreverence that in most cases stamps the fever of revolution. The town broke out into joyousness and revelry without any reflection or even knowledge as to how far there existed a reason for such festivities. French customs and French forms were adopted whereon to model the new government ; and a letter was addressed to Napoleon, expressing in servile language the gratitude felt by Venice " for the liberty which, thanks to the glorious French nation and the immortal Bonaparte, she now enjoyed." On

June 4th a great festival was held in the Piazza to inaugurate the reign of democracy. The "Tree of Liberty" was planted in the middle of the square, and beneath it the *Libro d'Oro* and all the insignia of ducal power and state, no longer required by an enlightened sovereign people, were burned ; and large tricoloured flags floated from the three masts standing in front of St. Mark's. Inscriptions in praise of Napoleon and the French covered the two columns of the Piazzetta ; one of them however being draped in black, as a tribute of mourning to Laugier and his countrymen, victims it was declared to the aristocracy and cruelty of Venice. Every trace recalling the past Government was as far as possible obliterated ; coats of arms, titles, and all allusions to rank and nobility were swept away ; the prisons were emptied of every culprit and criminal ; and the people in their zeal to eradicate all memories of their former rulers insisted on burning all the archives and documents of the Council of Ten, and of the Inquisitors of State on which they could lay hands. And while feasts, rejoicings, dances wherein all ranks joined readily, thanksgivings in the churches for the deliverance accomplished, marked the age of equality and fraternity in Venice, the cities and provinces under her sway flung off their allegiance on all sides, declaring equally their freedom and independence. The revolt began at Padua and extended to Torcello, Mestre, Chioggia, and Gambarare ; all asserting their right to be free, and have their own municipalities and administrations separate from those of Venice. In Paris the Venetian ambassador, Querini, was told to withdraw, the state which he represented having ceased to exist; Vienna declined to receive Vettor Gradenigo, who had been sent as the representative of the Republic; but Spain and the Porte still retained the Venetian envoys, as did also the Court of St. James, though under certain given conditions.

The French rule was not however destined to obtain a footing in the lagunes. The treaty of Campoformio signed October 17, 1797, handed Venice over to Austria together with Istria, Dalmatia, the provinces of Bergamo, and Brescia, and all that constituted the actual Dogado; while France retained the Ionian isles. This transaction doomed and destroyed the great Republic of Venice. The city, that had stood again and again as a barrier to Europe against the invasions of the Turk; that had proved herself in word and in deed "the safeguard of the West"; that had acted as the channel through which literature and culture and civilisation had flown into the Western hemisphere, this city was now disposed of like a bill of exchange by those whom the chances of war had made her masters.

The surrender of Venice to Austria was by no means a measure satisfactory to the French. They determined to leave her destitute and despoiled to her new masters, and erase all memories of her past greatness. For this intent they carried off all the money on which they could lay hands; the ships that were still serviceable they removed to Toulon, the rest they destroyed in the Arsenal; the *Bucentaur* was broken up and rifled; several works of art were burned, others were sold, and the larger part carried off in quantities to Paris, among them being the bronze horses. Venice, bereft of her chief monuments of history and art and glory, was vacated by the French on January 18, 1798; and the same day the Austrian troops entered and took possession of the desolate city.

MASQUERADERS.
(*From Yriarte's " Venise," op. cit.*)

CONCLUSION.

(1798–1866.)

THE story of Venice at the close of the eighteenth
and opening of the nineteenth century is so lost sight
of in that of Austria as to claim hardly any annals of
its own. Austrian victories that certainly appealed
in no way to Venetians aroused festivals and rejoicings
in Venice productive of the double advantage of keeping the citizens in a good temper, and of attracting
visitors to the town. Otherwise events ran smoothly,
though not happily, for sickness was rife in the provinces, depression and dejection reigned in most
minds ; and here and there a revolt, stifled as soon
as it was born, showed the discontent that lurked
under the silence of oppression. A change was consequently hailed with joy, and the Peace of Pressburg
was greeted with acclamations in Venice before any
proof could be had as to its gain or the reverse.
This peace, signed December 26, 1805, established
Napoleon's power in Italy ; and Venice was united
to his Italian kingdom, with a ruler appointed over
her, who was to reside alternately in Milan and in
Venice. This union was celebrated in Venice on

May 1, 1806, with solemn thanksgivings in the churches; Eugène de Beauharnais was proclaimed ruler, with the title of Prince of Venice; the town was to be declared a free port, and have free trade with all countries, England alone excepted.

In December, 1807, Napoleon himself came to Venice, when his orders and regulations in regard of the town were those of a wise and able prince. He endeavoured to revive the extent and efficiency of the trade and shipping of the Adriatic; he instituted laws for the administration of charity; he made rules for the enlargement and improvement of the ports, and busied himself greatly as to modern improvements in the town, laying out the public gardens, and so on. His dream was to restore Venice, in her quality of a French possession, to becoming once again a great centre for Eastern trade, but the state of European affairs and interests forbade the realisation of such a scheme, even backed by all the power and ingenuity of Napoleon.

In 1813 Venice underwent another change of masters, for as Napoleon's might began to decline, Austria asserted her claims to her former possession. From October, 1813, till April, 1814, Venice was blockaded; and on the dissolution of Napoleon's Italian realm she was ceded to Austria, and the following year formed into the Lombard-Veneto kingdom. Over this kingdom the Archduke Renier, brother of the Emperor Francis I., was appointed viceroy in 1818, and resided alternately between his two capitals, Milan and Venice. The Emperor Francis often visited the City of the Lagunes, to which he confirmed the free-trade grant accorded by Napoleon ; and for thirty years all was comparatively quiet and peaceful in the land. The heavy yoke of bondage and of foreign rule weighed though heavily in the town ; the demonstrations made on each occasion of a change of ruler were but the outcome of the agitation at that moment rife throughout Europe, an agitation growing ever greater, while the ideas which required only an opportune moment to transform themselves into facts were ripening from day to day.

On June 6, 1846, Pius IX. succeeded Gregory XVI. as Pope, and showed himself in favour of liberal ideas by according a widespread amnesty and initiating many useful reforms. In every part of Italy a desire for similar reforms arose, coupled with an ever-increasing hatred against the foreign lords. In France the dynasty of the House of Orleans had fallen, and the Republic been proclaimed. The effect of this revolution spread through Germany, from thence to Vienna, from where it communicated itself with hopes of deliverance to Venice. The Venetians rose in arms on March 17, 1848, rushed into the Square of St. Mark, and clamoured for the liberation of Daniele Manin [1] and Nicolò Tommaseo, two loyal and straightforward citizens who had been imprisoned by the Austrian police for having openly manifested patriotic sentiments. The prisons were attacked, the two prisoners liberated and brought out in triumph. Manin was proclaimed President of the

---

[1] He was not of the patrician family of that name, and consequently no relation to the last Doge.

Republic of Venice on March 22, 1848. The horrors of an insurrection were averted by concessions on both sides ; a capitulation was agreed upon, and the Austrians consented to vacate the city and retire by sea to Trieste, leaving in Venice Italian troops, as well as money and material for war. Throughout the whole of Northern Italy war was now the order of the day. Carlo Alberto, king of Piedmont, had declared war against Austria ; and from every part of the the peninsula soldiers flocked to fight for the Father-land. Fortune smiled at first on these efforts, but then hid her face. Pius IX. disapproved of war ; and the want of subsidies and organisation paralysed the movements of those who sought to carry on the struggle. The Austrians reconquered Milan, defeated the patriots in several places, retook the " Veneto," and threatened Venice herself. The dream of liberty so widely spread throughout Italy in 1848 had a rude awakening in 1849, and the overthrow of the Pied-montese army on the field of Novara (March 23, 1849) crushed for the moment the hope of Italian freedom. Carlo Alberto resigned his crown and went into voluntary exile in Portugal, where he soon died. All over Italy the old rulers retook possession of their dominions, Venice, however, being the last to surrender. Regardless of the desperate outlook of affairs she resolved to make a stand ; and the unani-mous voice of her people gave force and weight to the resolution. As in her story of bygone days Venice again appealed to the powers of Europe for help and support, and as of old the appeals met only with refusals. Venice was regarded by most of the powers as a city in revolt against her liege lord, the Emperor of Austria, and not as a spot from whence deliverance might yet spread through the land. The resistance she made singlehanded for seventeen months against Austria was worthy of her old traditions ; and not till famine and cholera had wasted their ranks did the citizens think of yielding. The courage and valour shown over the bombardment of Marghera was followed by equal bravery in defending the heart of the city, when the Venetians had to withdraw from the fortress. On July 29, 1849, the Austrians began to bombard the town of Venice, and when this had continued for twenty-four days, and human force and energy could do no more, it was resolved to capitulate. Manin and many of his associates were condemned to exile, and on August 27th General Gorzkowski took possession of the town in the name of Austria as civil and military governor, and a few days later Count Radetsky entered as field-marshal.

Venice was again reduced to a state of servitude, and remained in that state for seventeen years.

In 1853 the Crimean War broke out, and England and France invited Piedmont to join with them against Russia. Count Camillo di Cavour, the great Italian statesman, at once recognised the advantages that would accrue to Italy from such an alliance. Fifteen thousand Piedmontese were sent under the command of General La Marmora, and fought valiantly by the side of English and French troops in the Crimea, especially at the battle of Cernaia (August 16, 1855), where they played an important part. After peace was declared Cavour brought forward the question of Italian unity at the Congress of Paris ; and in 1859 Vittorio Emanuele II., who ten years previously had fought valiantly by his father's side at Novara, formed an alliance with Napoleon III., whereupon Austria declared war with Piedmont, which had now become the centre of the liberal Italian movement. Napoleon led the French army in person into Italy, and the united French and Piedmontese arms defeated the Austrians at the battles of Montebello, Palestro, Magenta, Solferino, and San Martino ; while other victories were gained in other parts of Italy by Garibaldi and his famous " Cacciatori delle Alpi." Venice dreamed that for her, too, the hour of liberty was at hand, but the peace of Villafranca (July 12, 1859) dispelled her hopes, while Lombardy, Tuscany, Modena, and Parma were united to Piedmont.

In 1860 battles for the independence of Italy were fought in the south of the peninsula. The kingdom of the Two Sicilies, after driving out the Bourbons, united itself to the other free sister state, and on the 18th of February, 1861, the kingdom of Italy, under the dynasty of the house of Savoy, was proclaimed.

War was declared in 1866 between Austria and Prussia, when this latter power, under the guidance of Count Bismarck, aimed at acquiring the supremacy of Germany. Italy, still faithful to the policy of Cavour, entered into alliance with Prussia and attacked Austria. The Italian arms were unsuccessful, and they were defeated at Custoza and Lissa. But the splendid victories of the Prussians over the Austrians, especially at Sadowa (July 3, 1866), brought the war to a close. Napoleon III. interposed between the belligerents, and by the treaty of Prague Austria was excluded from the Italo-German confederation. The " Veneto," which for diplomatic reasons was ceded to France, was through France united to the kingdom of Italy; and the seal of this union was set on November 7th of that year, when Vittorio Emanuele came to Venice. The " Re Galant'uòmo " was greeted with a pomp and ceremonial rarely seen even in Venice, and the rejoicings and festivals which proclaimed his presence left no doubt of the joy and welcome accorded by the City of the Doges to her sovereign and deliverer. Venice was made the chief town of a prefecture, and other changes were brought about in her administration which replace in an efficient though widely dissimilar form the famous councils under whose sway the story had been enacted of her rise, her greatness, and her decline.

.   .   .   .   .   .

The pride of the great Republic is over, her glory departed, but Venice herself still remains a lovely record of stirring times and events, and one of the fairest jewels in the kingdom of United Italy. The pomp attendant on the Doges, the dignity that surrounded the Great Council, the mystery that wrapt the tribunals of the Ten, and of the Three, are swept away, together with the romance and dread that belong to their histories. But the Ducal Palace still fronts the waves in its fairy beauty, while on its walls are enshrined in truly Venetian colours the chapters of that story which strangers of every race and clime flock continually to read. The Arsenal again sends forth ships of war from the site whence the *Bucentaur* once passed so proudly ; and the ring of modern industry and traffic re-echoes under the vaulted roofs where Venetian galleys were built in days of old. The names of Morosini, Mocenigo, Tiepolo, Zeno, linger yet about her palaces and waterways. The horses of Constantinople still paw the air on the portal of St. Mark's and the Winged Lion still points to the words, " Pax Tibi, Marce Evangelista Meus." May the peace that now encircles Venice prove fruitful and abiding, and endow her with a power and vitality whereby in days to come she may regain some of the glory and radiance of her mighty past ! In the world's stories there are many pages of interest and renown, but there are few which can boast of a splendour or a romance so absorbing and so wonderful as that which encircles the Story of Venice.

LION OF ST. MARK OF THE YEAR 1400.
(*From the Museo Correr.*)

INDEX.

465